WOLVES among SHEEP

The True Story of Murder in a
Jehovah's Witness Community

James Kostelniuk

3rd Edition

WOLVES AMONG SHEEP
The True Story of Murder in a Jehovah's Witness Community

All the events in this book are true. The author re-created some scenes based on interviews, letters, and eyewitness accounts.

ISBN-10: 1-926676-26-2
ISBN-13: 978-1-926676-26-5

Printed by Word Alive Press
131 Cordite Road, Winnipeg, MB R3W 1S1
www.wordalivepress.ca

WORD ALIVE PRESS
Just Write!

This book is dedicated to my wife Marge, to my mother Nellie, and to our dear friends M. James Penton and his wife Marilyn. I learn from you, respect you, and love you.

In memory of Kim, Juri, and Lindsay.

BOOK REVIEWS AND MANITOBA WRITING AWARD NOMINATIONS FOR *WOLVES AMONG SHEEP*

A compelling and heartbreaking read, the book makes complex connections between the author's life, the murderer's life, the lives of the victims, and the religion they all once shared. Kostelniuk untangles this web in clear, simple prose, writing in a tone profoundly free of anger.

—*Quill & Quire*

The book is the reconstruction of a murder, and of a man. It is a meditation on faith and forgiveness—and the limits of both.

—KEN MACQUEEN
The Vancouver Sun

No one will ever, could ever, accuse James Kostelniuk of [sensationalism]. His book is the antithesis of trash writing....*Wolves Among Sheep* is no easy read, but it is wonderfully intelligent and mature, with shining moments of grace and courage on one page, on the next acts of cruelty so casually delivered they knock the breath right out of you. Great true crime writing as it turns out—there's so little of it, who knew?—is just like real life. There's nothing as powerful, and nothing more sensational, than truth.

—CHRISTIE BLATCHFORD
National Post

This is a book that will follow you through the night while you are reading it and will remain with you, unsettling and harrowing, after you've put it down... No one who reads it will be quite the same again.

—HOWARD ENGEL
The Globe and Mail

Not since Capote's *In Cold Blood* have readers been so close to a killer... Through lengthy correspondence with the killer, generous police contacts and painstaking research, he takes us on a dark voyage into a killer's heart... But what makes *Wolves Among Sheep* stand out as a deeply gripping and profoundly heart-wrenching tale is neither the crime, nor the victims, but Kostelniuk himself. He is not a detached spectator sifting through a crime scene. He is the father of the murdered children.

—DARCY HENTON
Toronto Star

In an attempt to find closure in his life, he wrote *Wolves Among Sheep,* a riveting read that explores the darkest regions of religion and the human heart.

—ANDREW ARMITAGE
The Sun Times,
Owen Sound, Ontario

Kostelniuk tells his story in a clear and engaging style, transparently fuelled by equal measures of anger, sadness and regret.

—DOUGLAS J. JOHNSON
Winnipeg Free Press

But James Kostelniuk's story also strikes me, above all, as a profoundly human one. It is a sensitive, poignant, well-written, gut-wrenching account of nothing less than the great human struggle, the "agon" of life, and the triumph of sanity, light and hope over despair and darkness.

—DAVID ROBERTS
The Globe and Mail
From the foreword to *Wolves Among Sheep*

Kostelniuk's pain seeps through the pages. Any peace he does derive comes from writing about his children. *Wolves Among Sheep* is both therapy and their memorial.

—ANNA ASIMAKOPULOS
The Montreal Gazette

It is a rare occurrence when a published novel is used as a victim's impact statement in a parole hearing, but that is exactly what will happen with this book in the middle of February [2009].

—MARIANNE CURTIS
The Dawson Trail Dispatch

I believe the story that Jim tells is eminently worth reading because it shows that the "quality of mercy is not strained," and that it is possible to over-come evil, at least in ourselves, by manifesting love... Jim's course of conduct stands out as a bright example of Christian charity.

—M. JAMES PENTON
Author of *Apocalypse Delayed: The Story of Jehovah's Witnesses*

He has given the facts and allows his readers to judge those facts for them-selves. Secondly, he has shown the complexity of what has happened to a number of people and has demonstrated the intricacy of individual person-alities, thereby showing that there is so much bad in the best of us and so much good in the worst of us.

—ERNESTO VELA
James Kostelniuk's therapist

Wolves Among Sheep: The True Story of Murder in a Jehovah's Witness Community was nominated for the following Manitoba Writing and Publishing Awards on April 28, 2001:

- Eileen McTavish Sykes Award for Best First Book by a Manitoba Author.
- Alexander Kennedy Isbister Award for Non-Fiction.
- McNally Robinson Book of the Year Award.

Wolves Among Sheep was also used as a text in the Creative Communications journalism course at Red River College in Winnipeg for two years. Duncan McMonagle was the professor.

FOREWORD

WHEN JAMES KOSTELNIUK and I first spoke on the telephone, and when we met face-to-face in the autumn of 1996, he did not strike me as a man whose life had been utterly darkened. Soft-spoken and courteous, what struck me was James's enormous appetite for information, his thoughtfulness, his shyness and, ultimately, his ability to communicate in a way I had never before heard, with a profound depth of feeling that could only result from great suffering.

He told me his ex-wife and two small children had been shot to death in suburban Vancouver in 1985.

This in itself was shockingly sad. But then James began to reveal in haunting and exquisite detail his own story: the story of how he struggled over the years—successfully, I see now—to come to grips with this unimaginable loss and to find a small island of peace in a world torn asunder by grief.

That he had actually met with the killer of his family, Jeff Anderson, in an effort to understand why this horror had occurred—and pressed Anderson for detail about how he had pointed the gun, how far from their small faces—was to me most astounding. Anderson's own comments, you will see, speak volumes, for they are more multivalent and revealing of himself than he might have imagined: "As for victims, I've got the best."

In the months and years after our first meeting, James began to share with me drafts of the manuscript that became this book: the sum of his thoughts, feelings, correspondences, interviews.

And as I read I became even more astonished and gripped by it. I felt I was privileged to be given a special gift, a unique insight, as public a witness to a private sorrow. I had been taken "to the depths" and saw, not defeat, not shattered human remains, but triumph, victory. Certainly I have seen a "victim" standing in the rain at the serenely peaceful grave of his children. But I have also seen a very courageous man who is able to carry on and live life, not on the boundaries, as Paul Tillich put it, but at the center.

Victims of crime are rarely afforded much of a public voice. They get short shrift. Sometimes the courts offer them the pro forma chance to write a "victim-impact statement," which helps judges apply a fit sentence to an offender by taking into account the effects of the crime on others.

Some victims find this process cathartic. All too often victims choose silence. Sometimes, survivors of an especially horrible crime, such as murder, may justifiably choose a self-imposed silence—they do not wish their lives to become a public spectacle. I've had a few doors slammed in my face over the years and would not second-guess those who would wrestle with their grief away from the prying eyes and ears of a stranger. But on other occasions, unexpectedly, magically, the doors of grief are flung open and victims spontaneously decide to share their memories and their sorrow. Perhaps they unconsciously know that their burden may be lighter if their pain is shouldered by a wider community.

I don't know if that is what James intended to share with us in writing *Wolves Among Sheep,* but I suspect it is part of it. I know that even now the unanswerable questions haunt him: "Why did this happen? What could I have done to prevent it?" I also know this book was intentionally born of a feeling of responsibility, of doing right for Kim and for Juri and Lindsay.

Of course beyond this, recurringly, there is just a simple sadness: three innocent lives snuffed out. The survivors are left to pick up the pieces of their own shattered existence.

I truly believe *Wolves Among Sheep* offers unique and important insight into the psychological and spiritual travails of a father consumed by the guilt and existential crises of unimaginable loss.

But James Kostelniuk's story strikes me, above all, as a profoundly human one. It is as sensitive, poignant, well-written, gut-wrenching account of nothing less than the great human struggle, the "agon" of life, and the triumph of sanity, light and hope over despair and darkness.

The tangential issues it raises—with its profile of a pathetic, disturbed killer, the justice system's machinations, and the failures and foibles of an unusual religious sect—all these also are deserving of wide readership and careful consideration by all Canadians.

David Roberts
Bureau Chief
Manitoba and Saskatchewan
The Globe and Mail

PREFACE

I WAS AT HOME with my wife, Marge, when the RCMP officer arrived. He was dressed in plain clothes, and I guessed by his demeanor that this was not a routine call. I remember thinking that he didn't look like what you'd expect a policeman to look—that is, calm, and impersonal. In fact, he appeared very nervous, his face grim and flushed.

The officer looked like he needed something solid to sit on, and without thinking, I offered him a seat at the kitchen table. He took the chair gingerly, as though it might break. Marge and I sat across from each other and waited. We watched him reach for his jacket and take a piece of paper from his vest pocket. Looking down, he paused for what seemed like a very long time. I heard the paper rattle in his hands, and it was only then that I noticed that he was shaking. His whole body trembled, and I thought, "Something terrible has happened." Then I realized that I, too, was trembling.

Finally the words came, quick and precise. "Are you the father of Juri and Lindsay Kostelniuk?" I hesitated, thinking I could delay what he had come to tell me. But I knew, whatever it was, I had no choice but to hear it. I braced myself, and told him that I was.

"I'm very sorry to inform you that they and their mother, Kim Anderson, were murdered in Burnaby, British Columbia at about 12:30 p.m. today. Jeff Anderson, Kim's husband, is in police custody."

That day—August 29, 1985—would mark the end of my life as I had known it, and the beginning of unthinkable anguish and unending heartache. It would also mark the beginning of a relentless, almost obsessive quest for answers, one that would shatter my deepest beliefs and convictions, and force me to examine the darkest corners of human nature.

"Beware of false prophets, which come to you in sheep's clothing, but inwardly they are ravening wolves."

—Matthew 7:15 (KJV)

1

I GREW UP ON FARMS in southern Manitoba, a descendent of rugged Ukrainian and Polish immigrants who settled in boreal forest lowlands west of Winnipeg Beach. In memory, there are open fields of black loam plowed into long furrows and scattered with straw. Farm buildings, hedges, shelter-belts, and patches of bush occasionally break the flat monotony, and straight gravel roads and ditches run into infinity. The distant horizon is a thin, infinite line of blue haze. The sky is a vast dome, making everything under it seem small and insignificant.

Most of my childhood was spent on a farm near Clandeboye, Manitoba. My pre-school playground was nearby Medicine Creek, one of the many tributaries of the Red River of the North. I spent many hours exploring its sloping banks and nearby thickets of poplar, cranberry, wolf willow, and sponge-like humus. "Puppy," my American Eskimo, was my constant companion, his white coat constantly dirty from long days of digging for badgers and skunks. We ran for miles along that creek, which frequently appears as the artery of my dreams. At night, I am that little boy again, running along Medicine Creek with my dog.

In 1898 my great-grandparents, Woytko and Sylvania Kostelniuk, responded to Sir Wilfrid Laurier's campaign to settle the harsh, rigorous Canadian prairies with "a stalwart peasant in a sheep-skin coat." They and their five children traveled to Canada from Austria-Hungary on a ship called the *S.S. Italia*, landed in Halifax in early June, and continued their difficult journey westward by train, arriving in Manitoba several weeks later.

The "peasant" immigrants lured to Manitoba in those years settled their homesteads with great hope for the future and a better life for their children. But these small farmers were accustomed to the rich and open steppes of southeast Europe, and with only a few primitive tools and meager belongings, were ill-prepared for what faced them. Instead of the Promised Land that they had envisioned, they found themselves battling dense northern forest, plagued with mosquitoes, stones, and sloughs. After a generation of backbreaking toil and hardship, few of the original settlers who had come to the region with my grandparents remained on their homesteads, and their descendants have long since scattered.

However, Woytko and Sylvania Kostelniuk managed to endure. As was traditional, their youngest son Peter remained a bachelor and cared for his parents in their old age. Upon their death, the still struggling family homestead, located in what was known then as Foley, was divided between him and Stanley, the elder son. Peter remained single all his life, but Stanley eventually married a neighboring farm girl, Tekla Shewaga, who gave birth to my father, Michael, in 1916 and to his younger sister Mary in 1918. A third child, named Josef, was born in 1917, but he died two years later of Spanish Influenza.

From all accounts, Stanley and Tekla did not have a happy marriage. Their life was difficult; no matter how hard they worked, they could not seem to get ahead and fell deeper and deeper into debt. Mike, a third brother of Peter and Stanley, managed to buy his own farm, but also struggled to make ends meet. The Kostelniuk brother's dreams of having lives better than their parents grew increasingly remote, and disappeared entirely with the coming of the Great Depression.

At the time, many farm people sought solace and comfort in religion, which promised them a better life in the hereafter. Throughout the 1930s, an extremist religious sect known as Jehovah's Witnesses started to gain converts in Manitoba, especially among the province's immigrant farmers. The movement and organization were created in Allegheny, Pennsylvania in the late 1800s by a charismatic businessman who was called Pastor Russell. He and his followers preached a millennial message that appealed to those with little hope in their lives: Pastor Russell told them that the end of the world would occur within their lifetime, and that Jehovah's faithful would live to see the Promised Land.

There were many positive aspects to the sect: its members were encouraged to be peaceful, honest, cooperative, and the organization later went on to win a number of important legal battles that improved freedom-of-expression laws in North America. However, its emphasis on door-to-door preaching and conversion, rabid condemnation of all other religions and beliefs, outright scorn toward higher education, and what many viewed as a crazy belief in the coming Apocalypse brought frequent persecution and ridicule upon its members. The legal organization also demanded unquestioning obedience, chastity, and austerity from its members, and encouraged highly misogynistic attitudes towards women.

My father's uncles, Peter and Mike, became Jehovah's Witnesses in the early 1930s. By all accounts, Peter was a gentle and compassionate man, but Mike personified the stereotypical religious extremist: rigid, domineering, and misogynous. I often saw the more unpleasant aspects of Mike's personality in my father, and would later be dismayed to discover them in myself.

Tragedy entered my father's life in the early 1930s. My grandfather, Stanley, fell ill with tuberculosis and had to be quarantined away from his family in a distant sanatorium at Ninette, Manitoba. The family did their best to keep the farm afloat, but eventually lost everything due to unpaid taxes. Stanley died shortly thereafter, and in desperation his wife, Tekla, set fire to the house for the insurance money and ran off to British Columbia with a man she barely knew, abandoning her young children to fend for themselves.

Michael was only fourteen, and his sister Mary twelve. Mary was so crushed by her mother's abandonment that she attempted to drown herself in Lake Winnipeg, and failing that, took to the streets of Winnipeg. She was eventually rescued by a Polish immigrant three times her age, and agreed to become his common-law wife. Michael also managed to survive, but the harsh circumstances of his youth created the tough-skinned, hardworking, pragmatic, and often harsh man that I knew as my father. Although he eventually forgave his mother for her selfish act, he never lost his bitterness towards her. This aspect of my father's life had a large impact on my own psyche; it instilled in me a vivid awareness and fear of the consequences of family abandonment, and a deep need for reassurance, approval, and acceptance—especially from my father.

Michael was invited to live with his uncle Peter, whom he came to love and trust as a father. But money was scarce, and my father had to earn his keep by working for farmers during harvest and at other busy times of the year. He diligently saved his money and eventually was able to buy back his father's farm from the municipality, the farm that had been abandoned by his mother. He built another house in place of the one his mother had destroyed by fire, and in November of 1938, he married the daughter of a neighboring farmer—my mother, Nellie Walchuk—and together they ran a small dairy operation, shipping hand-churned cream and butter to the market.

Both my father and mother were dedicated Jehovah's Witnesses when they married; their parents on both sides were Witnesses. With the coming of the Second World War in 1939, many men like my father were exempt from military service by virtue of being farmers. But as one of Jehovah's Witnesses—who were neutral during the war and whose books and activities were banned in

Canada—Michael would have refused to enlist had he been drafted. If not for his exemption as a farmer, he might have gone to jail for refusing war duty.

In July 1940, my sister Jeanette was born. Money was still scarce, and in addition to the dairy operation, my father often peddled his bicycle many miles in search of extra cash-paying jobs. He once traveled thirty miles south to a village called Petersfield, where he found work on a local farm. Soon after that, my parents sold their farm in Foley and bought another one close to Petersfield. I was born in Winnipeg in August 1946. By that time, my parents had become alienated from and disillusioned with their Jehovah's Witness brethren in Foley, and quit going to meetings altogether.

When I was barely able to walk, I had the tendency to wander off by myself, away from the house and yard. After a winter snowstorm, as I played in the yard in my snow gear, I followed our red and white dog Butch out past the barn. The dog left me stranded and bogged down in a snow drift. My mother, frantic at discovering me missing, rushed out of the house dressed only in a light jacket, a skirt and a pair of shoes. Luckily, she had my trail in the snow to follow and found me in no time. But without the necessary snow boots, she wound up freezing her ankles.

Another time, later in the spring, I wandered off again, this time into a poplar bluff along a field. This disappearance was much longer in duration and more serious. The neighbors, concerned I would not be found before nightfall when the temperature would drop precipitously, organized a search party and the RCMP were called out with their police dogs. According to my mother, a dairyman from across Petersfield Road, Dennis Donohoe, found me sitting under a tree "without a care in the world, singing to myself." He carried me to the safety of my mother's arms.

One or two years later, when I was four years old, my parents sold their farm near Petersfield and bought another one near Clandeboye where I grew up. I have very pleasant memories of my father on that farm. I remember walking proudly towards him across a field one morning. I had caught a jack fish on the rapids at spawning time and was taking it to him as a gift. I'll never forget the expression on his face as he looked up, his face burnt from the wind and sun, and saw the full-sized jack fish in my hands. He laughed so hard he had to shut the tractor off. Stepping down from the tractor, the slippery fish wriggled out of my hands and fell at his feet in the soft earth.

On another occasion, I decided to move a rotting rowboat. I was a delicate little boy of five, but somehow managed to drag the boat from the water's edge, up the steep bank, over a gravel road, and into a ditch in front of our house—a distance of about 150 feet, mostly uphill. It took me nearly the whole day to get it to the desired destination. When my father came home that evening from working on the Canadian Pacific Railway, he asked my mother how the boat got there. When she explained what I had done, he stood on the roadside for the longest time, staring in stunned amazement, first at the boat and then at me. To this day, I don't remember why it was so important for me to move that boat.

My father loved me, and encouraged me in many ways, but he grew more and more puzzled by me as I grew older. He was a rugged, hard-headed, practical man who brooked no nonsense, and in his eyes I was a soft and dreamy youngster who needed toughening up. We were frequently in conflict over one thing or another, both attracted and repelled by each other. Yet I still longed for his approval and acceptance.

My father's disappointment in me stung me deeply, for I admired his strength and vibrancy and in many ways longed to be more like him. He was a man of strong emotions and passions, who loved to laugh and socialize with neighbors and friends. Like his father before him, he learned to play violin by ear, and from the time he was fourteen, provided old-time dance music for weddings and community banquets. Though he had no formal training in music, he played remarkably well—soulfully, like a Ukrainian gypsy. And though his music was also a source of extra money, he genuinely enjoyed performing and making people feel good.

As a child, I loved to watch people dance to my father's music, fascinated by the graceful, coordinated patterns they made as they circled the dance floor. I especially loved to watch my mother dance. Dance was an important part of the cultural and social life in our community, and she loved it. She was a colorful and flamboyant young woman who was more in love with the musician in my father than the farmer. After they married, she did not adapt well to being a farmer's wife, and I often sensed the keen disappointment they felt in each other throughout their marriage.

I was closer in temperament to my mother, and I now think that my father sometimes resented our relationship. The more distant my parents became from each other, the closer my mother and I grew. She shared her most intimate thoughts and secrets with me, and I cherished our time together. I have fond memories of the colorful house dresses and wide-brimmed hats she wore as she fed the chickens, gathered eggs, or worked in the garden (she sewed her own dresses and was an avid gardener). Every evening, just before nightfall, when the white leghorn chickens would fly over the fence to roost in the trees, I would help her pull them down from the branches so the hawks wouldn't get them. I remember how they looked like ghostly white spirits as we picked them from the dark foliage, still asleep, and carried them off to safety.

My sister Jeanette was six years my senior, and we could not have been more different. I was fair-haired, respectful, and well-behaved; she was dark, rebellious, and wild. She was a popular teenager in the 1950s who rode around in fast cars with her friends, smoked cigarettes and drank lemon gin at dances. She and her girlfriends were admired by the other kids at school, and I was envious of her popularity. I would watch her and her boyfriend with fascination: Jeanette had pretty, dark hair, and eyes that flashed with emotion, and her boyfriend, Pat Ryan, was devilishly handsome, with sideburns and a Waikiki wave in his hair. As I grew into puberty, there was a part of me that yearned to be like them, to be rebellious and bad.

But that yearning conflicted with the part of me that needed approval of the adults around me, the part that wanted to be good. It also conflicted with my growing interest in religion—an odd preoccupation, given that my parents neither attended regular church services nor provided us with any formal religious instruction. My father's uncle, Mike, frequently pressured him and the rest of us to return to Jehovah's Witness meetings. But by that time, my parents had lost all interest in religious matters, preferring a life of hard work by day and a somewhat hedonist lifestyle at night, and neither encouraged nor discouraged my leanings.

My earliest concepts of God were closely associated with the abundance of nature that surrounded me. When I was about three, I overheard my father telling my mother that he was going to help a neighbor move some fuel drums. It was a warm spring morning, and before he left, he cheerfully expressed the hope that God would give him a sunny day, so that he would be working under the sun. Later that morning, I took a walk down the long lane from the house to the letter box stationed by Petersfield Road, as my mother was expecting a large can of strawberry jam from the general store in town. As I waited for the delivery to arrive, I would look into the blazing sun for as long as I could, then delight in the pulsating, visual aftereffects when I turned away. Through the dancing lights before my eyes, I gradually began to make out the figure of my father in the distance, pushing bright, shiny drums under the sunny sky he had hoped for. In that moment, my father, the sun, and God became inextricably linked in my consciousness.

The moon and stars held equal enchantment. I would watch for the planet Venus to appear after sunset, and often played in the moonlight by myself, watching moon shadows. Captivated by the soft light of stars against the night sky, I would wonder why God created light and darkness, and why things lived and died.

My first job on the farm was to feed and water a large flock of chickens before breakfast. Laying hens have very short life spans—no more than three years or so—and now and then one would die of old age. I remember holding those poor birds in my arms, feeling pity for them as their lives ebbed away. My parents had taken me to several funerals by that time, and I was deeply impressed with the rituals of death. As the chickens were my responsibility, I felt I should see them properly into the next world. I would place the dead bird in a shoebox lined with Kleenex and dig a grave in a special place behind some bushes. There I would conduct a funeral ceremony, usually attended by one or two neighbor children. We would solemnly bow our heads, say a few words for the departed soul of the bird, then lower the coffin into the ground with pieces of string. Each grave was marked with a cross made from old window frames painted white. My parents had no idea about any of this until my Uncle Carl happened upon the area one day and asked about the cemetery behind the choke-cherry trees.

I was also fascinated by fire. Farmers often burned stubble after the harvest which kept burning in long rows of flame into the night. The sight of a prairie brushfire always excited me, and I would watch the spitting flames of a campfire for hours. Fire seemed to have a mysterious life of its own, and I associated that mystery with God. It was only later that I encountered the story of Moses and the burning bush, and the pillar of fire that led the Israelites out of the desert—though it was from watching Cecil B. DeMille's *The Ten Commandments*, and not from reading the Bible.

When I first saw *The Ten Commandments* at the Garry Theater in Selkirk in the winter of 1957, it had a dramatic impact on my concept of God. Although I found the glamorous Egyptians much more attractive than Charlton Heston's Moses and the dull Israelites, the film's depiction of a powerful, angry, almost human and *physical* God, left an indelible imprint on my consciousness. Soon after, we began to study ancient Egypt and Israel in school history, with a textbook, *Builders of the Old World*, that made frequent references to the Bible. It was then that I began to read the Old Testament—Exodus, Numbers, Leviticus—and began to internalize the idea of God as an all-powerful Jehovah of Armies, who was more fearsome than loving.

By the time I was twelve, I had read the entire Bible from cover to cover. The absence of formal religion in our home made me curious about the churches that my fellow schoolmates attended each week, which led me to join (without my parents) a local congregation of the United Church of Canada. I regularly attended Sunday school and sang in the children's choir, often daydreaming of one day standing in the pulpit preaching to the congregation.

However, my life took an abrupt turn in 1960, the year I turned fourteen and began to attend high school, commuting by bus to the local town of Selkirk. Having lived on a farm all my life, I felt like the proverbial country yokel, and did not fit in with the other students. It was a severe blow to my self-esteem; I felt desperately awkward and out of place. Around the same time, my parents— seemingly oblivious to my own difficulties—went through a kind of midlife crisis and suddenly found religion—again. At the urging of relatives on both sides of their families, they started attending Jehovah's Witness meetings. And, although my father would never become a devout Witness, my mother embraced her new faith with great passion.

Over the years, I had listened to many conversations about Witness doctrine between my Uncle Mike and my father, who frequently tried to persuade him to return to the Society. I knew that its doctrine was in radical conflict with what I was being taught by the United Church—that Witnesses were taught to shun the outside world and fraternize only with fellow Witnesses—and that they were frequently "disfellowshipped" for going against or even questioning Witness teachings. More importantly, I was also aware of the rules concerning disfellowshipped members, which by 1960 had become extremely harsh in an effort to keep the organization clean. Witnesses in good standing were not allowed to speak to or associate with disfellowshipped persons, even if they were close family members. They were taught to view all such individuals as eternally damned; a Witness parent could not even attend the funeral of a disfellowshipped child without the risk of being ousted from the community.

Although my parents did not openly pressure me to join them in their return to their chosen faith, I felt that I had no choice. Still feeling deeply insecure about my social isolation at school, I feared my parents' increasing involvement with Jehovah's Witnesses would lead to their eventual abandonment of me as a non-believer. Although Witness doctrine went against everything I believed at the time, I soon began to convince myself that my parents and other family members knew better, and that one religious organization could not be much different than another, as long as I continued to love and serve God.

In early 1961, I stopped attending United Church services in our rural community and started to accompany my parents to Jehovah's Witness meetings in nearby Selkirk. And in July of that year, my mother and I attended an international convention in Vancouver. It was there that I publicly declared myself "a sinner needing salvation from Jehovah God" and allowed myself to be submerged in water and baptized as one of Jehovah's Witnesses.

2

THOUGH INITIALLY AMBIVALENT about becoming one of Jehovah's Witnesses, I soon embraced the Witness lifestyle with great enthusiasm, as its duties and doctrines quickly helped to fill the empty holes of my confused adolescence. Where I used to feel ashamed for being different and longed to fit in, I now felt proud to be set apart as one of Jehovah's chosen few. Where I used to feel like a child under my father's ridicule, I was now treated seriously as an adult. Where I used to feel a lack of focus and ability, I now discovered a talent for preaching and speaking to people's hearts. And where I used to be afraid and uncertain about the future, like other Witnesses I now looked forward to the coming Apocalypse within a few short years.

Although there were a few Witnesses in our congregation around my age, most were older, rather stodgy individuals. Nonetheless, I found them to be very kindly people who showered me with a great deal of love and affection. I now know that love bombing is a common technique of cult-like groups and organizations, but at the time the attention was like a soothing balm to my bruised ego.

I was able to avoid questioning Witness doctrine at first, as being a dedicated Jehovah's Witness didn't leave much time for idle thought. In addition to attending Kingdom Hall meetings three times a week and reading the Society's numerous publications, we were required to devote a certain number of hours a month to public evangelism. Although I was initially reluctant to undertake the required door-to-door preaching, and disliked rejection and the confrontation it often involved, I soon found that it brought out sociability and a gift for the gab I didn't know I had, as well as a genuine desire to teach and help others. This preaching and teaching activity did much to raise my self-esteem and confidence, and also earned me the respect and approval of my fellow Witnesses.

However, this newfound confidence inevitably seeped into my secular life as well, to the detriment of my religious vows. Though taught to shun the outside world, I soon began to develop interests and relationships that were in direct opposition to my life as one of Jehovah's Witnesses.

I had a burning desire to understand the human psyche (my own in particular), and spent many hours in the school library reading the works of Freud and Jung. It was there that I met Victor Colonval in the fall of 1964. He was an older student who had done a stint in the Navy and had then returned to school to finish his diploma. Very intelligent and strikingly handsome, he had a sophistication and knowledge of life that I envied. Of French Canadian and Métis background, he had spurned his traditional Roman Catholic upbringing in favor of agnosticism and a kind of bohemian self-education. He had a bold, almost arrogant confidence in himself that I lacked and admired, and had a grand aspiration to be a writer. With his daring wit and facility with words, I never doubted that he would achieve that goal.

Victor knew that I was a Jehovah's Witness, but rarely mentioned it. I think he saw potential in me and thought of himself as my mentor. He encouraged me to be less passive in life and dismissed my interest in psychology, telling me it was necessary to read great literature in order to understand human behavior. When he lent me his well-worn copy of Hemingway's *A Moveable Feast*, I was instantly hooked by the book's clear, masculine style, and sometimes startling imagery. With Victor's encouragement, I went on to devour the work of other writers of the lost generation, and then the Russians: Dostoevsky, Tolstoy, Turgenev, and Chekhov.

My other worldly friend was Richard Pochinko, a charming and talented young man heavily involved with the school's drama and social committees, whose aspiration was to be an actor. When I introduced him to Victor, the three of us became fast friends, sharing a passion for books, jazz, films, and lively conversation. When I was with them, I felt very sophisticated and my life as one of Jehovah's Witnesses seemed far away.

Like any other adolescent, I also began to develop a keen interest in girls and sex. But although I had dated a number of young women (both Witnesses and non-Witnesses), I did not have a steady girlfriend until I was seventeen. Deeply affected by Witness teachings about the sin of premartial sex and fraternization with non-Witnesses, I jumped from girl to girl in an effort to avoid temptation, and as a result earned a reputation for being a flirt.

However, that changed when I met Bev Robson, a pretty red-haired girl of Irish-Canadian background, with a strong, fiery personality and an independent mind. An avid reader of Ayn Rand and a passionate feminist before her time, she was hardly the right kind of girl for a good Jehovah's Witness boy to be associated with, but I was drawn to her intelligence and liveliness, and we soon became a steady item.

Despite the improvement in my social life, however, I continued to experience a great deal of conflict and confusion. My life was now firmly divided: on one side I played the part of a devoted Jehovah's Witness who regularly attended Kingdom Hall meetings and preached the Word of God; on the other I was becoming an increasingly sophisticated teenager, intensely curious about the world. The longer I maintained this double life, the more anxious and confused I became. When I was with my fellow Witnesses, I felt wracked with guilt for my sinful lifestyle and dishonesty, and when with my school friends, I was ashamed of my religious affiliation and scornful of its teachings.

My anxiety and ambivalence often caused me to behave capriciously. After Bev and I had been going out for several months, I suddenly broke it off and began dating her cousin Sandra Ingram, a beautiful, intelligent, artistic girl with a perfect oval face and bright blue eyes. Her background could not have been more different from mine—her parents were well-off, conservative WASPs—and I knew the relationship could never work, but nonetheless I fell desperately in love with her.

Sandra and I went steady for several months. But even though we shared a lot of interests and enjoyed going to jazz clubs together, I remained anxious about the class difference between us. I kept waiting for her (or her family) to tell me that I wasn't good enough. And although we often made out, I was still deeply afraid of sex and had even started to question my sexual orientation. Perhaps to compensate, I started to flirt with other girls, even though I was supposed to be going steady with Sandra. Then, instead of spending the Christmas holidays with Sandra, I decided to take a trip to New Orleans with my friend Lyle, an older Witness friend who had a flashy car and also led a bit of a double life.

When I came back from our fun-filled trip to New Orleans, my life seemed to spin out of control. One day I made the mistake of making a pass at one of Sandra's girlfriends, and as a result she broke off our relationship. I was devastated, deeply ashamed and confused by my own behavior. Then I found out that my two best friends, Victor and Richard, had taken off to Toronto together without even saying goodbye. I felt both betrayed and hurt that they hadn't invited me to come with them.

Meanwhile, I was also failing most of my classes. I had always been a bright student, and did well in school before becoming one of Jehovah's Witnesses. My father, who had secretly wanted a higher education for himself—but lacked the means to do so—had often helped me with my homework and encouraged me to pursue a university education. However, Jehovah's Witnesses strongly discouraged higher education as a source of temptation and distraction. As a result of that influence, as well as the many Witness and non-Witness extracurricular activities in my life, I lost interest in my studies and became an academic underachiever.

After these events, I felt completely alone and adrift. I couldn't pretend to be a devout Jehovah's Witness anymore, but I was also afraid to try my wings in the real world, alone, without family or friends. And there was the nagging thought: what if the Witnesses were right? What if the end was so near that I would never grow old? What if, failing to conform to their program, I was damned to eternal darkness?

Between January and August of 1965, I fell into a deep depression and began to experience bizarre physical symptoms: frequent headaches, low-grade fevers, pain in my face and neck, swollen lymph nodes. Eventually, I was placed in a hospital isolation ward for two months. At first, the doctors thought I might have Hodgkin's disease, but all of the tests came back negative and the symptoms gradually began to subside. Finally, towards the end of summer, a surgeon came into my room and told me there was nothing physically wrong with me: "Get out of this hospital bed and do some living, son." It was the worst news he could have given me, because at that point, living was the last thing I wanted to do.

I did not return to school that fall, which made my father very angry. He had always wanted a better education for himself, and felt that I was squandering my opportunities. As time went on and he realized he could not persuade me to return, he then pressured me to settle down and take over the family grain farm. But, like many young men of my generation, I wasn't interested in being a farmer. I was nineteen years old, feeling restless and adventuresome, and still believed that my future involved a religious vocation of some kind.

I helped my father with the harvest that fall, for which I was paid $65. Then, without telling my parents, I used the money to buy a one-way bus ticket to Vancouver. I sent them a greeting card about a week later to let them know I was staying with my Aunt Doris and Uncle Jim Walchuk (my mother's non-Witness brother) and working in a furniture factory.

I was deeply confused about my spiritual life. I continued to attend Witness meetings in Vancouver, and made a number of new friends there, but deep down I knew that my spiritual yearnings could never be expressed and satisfied through an organization like the Jehovah's Witnesses. I also had enough knowledge of psychology to know that my recent bout with illness was rooted in deep inner conflict. As a result, I sought out the help of a hypnotherapist, whose sessions helped calm my fears and bring me to a more peaceful place. The therapist also introduced me to the writings of former Christian Scientist, Joel S. Goldsmith, a faith healer and mystic whose teachings could not have been further from those of Jehovah's Witnesses. I devoured Goldsmith's writings like a starving man; its emphasis on self-trust and an inner knowledge of God made me feel better than I had for a long time, and I experienced a oneness with God that I had not felt since I was a child.

However, because of my family ties with Jehovah's Witnesses, I still had a desire to fit my spirituality into that particular faith, and after a few weeks I began to think of returning home to Manitoba. My therapist warned me that going back home and continuing with the Jehovah's Witnesses was like "a horse running to the burning barn," and urged me to stay in Vancouver until my new sense of self became more stable. Unfortunately, I did not heed his advice.

After returning to Manitoba, I became involved in a serious relationship with a non-Witness girl, Mae Taylor, who I had met previously in high school—only now Mae was a voluptuous, sexy woman of experience. Although a year younger than me, she seemed much older and sophisticated. She worked for the local hardware store in Selkirk and had been living alone in a two-room apartment above a dress shop since her family had moved to Alberta the year before. She liked to wear Western-style clothes, which suited her gorgeous figure, and had a warm, sincere personality.

We were both very lonely, and became sexually involved (my first) soon after we met. I moved in with her the first night we made love, and after that we couldn't get enough of each other. I worked in Winnipeg during the week and returned to her apartment on weekends. My parents and my friend Lyle did not let on that they knew anything about this arrangement, so they were not obligated to inform the Witness elders of my sinful lifestyle. In fact, Mae and I frequently spent weekends at my parents' farm during the summer of 1966, where I would sneak into Mae's room at night to make love.

Soon I began to think about marriage. My mother was extremely fond of Mae, and they were alike in many ways. To test the waters, I took her to a Witness meeting at the Kingdom Hall in Selkirk, where she was treated very hospitably by one of the prominent elders. She seemed to feel at home there, and with her natural love of traditional family life, I began to think that she would make a good Witness wife. Mae had told me how badly she wanted to have children, and would hide my condoms under the bed in an effort to get pregnant. Not surprisingly, one day she announced that she had missed two periods in a row.

I pretended to be happy about the pregnancy, but was actually extremely distressed. I knew that I was not ready to be a father, but could see no way out of the situation, so I proposed marriage and she accepted. When Mae's period arrived a couple of weeks later, I could not hide my relief. Our relationship ended badly when I told her I was not ready for marriage, and did not want to follow through on our plans. Deeply hurt, she left to join her parents in Alberta, where I heard she later married and had several children.

I missed Mae terribly after she left and knew I had let her down badly. Feeling like a hopeless failure, I immediately got involved with a troubled Witness girl named Tracy, who had been flirting with me for several months. Tracy had extremely strict and repressive Witness parents and was desperately looking for a husband as a means of escape. We had a brief and confused sexual relationship (her first), after which she became very clinging. The relationship frightened me, and I soon left Manitoba to take a short-term job with a newspaper in Kamloops, British Columbia.

After my departure, Tracy's life spun out of control. In the few months I was gone, she had a string of sexual relationships and contacted VD. When her parents found out, she was brought before the Witness elders, who told her she must either confess her sins and recommit herself to Jehovah or be disfellowshipped. Deeply repentant and frightened, she told them the story of her sad decline, which began the night I "seduced" her.

As a result, when I returned from Kamloops in the summer of 1967, I was also called before the Witness elders. My father, who by this time did not agree with many aspects of Witness doctrine and teaching, attempted to defend me against their formal charges of fornication, but my mother was deeply ashamed by the scandal and stayed away. The elders offered me a choice: to confess my sins and recommit myself to Jehovah (in which case I would be placed on probation for a year under the guidance of an elder) or be disfellowshipped, and perhaps eternally damned.

I was between a rock and a hard place. I had sabotaged several relationships with non-Witness women, and had not made much of myself in the world. I was also still deeply ambivalent about Jehovah's Witnesses, and had begun to question much of their doctrine, especially the prophesied Apocalypse of 1975. However, I could not face any more loss and failure in my life. After much soul searching, I convinced myself that my conflicts had been the result of spiritual immaturity, accepted the elders' censure and probation, and made the decision to recommit my life to Jehovah.

In the spring of 1969, I returned to Vancouver as a full-time evangelist, or what the Witnesses call a pioneer. Since my fall from grace, I had worked hard to become a model Jehovah's Witness. All of my friends were Witnesses, I kept myself separate and apart from the world, and I considered secular work to be secondary to my career as a spiritual salesman: preparing talks, conducting home Bible studies, preaching from door-to-door, and selling *Watchtower* publications.

Most importantly, I no longer fraternized with non-Witnesses, especially women. The Witnesses taught that to marry a non-Witness was to be "unevenly yoked with an unbeliever." Any marriage prospects for an earnest and zealous Witness like me could only be found in a pool of like-minded Christian associates.

3

I MET KIM EVANS in the spring of 1972 at the house-moving party of a young Witness friend. I was twenty-five, still single, and looking for a compatible Witness girlfriend. Kim was just eighteen, a recent high school graduate.

When I arrived at my friend's apartment, most of the furniture had already been moved and Kim was sitting on the hardwood floor with her back to the wall. When I was introduced to her, she stood up shyly and awkwardly, her straight, light brown hair framing a pleasant face. Despite her slim, childlike figure, I was struck by her mature voice, intelligent slate-blue eyes, dark brows, and healthy, radiant skin. Though seemingly timid in a folksy way—a style typical of girls then—she had a gentle poise and quiet dignity that suggested deeper waters.

I wanted to approach Kim when the music started and the dancing began, but she kept a silent vigil against the wall, and would not meet my gaze. It was springtime, and the smell of cypress wafted through the open balcony doors. I remember feeling happy and joyful as I danced with other girls at the party, but Kim was always on the periphery of my mind. Later she would say she had been very conscious of me as well.

Kim didn't enter my thoughts for the rest of that spring and summer. I went on to have a relationship with a sixteen-year-old Witness girl named Coleen Pritchard, but that didn't last long. Her father was concerned about her being involved with an older man, and twenty-five years later, I can understand his apprehension. At the time, though, I experienced it as a personal rejection and quickly rushed into another relationship, this time with a Witness girl just two years older than Coleen named Linda Orge. But her father, who was not a dedicated Witness at the time, objected to me also, for reasons other than the age of his daughter and that liaison ended as well.

I started to wonder if there was something wrong with me, whether my tarnished reputation had somehow followed me from Manitoba. By now, I was a dedicated Witness who took his vows very seriously, held a responsible job, and had no alcohol or substance abuse problems, so I couldn't understand why Witness (and non-Witness) parents would object to my dating their daughters.

Kim re-entered my life when my self-esteem was at its lowest. She unexpectedly appeared at a meeting of the Marine Congregation of Jehovah's Witnesses, which I was attending in the summer of 1972. Although it was only our second meeting, she smiled warmly and addressed me in her rich womanly voice like an old friend: "Jim! How are you? Where have you been?" She made me feel like I was the most important person in the room, and I was impressed by her all over again.

She told me about her one-room basement apartment in Burnaby and I told her about my place near Broadway and Granville. As we talked about our summer activities, she confided in me about an ex-suitor from my congregation who had become a pest and wouldn't leave her alone. At that moment, she projected an attractive vulnerable quality, and I felt a sudden desire to rescue and protect her. We exchanged telephone numbers and quickly began a relationship.

After a week of talking on the phone, Kim started to visit me at my apartment. Her visits were quite innocent, as we were both devout Jehovah's Witnesses who believed that premarital sex was a serious sin. Over the next month, most of our time together was spent fulfilling our duties as full-time Witness pioneers, preaching the Witness message from door-to-door, as we both held part-time jobs as well. But we were both lonely for companionship, and looked forward to seeing each other in any context. When not preaching or working, Kim and I often took long walks under the boulevard trees, talking late into the night. When it rained, we would stand huddled together under the broad sheltering boughs of the trees and wait for the rain to subside. Or we would go to the Vancouver Planetarium or a local coffee house—we were both quite poor and couldn't afford much else. We didn't go to bars, nor did we drink much alcohol, but there were times when we would visit the enchanting, vine-covered Sylvia Hotel along English Bay to indulge in B.C. apple ciders.

Kim was unlike anyone I'd met before, and I thoroughly enjoyed being with her. Sometimes she was teasingly competitive and witty, while at other times she was really sweet and thoughtful. She seemed to enjoy my company too.

Still, I was initially uncertain about Kim's feelings towards me. During the first month we were seeing each other, she treated me as no more than a special friend and did not seem to be interested in a romantic relationship. This coolness only deepened my interest, and I longed to explore the deep waters beneath her placid and playful surface. But despite my previous experience with women, I could never seem to get up the courage to kiss her, for I had begun to think of her as the perfect Witness woman, superior to me and a little hard to get. In the end, it was Kim who finally took the initiative. As we waited for her bus to Burnaby one evening, she surprised me with a sudden kiss on the lips. Then she boarded the bus and was whisked away to her home in North Burnaby. I was delighted, of course, but continued to be uncertain about her feelings; though the kiss was affectionate, it lacked the passionate feeling I had come to identify as love.

Late summer turned to autumn and Kim, in high spirits, waded through leaves that had fallen from the bigleaf maples and horse chestnut trees. She fell spontaneously into a pile of leaves, covering herself with them and laughed. Leaves were fun and there were millions of them on the boulevards.

The people of the Marine Congregation of Jehovah's Witnesses were rather stodgy for an unmarried couple as young as we. To them, we must have seemed like children, sweet and earnest but not very wise. Still, we got a kick out of visiting the "old folks" from time to time. After awhile, age difference didn't seem to matter, though some of our friends were in their late seventies and eighties.

One evening that fall, we walked to an elder's home near Kitsilano Beach Park, along the oceanfront. The homes were older, solid, and respectable. We knocked on a side door and a small, hospitable woman with a surprisingly deep voice and playful eyes greeted us. She offered a seat on the sofa by a darkened window. Night had fallen early. A very tall and lean man entered the room, a little unsteady on his feet. Kim had said she'd known him since she was a little girl in the Marine Congregation, back in the days when her mother was separated from her father and single. Kim liked the man and he adored her like a granddaughter.

The woman of the house brought tea, sat down, and looked at us appreciatively. Kim bantered with the old gentleman teasingly, something she liked to do with men. He had a certain befuddled charm and retained quite an eye for the ladies. As I watched the two of them, I noticed how stunning Kim was. She was enjoying herself immensely and conveyed an engaging, warm personality. She glowed in the lamplight. Her light brown hair was pinned into a French twist that showed off her long, elegant neck, making her appear more sophisticated than she really was. It struck me that I had never before seen a woman look more gracious and sound more intelligent.

Over the next month, Kim began to open up and reveal more about herself. She explained that she was a second-generation Jehovah's Witness, rather than a convert to the faith, and had never known any other life. She also revealed that her parents had divorced when she was quite young and that her mother, Jackie, had later remarried. At the time, I sympathized with how ashamed she must have felt about this, for Jehovah's Witnesses do not permit remarriage except in the case of adultery. That meant that her father must have been unfaithful, a fact that would have been common knowledge to the congregation in order for her mother to be allowed to divorce and remarry and still remain a member of the fold.

I did not learn the full story until much later. Her parents' divorce did not, in fact, involve adultery, and it was not until her mother later married her current husband, Norman Cole, that the family became a source of gossip. For a period of months, they were openly shunned by the congregation, for Jackie was considered to have unlawfully left her marriage and to be living in sin with another man. Although she was eventually exonerated by a prominent elder of the congregation, James Cameron, a cloud of shame hung over the family for most of Kim's childhood.

One evening, after a typical Vancouver rain in November, we took a walk to a restaurant located in the H.R. MacMillan Planetarium, where we had supper together. I didn't own a car or have to maintain a house, so costs were low, and I was able to save for small luxuries and outings from money earned as a janitor at two ladies' dress shops on South Granville Street.

As we approached the planetarium, we saw the Zodiac/Cancer fountain out in front which reminded me of a crab nebula, glistening with water. The décor inside the building was of glass and metal, the atmosphere grand and futuristic.

After we had dined on our salmon dinner, topped off with a cheesecake desert that Kim said was to die for, we looked out over the Vancouver skyline. City lights were reflected in the inky darkness of English Bay. She spoke glowingly of how she had helped her mother raise her little half-brother Reeve and half-sister Cindy, children from her mother's second marriage who were at least ten years younger than she. There had been happy times and difficult ones. She described her little brother as being hyper. He had accidentally put his arm through a window and cut his elbow badly. Her mother had panicked while Kim had forced herself to remain calm in order to staunch the flow of blood—something very important among Jehovah's Witnesses because of their abhorrence of blood transfusions. I was impressed. She seemed so sensible for her age. It was evident, too, that she loved caring for children. How, I asked myself, could a woman barely nineteen have such deep maternal feelings? The thought of having children had not crossed my mind before, not seriously. Now, listening to Kim, I began toying with the idea of having children with *her*. It surprised me. Ordinarily, such a thought would have driven me in the opposite direction. But now, I began to think of Kim as the ideal Witness wife.

Although Kim's father, Ken Evans, actively participated in her life after the divorce, and the scandal of her mother's remarriage eventually faded, I didn't realize how traumatic these events were for Kim. Despite my initial impression of her as a poised, mature, and self-confident young woman, I would later discover a quite different Kim, a childlike girl who was deeply insecure and, as a result, extremely rigid in her attitude and prone to unexpected outbursts of anger.

Every week, several young Witness men, all young and single, would come to my apartment to study our official magazine, *The Watchtower*, in preparation for the regular Sunday meeting. After a time, Kim began to attend those informal sessions also. She said she preferred the company of men, and she liked my friends. We were birds of a feather. We eventually started talking about 1975, the year that Witness leaders and publications were proclaiming as the end of the world as we knew it. In that year, Jehovah's Witnesses expected the current political, religious, financial, and social orders to be destroyed and replaced by Christ's Kingdom, which would reign for a thousand years. We believed that we were engaged in an evangelical harvest of grand proportions. Like all young Witnesses, we talked about these coming events with great excitement and did not notice when Kim quietly left the room.

Suddenly, our discussion was interrupted by a great clattering in the kitchen. Without warning, Kim stormed into the living room to complain that I had allowed some oysters to go bad and that they were stinking up the whole apartment. Before I had a chance to respond, she stomped back into the kitchen and proceeded to clean the refrigerator with a great deal of noise and complaint—which quickly ended the meeting in my apartment. I had not seen this side of her before and was deeply embarrassed by her behavior in front of my friends. Though she later apologized for the outburst, it was a disturbing incident—and not an isolated one.

Around the same time, my parents came to visit me in Vancouver. I was naturally anxious to introduce them to Kim, and really looked forward to the occasion. To my great disappointment, Kim seemed to take an immediate dislike to my father; she was very cool towards him the entire time, and later ridiculed his peasant appearance. At first I blamed myself for having prejudiced her against him, as I had talked extensively about the many conflicts between us over the years, as well as the degree to which my father questioned Witness doctrine. However, I couldn't help feeling that Kim simply considered him rough and uncouth.

Nonetheless, Kim and I continued to see each other. After knowing her just a few months, I began to seriously think of marriage. In an attempt to get her to reveal her feelings for me, I phoned her one night and lightly posed a question: "How does anyone know if they're marrying the right person?" To my surprise, she answered my question with great seriousness, basically repeating the Witness party line on the subject. She asserted that she did not believe in romantic love; compatibility and a mutual purpose were the only important considerations when choosing a spouse. Love would come later as a natural byproduct of shared experience.

Although I was initially taken aback by her bluntness, her response seemed so sensible that I momentarily forgot how unrealistic it was in light of everything I knew about relationships. I also did not stop to consider the implications of her non-romantic view of marriage. I simply assumed that Kim was trying very hard to follow the strict, Victorian ideas of love, sex, and marriage that she had been taught as one of Jehovah's Witnesses, and wanted to avoid making the same mistakes as her mother. Witness elders considered young men and women too immature to make marriage decisions for themselves, and touted the superiority of arranged marriages. I concluded that Kim was keeping a lid on her feelings for me until we were husband and wife, and consoled myself that if we were to wed, at least it wouldn't be by arrangement.

A few days after that conversation, Kim and I took an evening walk not far from my apartment. It was time to pop the question. But I hesitated, so nervous and unsure of how she would respond. After I asked her to marry me, we kept walking in silence down the empty sidewalk for several minutes. It had just finished raining. The only sound was of water dripping from the trees above. She carried a black umbrella; it was closed and she held it suspended like a walking stick. If she wasn't going to speak soon, I thought I would die. Finally, she stopped in her tracks and turned to me. With touching sincerity and plainness she said, "Yes, I'll marry you, Jim." In those few minutes of silence leading up to her acceptance of my marriage proposal, the world had stood still. She must have considered all of the ramifications and come up with a logical decision.

I thought I would feel overjoyed, but instead I felt only relieved. After returning to my apartment, we sat on the sofa and listened to an old-fashioned Andy Williams record. She looked at me soulfully, trustingly, and smiled. She told me how happy she was—yet something was wrong. I felt odd in that old, wallpapered room and went to open a kitchen window; the air was stifling and humid. Was this the way it was supposed to be, I wondered? Something was missing. I was only vaguely aware of how little I knew Kim. I tried to push these

21

qualms away, but the events of the following week did nothing to calm my unease.

A couple of days later, Kim and her girlfriend Darlene were spending an afternoon at my apartment while I attended a private meeting at the Kingdom Hall a few blocks away. When I returned, I could see that Kim had been crying, but neither she nor Darlene would tell me why. I was very concerned and insisted on knowing what was wrong. After a few awkward moments, Kim finally blurted out, "Jim, I know I'll ruin your life if I marry you." I was shocked, but dismissed her outburst as temporary cold feet. As the presumably more mature person in the relationship, I tried to ease her fears, and later we were both able to laugh and make light of the incident.

The next day, I decided to take Kim to my workplace and show her around. As a part-time janitor at Chapman's Ladies Wear on South Granville Street, I had access to the building when it was closed, and we were the only ones there. Feeling like naughty children, we made ourselves at home on the plush, maroon carpet where the floor level was split by a single stairway. It was a rich, sensual atmosphere, with expensive and colorful garments hanging all around us in the half-light and a hint of perfume in the air. I pointed out to Kim that some of the garments were quite sheer, and, feeling amorous, turned to kiss her. It seemed like a perfectly natural thing for an engaged couple to do, but soon after I began to caress her, Kim stopped me, recoiling from my advances. "No," she said, "this is wrong. We shouldn't be doing this here."

At first I thought she meant that the owner might object if he saw one of his employees making out in his dress shop, but then I realized how seriously Kim took the Jehovah's Witness rules about dating and courtship. Not only did those rules forbid premarital sex, they also strongly discouraged physical contact of any kind. While I understood Kim's desire to be good, her behavior puzzled me, as I had never known any other Witness woman to follow the Society's beliefs so strictly. I respected Kim's desire to remain a virgin until marriage, but I wanted us to be in love and to act like we were in love. Sometimes her agreeing to marry me seemed more like a logical business decision on her part. Nonetheless, I pushed these doubts to the back of my mind and reasoned that Kim was saving her passion for our wedding night. I didn't have the sense to realize that, in a romantic sense, if there were no clouds it wasn't going to rain.

The next evening, Kim told me that she had finally got up the courage to tell her parents about our engagement. We were having a meal at the Black Cat Café, just down the street from my apartment. When I asked how her parents had responded, she became visibly upset. Apparently, both Ken and Jackie (who usually didn't agree on anything) had reacted very badly to the news of our engagement. They told her we had not known each other long enough and should take more time before marrying. As Kim's eyes began to brim with tears, it occurred to me that she seemed more childlike every day.

However, instead of consoling her, I merely felt annoyed. I had worked hard all day and had looked forward to a pleasant dinner with my fiancée. And now this! To my surprise, Kim suddenly seemed to gain emotional strength and asserted that we should marry regardless of the wishes of her family. She had just turned nineteen (on October 20), she declared, which in British Columbia was old enough to marry without parental consent. I felt encouraged by her spunk, and began to think that her feelings for me might run deeper than her previous behavior suggested.

A few days later, Kim told me that her parents were becoming increasingly hostile towards me and the idea of our marriage, and were pressuring her to break off the engagement. She reported that her father, whom I had met only once, considered me "a bum who wouldn't amount to anything." For her part, Kim's mother, who had never met me, referred to me alternatively as a "Don Juan type" and "dull." Kim also reported that some members of her congregation in North Burnaby had spoken negatively about me, no doubt having heard of my earlier censure in Manitoba. I was very surprised and taken aback by Kim's parents' intense opposition to our marriage, and very hurt that Christian brothers and sisters whom I hardly knew could be so critical.

But I was determined not to allow this relationship to be derailed like the others. I asked Kim's mother if I could pay her a visit, to demonstrate to her that I was a responsible and respectable person who cared about her daughter. There were two things that surprised me about Jackie. First, her voice on the telephone sounded remarkably like Kim's. Secondly, she invited me to come to Burnaby the next afternoon—something I hadn't expected. When she met me at the door, I realized that I had met Jackie a few years before, at a Witness event in Kitsilano. Her attractive appearance and kindness towards me had made a lasting impression. This was different, though: I was now asking for her daughter's hand in marriage.

The first thing she said was, "Jim, this engagement between you and Kim is too sudden!" Until then, I hadn't realized how truly concerned Jackie was, as a parent, and I, too, began to wonder if we were moving too fast. During the rest of my visit, Jackie talked to me very frankly about Kim. She told me I didn't realize how young and immature Kim was, and what a problem she had been as a teenager. Kim was often moody, sleeping in until all hours of the day and, as a result, missed meetings at the Kingdom Hall and almost failed to graduate high school. Moreover, she was not ready to be a wife, as she had not mastered basic domestic skills like housekeeping and cooking. Jackie also referred to Kim's frequent tantrums and the fact that she was not liked by many of her Christian brethren. She questioned why a twenty-six year old man like me would be attracted to such a young and immature girl.

Jackie's bluntness made my heart sink; much of what she said had finally made sense to me. But I put on a brave face and told her that I was determined to stick with Kim, despite her faults. Surprised by my response, Jackie studied me hard until she was sure I meant it, then leaned back in her chair and spoke seriously: "Jim, Jehovah always disciplines the ones He loves. If you marry Kim, He may see fit to do that through you." Her words shocked me—and would later come back to haunt me—but I stood my ground and reiterated that Kim and I intended to follow through on our marriage plans.

After that, Kim began to change. To begin with, she was impressed with the way I had confronted her mother. To her, I had navigated a difficult passage that had threatened to wreak havoc on our relationship, and she told me so. Although she still worried that something untoward might happen to us, she was becoming more confident. She bought me a poster of a kitten hanging on a horizontal pole by its front paws, with a look of panic on its face. On the bottom of the poster was a caption that read: "Hang in there, Babe."

Kim was also showing more outward affection for me. On one occasion, she brought me some soup and sat with me while I was sick with a cold. When she wasn't with me, I was heartsick.

About a week after my visit with Jackie, Kim told me that her mother's attitude towards me had begun to change. Indeed, Jackie had been impressed by my courage in confronting her and was more willing to accept our engagement, albeit reluctantly. However, there was still one more hurdle to overcome: Kim's father, Ken Evans.

A devout Jehovah's Witness at the time, Ken was also a coldly rational, hard-headed businessman. When Kim and I visited him to discuss his opposition to our engagement, he remained very calm and controlled but made it clear that he intended to dissuade us. Like Jackie, Ken questioned my interest in her and said that, although Kim at times acted and sounded mature, she lacked experience. He then asked frankly why we were in such a hurry to get married. Unable to answer that question, even to myself, I told him that if we married before the end of the year, I would be able to claim Kim as an income tax dependent. Remaining unconvinced, Ken offered to pay me the cash difference if we postponed the wedding, then insisted that we take a marriage compatibility test he had devised. Ironically, the test results indicated that Kim and I were a perfect match, and we left his house with an even greater sense of resolve. In fact, we felt elated that we had bested Ken, and congratulated one another, especially on having passed his homemade marriage test.

It wasn't long after our visit with Ken that Kim asked the question that must have been bothering her for at least as long as her parents had been comparing my worldliness with her innocence. Kim asked, quite timidly—uncharacteristically for her—if I was still a virgin, while her own virginity was without question. I had sensed that she would ask this question, sooner or later, because it probably had been asked by others. Without hesitating, I replied that I had had relations with another young Witness woman, but that the relationship had ended years before. I added that I had been put on probation because of it and had resolved to serve Jehovah. I detected some hurt in Kim's eyes, and sympathized with her need for exclusivity and purity. But she soon recovered and accepted me, tarnished but still desirable somehow, and the subject was never mentioned again.

I couldn't wait for our wedding day, and grew anxious that Kim might reject me at the last minute. Every night I waited for her phone call, and then would talk with her for hours. After our conversations, I would usually feel lonely and isolated, and would often lay awake most of the night, listening to the sounds of winter outside my window: the steady pelting of rain, the swish of cars on wet pavement on Broadway, and the deep base notes from the foghorn across the harbor. Confused and alienated, I longed to have Kim by my side always, to drive the blues away.

A few days before our wedding, I noticed a girl approaching my apartment as I walked down Broadway. She didn't look at me. Her clothes and hair were unkempt and she loped gracelessly down the street with a bag of dry cleaning slung over her shoulder. It was not until she was almost at my apartment building door that I realized the girl was Kim. In that moment, I realized that I did not know her at all. I realized I was making a terrible mistake.

Another rock and a hard place: not only could I not face the shame of yet another failed relationship, but an engagement between two Jehovah's Witnesses was considered a serious, binding agreement. If I were to break that agreement, I would once again be subject to stern congregational discipline. That meant that I would be removed as a Witness pioneer, shunned, and possibly even disfellowshipped. Though I could feel the parameters of my life shrinking dangerously tight, I believed I had no choice but to continue down its narrow tunnel.

JAMES KOSTELNIUK AND KIM EVANS were married on a cold rainy day in late January 1973, in a plain and poorly heated Kingdom Hall. The elder who solemnized the marriage conducted the usual Witness ceremony, with its special emphasis on the bride's obligation to be "an obedient, Christian wife," while the bride and groom stood, nervous and unsmiling, before the congregation. It was supposed to be the happiest day of their lives, but as they took their vows, they saw only fear in each other's eyes.

After the wedding, the guests attended a modest reception at an equally modest hotel on East Hastings Street in North Burnaby. The groom's father was not in attendance because he felt unwelcome by the bride. The bride's family snubbed the groom's mother and sister, causing tears and recriminations, and the bride refused to cut the wedding cake. After the reception, the couple returned to their apartment, where they shared a bed for the first time. Unable to consummate their marriage, afterwards they tried to reassure one another.

It was the beginning of their married life together.

4

TWO DAYS AFTER OUR WEDDING, we rented a car, a red Maverick, for our honeymoon trip to Lincoln City, Oregon, a day's drive away. When we reached Portland, the sky was overcast. Traffic sped over tiered freeways that looked grimy and alien. Night fell and we rushed on to the Pacific coast. Approaching the ocean, the road sloped and we entered a deep fog. Roberta Flack's angel-in-the-night voice chanted *"Killing Me Softly with His Song"* on the car radio. It became our honeymoon song. Arriving in Lincoln City, we rented a motel on the beach where we could hear the ocean waves roar.

After getting settled, we took a walk along the breakers where some logs and driftwood had been tossed ashore. The mist we had driven through earlier had cleared and Kim looked up at the stars. Then she looked at me and her face was wet with tears of joy. She loved the magnificence of nature and at that moment was grateful to share it with me.

When we returned to our motel room, I tried to ignite some pressed logs in the fireplace, but at first I failed. The humidity permeated everything and the logs were damp. I finally managed to get a flicker going and went to bed.

The king-sized bed we slept in seemed so big that we felt lost in it. I wanted Kim to respond to me with abandon so I could stop worrying and forget my feelings of inadequacy. I was in a troubled state of mind when I finally drifted off to sleep.

In the middle of the night, I was awakened by the rhythmic sound of the sea. I felt as though we were immersed in the heart of the primordial ocean; it was the most erotic, floating, and dreamlike sensation I had ever felt. Kim stirred in her sleep and I put my arms around her. She came around, passive but willing. We had finally begun to relax and act naturally.

The following morning, Kim dressed in a long, turquoise-colored housecoat with gold trim and watched the breakers roll in from our front window. She loved the marine hues of aqua-blue and green. Like a true British Columbian, water was her element. She spent the rest of the morning putting recipes on file cards. Apparently, she was serious about becoming a homemaker.

That day, we drove south along the Oregon coast. The evergreens along the cliffs were bent back in unnatural contortions by the wind. Beyond the trees, the view of the ocean was breathtaking. When we got to Newport, we went to an indoor swimming pool where Kim showed me what a skilled swimmer she was.

During the six days of our honeymoon, both Kim and I began to relax even more with one another. On a visit to a sauna one day, she disrobed unselfconsciously. She was a tall, sculptured beauty with long, graceful limbs.

I now realize what was happening during those few days of our honeymoon. For the first time in months, Kim and I were out from under the terrible stress of the lives we were living. We had been burning the candle at both ends. We had kept up our pioneer evangelism while we conducted five or six home Bible studies per week with prospective converts. I had been working both day and night, spending every spare moment courting Kim and working through the complications of dealing with her judgmental family. As for Kim, she was no better off. She had kept up her pioneering as well, had worked part-time at a Willson's Stationary Store, and was under as much emotional strain, if not more, than I was over our marriage plans.

To a certain extent, we were victims of our own religious zeal, and it was that zeal which was causing so much stress. Nonetheless, I have a feeling of bitterness towards the Watch Tower Society over what had happened to us prior to our wedding and in the years that followed. What is central to the belief system and day-to-day routine of Jehovah's Witnesses is their preaching work. Since the 1920s, the Society has virtually dragooned every Witness—young and old, male and female—into a proselytizing work of major proportions. To accomplish this work, the Society has demanded great sacrifices on the part of loyal Witnesses, particularly young, single men and women. Rather than encouraging them to learn anything more than basic occupational skills in high school or take further studies at university, the Society has held that they should become self-supporting pioneer evangelists at seventeen or eighteen years of age.

In other words, we existed in a highly legalistic system which paid practically no attention to our personal needs. We were like troops attacking an enemy beachhead, the first to be sacrificed in a spiritual battle for the minds and souls of men and women. Unfortunately, our commanders—the Brooklyn leaders of the Watch Tower Society—showed little interest in how we might be wounded or even destroyed spiritually.

After our brief honeymoon, Kim and I returned to our spiritual battleground in Vancouver while we tried learning to live together as man and wife. We resumed our duties as pioneers while we acted as residential caretakers of our apartment block. In addition, we worked together as nighttime janitors. In a few weeks, we were exhausted.

In spite of that, we kept up the steady grind. We were so devoted to Jehovah that we prayed for strength every night at bedtime, holding hands. Rather, *I* prayed for both of us. Women were rarely allowed to pray aloud in the presence of a dedicated male Witness.

One day that spring, Kim and I walked to Kitsilano Beach. It was one of those mornings that sparkled after a wind had driven the clouds farther inland, a day to appreciate life and expect better things to come. We sat on the lush grass and looked out to sea where the rust-colored freighter ships were anchored in the harbor. Bright sails of smaller craft danced on the water. Yet, I didn't feel right with the world. I looked over at Kim. I know it's an old cliché, but she was so obviously young and beautiful. And she was *willing*. Yet, at that moment, it struck me that I had married the wrong woman. Remembering what Kim had said about romantic love before I had proposed to her, that she didn't believe in it, that love would come later as a natural byproduct of shared experience, didn't inspire much confidence in me then. I wanted to save my marriage, although I didn't have the foggiest idea how to do so. Love was a powerful mystery far greater in strength than my will, much to my distress.

It wasn't long before another problem cropped up. Kim was dissatisfied with the Marine Congregation; it was a reminder of her unhappy past when she and her mother had attended there. Childhood ghosts haunted the place. James Cameron, the powerful elder who had helped Kim's mother over some personal difficulties, had died the year before, and Kim found no one else to turn to as a spiritual father figure. With contempt, she referred to the entire congregation, and the elders in particular, as deadwood, meaning that they were spiritually impotent—unable to inspire or convert anyone. She became so frustrated that during one meeting she strode to the back of the Kingdom Hall where she stood like a judge, arms folded across her chest with a look of scorn on her face. Her disgust was so obvious that after the meeting one of the elders approached me and asked if there was something wrong with my wife, suggesting that she was not showing proper subjection to male headship. I refused to talk about it. I understood Kim's frustration, and didn't want the elders meddling in my personal affairs.

Kim and I were married for almost six years, most of them not very happy. We tried hard to make the marriage work, but our relationship rested on a shaky foundation.

At home, Kim was to prove a very practical household manager and eventually an excellent mother to our children. I more than fulfilled my duties as a breadwinner and provider, but was to fall far short of Kim's image of the ideal Witness husband. According to Witness doctrine, the man of the family is to be its spiritual head, guiding its members along the straight and narrow and keeping them faithful to Jehovah. Instead of providing the stabilizing influence Kim craved in her life, I eventually began to express deep dissatisfaction and doubt about the Jehovah's Witness faith, and threatened to draw her and our children further and further away from what she saw as its safety. Looking back, I realize that Kim had every reason to feel I had misrepresented myself to her.

On the other hand, my naïve and unfounded hope for a passionate relationship with Kim quickly evaporated. With the exception of the times she wished to conceive, Kim's interest or pleasure in our sexual relations was half-hearted. She made it clear that she was only participating in lovemaking to accommodate my needs and because it was her duty as a Christian wife. At first I thought her lack of interest was due to inexperience or my failure as a lover. I gradually came to realize that Kim genuinely believed that sex was a necessary evil at best, and a mortal sin at worst.

Her belief was not surprising in view of Witness teachings on the subject, which, even in the 1970s, condemned all but the most unavoidable sex acts, even between married persons. In a December 1972 issue of *The Watchtower*, the Society's leaders asserted that when Jesus taught that divorce could be justified in the case of *porneia* (usually translated as "fornication"), he was not just alluding to sex outside marriage. According to the Society, *porneia* could be interpreted to mean any kind of illicit sex. Therefore, the sin of *porneia* could also occur between husband and wife.

To the embarrassment of many, congregations were given detailed lectures on what was and wasn't allowed in the marriage bed. As a result, many began to regard sex with abhorrence. Witness wives feared that they might unwittingly commit sin during lovemaking, and couples felt the need to detail their sexual intimacies to elders in order to ensure they weren't doing anything wrong. Witness men were often disfellowshipped, and their wives granted divorces for having committed *porneia* with their husbands.

Eventually, it got to the point where elders didn't know how to deal with some of these situations, and after much complaint the Society's leaders suddenly reversed their position in a February 1978 issue of *The Watchtower*, stating that "the Bible does not give any specific rules or limitations as regards the manner in which husband and wife engage in sexual relations." At no point, however, did the organization express remorse or apologize for the many marriages, families, and reputations that were damaged or destroyed by the earlier teaching.

In the early months of our marriage, I tried hard to remain a dedicated Witness pioneer. But in the end, we decided to give up pioneer evangelism in order to concentrate on our married life. This decision was an enormous relief for me, as I had grown weary of door-to-door preaching, day after day for three years, and had begun to question its effectiveness as a means of spreading the word. Our circuit overseer supported our decision to quit the pioneer work and gave us his sympathetic blessing. Nonetheless, Kim was devastated that she could no longer call herself a Witness pioneer.

Looking back, I realize that Kim's entire self-esteem had rested on her achievement of pioneer status in the Witness community. As a youngster, she had a great fondness for animals and had dreamed of becoming a veterinarian; when she graduated from high school, her father offered to send her to veterinary college. However, by that time she had been thoroughly indoctrinated by Jehovah's Witnesses, who strongly discouraged higher education and instead encouraged young people to become full-time pioneer evangelists. These beliefs had affected Kim and she turned her father's offer down, announcing that her goal in life was to serve Jehovah.

When Kim had to acknowledge that she did not have the strength to continue the demanding work of being a Witness pioneer, she felt that she had failed in her chosen career. She was a bright and intelligent young woman, and had developed public speaking skills that she was proud of, but she also belonged to a highly chauvinistic religious organization, and as a woman, had little opportunity to use her talents and abilities effectively. She had sacrificed the opportunity for achievement in the real world, and had then failed to live up to what was expected of her as a Witness pioneer. Within the context of her life as one of Jehovah's Witnesses, all she had to look forward to was being a dutiful wife and mother.

Kim had always been deeply conflicted about her status as a Jehovah's Witness woman—the sex once referred to by a Witness leader as "a hank of hair and a bag of bones." She had a deep and sincere desire to please Jehovah, which meant being a submissive and dutiful Witness wife who bowed to the wisdom of her husband. But she was equally resentful about having to obey male elders who she regarded as her spiritual and intellectual inferiors, and she frequently challenged their authority in subversive ways.

That conflict manifested itself in our marriage. I did not take naturally to being a dominant husband who demanded obedience from his wife, and as a result, Kim would frequently accuse me of being weak. At the same time, she maintained a stubborn, headstrong control over our lives, and would not be opposed once she had made up her mind about something. At times, her defiant attitude translated into a refusal to face the reality of a situation, and any attempt to reason with her would only cause her to dig her heels in further. Friends and family commented on her "cockiness," and expressed the fear that it would get her into trouble some day.

Soon after we stopped pioneering, Kim became depressed in a way I had never seen before. She began to sleep a great deal, stopped going to Kingdom Hall meetings, and lost so much weight that I feared she might be seriously ill. She frequently told me that she felt like "a drowning person about to go down for the third and last time." The degree of her despondency alarmed me, and the temporary relief that I had felt after quitting pioneer work soon turned into a restless anxiety.

One day, I suggested that we move from Vancouver and start a brand new life away from the Marine Congregation. To my great surprise, Kim supported the idea. In July 1973, we packed our bags and took a trip to the Cariboo Plateau, a rugged area of timber, saw mills, and scattered lakes about 350 miles northeast of Vancouver.

In the village of 100 Mile House, south of Williams Lake, I quickly landed a couple of janitorial contracts. Our future, financially, seemed to be heading in the right direction. Kim returned to Vancouver alone to spend two weeks finishing our work there and packing for the return trip. In the meantime, I started working at the newly constructed Cariboo Mall the next day. I found a small, furnished apartment in 100 Mile House and waited for Kim's return. It didn't take long to realize how much I missed her.

Shortly after she arrived at the dusty little bus depot in the village, I saw her sitting on a trunk surrounded by several cardboard boxes. I was excited and happy to see her. She looked back at me with a confident little smile, as if to say: "Yes, you *did* miss me after all, *didn't you.*" We would soon grow close living in a place where we knew so few people, and the move seemed to improve Kim's spirits.

There was a brief heat wave in the Cariboo in mid-July. Autumn followed quickly and the nights grew cold. Winter arrived with a suddenness seldom seen on the coast and dumped generous snow flurries on us. Cloud covered the sky most days and, depending on which way the wind blew, it alternately snowed or melted. Ordinarily, it was a time when Kim felt low—very low. But she surprised me one evening as we crossed an open field on the way to the Cariboo Mall; she was suddenly joyful—invigorated, in fact. Wearing a red toque, a long winter coat, and a blue and white scarf, her rosy cheeks radiated the health that had seemed so lacking before. She spoke to me of love, something rare for her, and cheerfully insisted that all she wanted to do was make me happy.

Later, she spoke optimistically about the future, and before long announced that it was time to do what meant so much to her: have a baby. I protested that we were not ready to have a child, financially or otherwise, but Kim was determined. She threw away her birth control pills and, for the first time in our marriage, actually initiated sexual activity. I started to think we had achieved a sexual breakthrough and didn't struggle against her agenda.

We finally bought our first car, a black 1968 Mercury Cougar with an all white interior. With it, we were able to move sixteen miles southwest of 100 Mile House to a mountain village called Lone Butte. It wasn't much of a place. Our new home was a quaint cottage located in a remote area at the end of a long mountain road, and was meant to be our refuge from the trappings of civilization. The road there climbed in altitude and wound through conifer forest over some of the loneliest country I'd ever seen. I clearly remember my feelings the first time we drove to Lone Butte on a cold, clear winter night. The moon had never been brighter and the stars seemed close enough to touch. I thought of Kim, sitting right beside me, and of our difficulty in connecting emotionally. *Just love her,* I thought, *and everything will be alright.*

I fantasized that Kim and I would finally get to know each other in such a secluded environment and in the first couple of months we did become closer. But that temporary intimacy was soon disrupted by Kim's increasingly unpredictable moods. I never knew what to expect from her from one day to the next. One minute she was sweet and loving, begging me to have patience with her; the next she was coldly critical and complaining. It was an emotional roller coaster that kept our relationship continually off-balance.

Despite this, life in that rustic cottage was quite idyllic for me. I remember getting up on chilly winter mornings to stoke the fire in the woodstove and taking long walks in the nearby woods during my time off. One morning, I stopped beside a ridge of pines to watch a bulldozed slash-fire. I had often passed the area on my way to work, and had wondered why the piles of brush smoldered continuously without being consumed. As I approached to take a closer look, I was amazed to see that the pile of burning slash glowed and radiated under a mound of snow, with a weird, constant glimmer. That unusual image of fire and ice reminded me of Kim, and I wondered if I would ever penetrate her strange nature.

Spring came to the Cariboo Mountains in 1974 and the snow melted quickly. Main roads like Highways 24 and 97 were passable, but the bush roads had turned to slush and logging operations had to be suspended for the annual spring break-up. I continued to work nights in the village of 100 Mile House while Kim stayed at home. She spent most of her free time reading mysteries—novels by Helen MacInnes. At that time, she also read books on natural child birth. By April, Kim announced that she was pregnant.

After spring break-up, the logging roads dried up. We got into our car and drove to see where the roads went. They wound endlessly, crisscrossing the forest like tangled threads. At times, we felt lost and stopped the car to look around. At other times, the roads dead-ended at a lake and we had to turn back.

Because Kim was pregnant, she slept on her side with the windows open in summer. I often slept with my arm around her waist. She would guide my hand to where I could feel new life stirring. Our intimacy, and my sense of wonder, grew.

In June, we traveled in our car to Manitoba to visit my parents on their farm. Heading east along the Trans-Canada Highway beyond the Rocky Mountains, the drive across the prairies became hot and tedious. For long stretches of the journey, Kim rested curled up on the white faux-leather upholstery of the back seat. Hot weather never agreed with her and being five months pregnant didn't make it any easier.

Shortly after we arrived, my father made every effort to put Kim at her ease and erase the memory of their previous meeting, but it was to no avail. She continued to be cool towards him and uncomfortable in his presence. He also made the mistake of expressing misgivings about certain Witness teachings, a blasphemy that Kim could not tolerate. She ended up speaking rather sharply to him on some religious subject, an incident that forever ended the chance of a relationship between them.

We slept upstairs in a small, unfinished and unpainted room that had been mine as a child. That first night, Kim woke me in the midst of a nightmare, the only one I'd known her to experience. While she screamed and gasped, I held on in an effort to wake her. Gradually coming out of the dream, she spoke to me briefly. I asked what terrible thing she had dreamt, but she wouldn't discuss it.

The next morning after breakfast, we sat side by side on a hammock suspended between two large maple trees. Kim stated that she felt an unsavory sense of conflict in my parents' house.

Later that day, we moved to the summerhouse, about a hundred yards from the main house. A shady little cottage, it had screened windows permitting generous air-flow throughout. It was adequately equipped with an ancient wood-burning cook stove, a small GE refrigerator stocked with beer, a radio, a Form-ica table, and a big bed.

One afternoon while Kim was in the garden with my mother, my father visited me while I rested in the summerhouse alone. He had built it from sal-vaged lumber as his retreat from my mother's cluttered world of gardening, houseplants, sewing materials, and television soap operas.

Although for the most part my father was a cheerful man who enjoyed people, he did have regrets. His marriage was anything but picture perfect. He said that after thirty-six years, he still didn't understand my mother. "A woman will make you or break you," he said, repeating the words for emphasis. I knew then that he was talking about someone other than my mother—and it was Kim.

"But dad, she's my wife," I protested.

"I know," he said, softening his tone. "Just remember what I'm telling you, son."

One sunny morning, Kim and I took a walk down the gravel lane in front of my parents' house. Heading south, we followed a tall hedge of golden willows along one side of the road and some poplar thickets descending the bank of Medicine Creek on the other. For a quarter mile I speculated, rather whimsic-ally, on the prospect of moving us back to Manitoba permanently. I felt at home there, close to my aging parents, and thought—quite foolishly in light of every-thing that had taken place over the past two days—that Kim might feel the same way. But when we arrived at the crossroads overlooking an open field, she stepped into the quiet intersection and with one sweeping gesture she laughed and said, "But look at this country. There's nothing to it."

My own son was born three months later at the 100 Mile House Hospital, where I was allowed to stay with Kim and watch the delivery. At first he was just a purple bundle of flesh, a strange appendage of his mother's body. When the doctor removed the mucus from his mouth, he gasped and cried, and became a cooler pink. As a nurse cleaned out his eyes, the little bundle of flesh seemed to look right at me, and at that moment he became a distinct human being. As I gazed into his blue eyes, I felt a depth of love and wonderment beyond description. We named him Juri Michael Kostelniuk, after my father and the first man to orbit the earth, Yuri Gagarin, the Russian cosmonaut.

Kim was overjoyed—the happiest I had ever seen her—and she made light jokes with the hospital staff, not her normal disposition in public.

I drove home alone to Lone Butte. I was cheered in a way I had never felt before. Clearly, having a child was the best life had to offer. Our black and white Malamute Husky pup Nikki was outside the cottage, waiting for me. He looked up curiously—one of his eyes blue, the other brown—with the most benevolent animal intelligence.

It had grown cool inside the cottage, so I lit a fire in the box stove. I fed Nikki and stepped outside. Darkness had fallen. There was a bright scattering of stars. The wind caressed the pines with its ancient murmurings. From inside the cottage, the local radio station played country music. It was the sad sound of a faraway, heartbroken world. That night, however, I was immensely happy. I felt lucky. The feeling of alienation that had persisted for so long had finally lifted.

Kim took naturally to motherhood. She had learned all about child-rearing when she cared for her younger siblings, and now she passed that knowledge on to me. I took an active part in Juri's daily care, changing his diapers, feeding him, and holding him in the crook of my arm while he slept. I experienced the growing bond between us as more than just a feeling—it seemed like an actual physical organ deep in my chest that grew a little larger everyday. Until then, I hadn't known that such powerful emotions existed.

My son's birth awakened other emotions in me, feelings I had not experienced since I was a boy. I began to hike for miles through the many trails near our cottage with Nikki, and again became fascinated with the night sky all over again. I remember that medieval men had viewed the stars in the firmament as windows into heaven, and felt a great longing to know God through the wonder and glory of natural things, and to teach my son that knowledge.

A few months after Juri's birth, Kim again experienced a debilitating depression, one that lasted for weeks. During this depression, she would sleep in long after I left for work, take a nap with Juri in the afternoon, and go to bed soon after I came home. Our rustic cottage was not a very practical place to raise a baby, so in January 1975, we moved to a better-equipped house just northeast of 100 Mile House. It was a great improvement, with indoor plumbing and an oil-burning furnace, and I hoped the move would lift Kim's spirits. Unfortunately, the new house sat at the bottom of a deep gorge along a frozen creek, surrounded by tall snow-covered spruce, and Kim said it made her feel trapped—"like a wild mustang boxed in a canyon."

Though Kim's depression eventually lifted, there would be others, and for the rest of our marriage she would experience tremendous mood swings. She had a lot of free time when I was at work, which she spent looking after Juri and the house, and reading mystery novels. When Kim was down, I had to assume a lot of her domestic duties, which I found exhausting at the end of a long workday. But when Kim was up, I experienced her as a whirlwind of unfocussed energy who constantly complained about my failings as a husband and father. The odd time we were with Witness friends our own age, she would unwind and be truly joyful, talking and laughing hysterically, but there were too few of those in-between times.

Looking back at what Kim's mother had told me about her teenage years and the pattern of her behavior before and after our wedding, I realize now that Kim probably suffered from bipolar disorder—or what used to be called manic-depression, and I wish I had been more understanding. But I was not much healthier myself, psychologically speaking, and at the time she just frustrated and exasperated me. The stress of her changing moods and constant criticism fed my own simmering anger, and I was frequently bad-tempered and impatient with her. Soon Kim and I began to argue and bicker with one another on an almost daily basis.

One morning after a particularly heated argument, Kim suggested that we take "separate vacations" and expressed a desire to visit her mother in Burnaby. I agreed that it might be beneficial for her to get away, and so we arranged for her to take the car and for me to take a few days off from work to look after Juri. After she left, I worried about her safety on the icy mountain roads and even wondered whether she would bother to come back. But looking after Juri soon kept me too occupied to worry, and I felt thankful for the opportunity to spend time alone with my son. While Kim was away, I fed him, changed him, bathed him, and rocked him to sleep. I would frequently check his crib during the night to make sure he was comfortable and breathing normally. During the day, I delighted in his playful responses and the way his eyes lit up in recognition of me.

Kim seemed a different person when she returned from Burnaby. Up to that time, she had let her hair grow long. But while away, she had her hair cut in a very attractive, sophisticated style, and told me that she had had a very "healing" visit with her mother. For a while, she seemed more mature and self-confident. I began to feel hopeful that our difficulties had been a temporary phase and things would soon improve between us.

However, our religious differences began to deepen. In April 1975, I watched the Vietnam War come to a close on the evening news. The war and all of its atrocities had long been repugnant to me, but Jehovah's Witnesses almost seemed to view its ending with disappointment. According to Witness doctrine, war was actually the *hope* of mankind; many believed that its potential for mass destruction would trigger the political and social collapse of the world, signaling Armageddon and the dawn of Christ's Kingdom. Since 1966, the year 1975 had been predicted as the probable date of the end of the world, and Witnesses were disappointed that the world seemed to be moving towards peace instead.

Throughout their history, Jehovah's Witnesses had looked to specific dates—1874, 1910, 1914, 1918, 1925, and others—as being the day of great reckoning. As each date passed without the expected Apocalypse, the Society's leaders would set a new date for the faithful to look forward to. With the ending of the Vietnam War, I started to realize that 1975 was not going to be any different, and I tried to convince Kim how foolish these expectations were. She refused to question or even discuss Witness doctrine with me. Time after time, she turned her back and told me to take whatever questions or doubts I had to the elders, not to her. Because I knew how strongly Kim felt about her faith, I decided to leave Juri's religious education in her hands.

In August 1975, we purchased a house just north of 100 Mile House, in a suburban community referred to as the 108 Mile Recreation Ranch. That autumn, Juri stood in his crib for the first time, clinging to the railing and laughing like a little show-off. Not long after that, he took his first steps and spoke his first words, and soon became a walking, talking, running machine. Though he eventually developed into a quiet and reflective boy, he always had endless energy when it came to spending time with his dad. The highlight of both our days was when I arrived home from work in the afternoon and we could go off together on one of our adventures. We took walks together outside. At first, when he was still quite small, I would carry him past the backyard fence to a pasture where there were rolling hills and bluffs of tall poplar and trembling aspen. Horses grazed there. I used to rest on my back under the trees and watch the magnificent cumulus clouds roll by. Leaves rustled in the wind. Looking over at Juri, singing to himself on a blanket, I realized how truly happy I was.

I tried to involve Kim in our daily outings, but she preferred to stay home curled up with one of her mystery novels. Juri and I would go off to explore the neighborhood and surrounding countryside. We would pass the small fire hall at the end of our street, where the volunteer firemen would sometimes let Juri sit in the old fire truck. Beyond the fire hall was an attractive elementary school that I expected Juri to attend when he was older. Then came the community hall and an outdoor pavilion, where the local kids played basketball in the summer and hockey in the winter. Farther along one of the winding roads was a small church that reminded me of the one I had attended in Clandeboye.

On these walks, Juri and I would smile and wave to the familiar faces of our neighbors, who always greeted us in return. For the first time since my childhood, I felt part of a normal community and was happy that my son would be growing up in such an environment. I felt like a child myself, waking up to a shining, brand-new world. I had become so tired of being aligned with a small, despised minority group and weary of compensating my feelings of isolation with self-righteousness. I realized that I no longer cared whether the Witnesses were right or wrong about the evils of this world. All I knew was that suddenly the world didn't seem so bad. In fact, it was becoming downright appealing.

Kim did not agree, of course, and continued to talk of our need to maintain vigilance as Jehovah's Witnesses. It seemed that the happier and more content I grew in that community, the more critical and suspicious she became of me. Her vacillating moods and escalating criticisms made our home a very unwelcome place, and my hikes with Juri soon became a means of escape. As a result, Kim often felt ignored and abandoned, and began to resent the time that Juri and I spent together. One day, after a particularly pleasurable hike with Juri, I said to her, "You know, all my life I've been lonely, but with Juri I don't feel that way anymore." She looked at me with surprise and hurt in her eyes, and I realized with regret what I had just expressed.

On some days, Juri and I would get in the car and drive around the country-side within the greater development. Sometimes we would drive to a nearby lake used for community swimming and climb a nearby hill just so we could look deep down into the jade-colored water. Other times we went to our special place—a ridge overlooking a crystal lake not far from our house. Often, in the night, we could hear the haunting sounds of loons calling from that lake. I would tell Juri how the area used to be a real ranch, pointing out the stout old cedar tree where ranchers would have tethered their horses. Once Juri asked where the ranchers were now, and I told him they were "long gone, probably dead." I still remember the look of confusion on his face as he looked up at me, pale and uncomprehending, unable to understand the difference between "gone" and "dead."

Next to the cedar tree was a deep gorge. Stones had been piled at its edge years before, presumably to clear the pasture. One day, I decided to show Juri how exciting stones could be and tossed several into the deep ravine, like eggs from an Easter basket. Together we watched clouds of dust rise from the shadows as the stones silently hit the bottom. Juri laughed and shrieked with delight, and was soon heaving heavy rocks into the ravine all by himself.

By the fall of 1976, we learned that Kim was pregnant again. During her pregnancy, I began to discover serious flaws in our new house, and had to spend endless hours attending to repairs. When large snowfalls arrived in November, the melt on our roof poured through the ceiling like rain. Climbing up onto the roof to shovel off the ice and snow, I discovered large patches of rotting wood caused by poor ventilation in the attic. The plumbing under the house froze in winter, and when I squeezed into the crawlspace to investigate, I discovered that the water pipes had not been properly insulated. Worst of all, the septic tank was plugged—which would not be a pleasant situation when the March thaw arrived.

I felt angry that we had bought such a lemon of a house, but that was not the only reason for my increasing irritation. For some reason, the problems with our house made me more and more frustrated with our lives as Jehovah's Witnesses. Why hadn't we put aside savings for repairs like this? Why were we so trusting, living in the moment, waiting passively for Armageddon to arrive? Why hadn't we made plans for the future? Kim's only response to these questions was that Jehovah would always provide, as long as we continued to serve him faithfully. But for some reason, those familiar words no longer reassured me.

Kim and I looked forward to the birth of our new child with great anticipation, and our daughter Lindsay was finally born on April 12, 1977—on my mother's birthday. She was a beautiful baby with the brightest, bluest eyes I'd ever seen, and I fell hopelessly in love with her. Lindsay would come to express her entire personality through those eyes, which were truly windows to her soul.

Juri couldn't wait for his new little sister to come home, but he was also very happy to have me all to himself while Kim and Lindsay were in the hospital. I bought him a new, red and white tricycle on the way home one day to make sure he wouldn't feel left out when Lindsay came home. But to my surprise, he paid no attention to it and instead stayed close to me the entire time, wanting to be involved with everything I did. The memory of those intimate evenings with Juri, reading books and telling him stories, is very dear to me.

We settled into our normal routine after I brought Kim and Lindsay home, but our house problems continued unabated. One day, I started to dig a trench outward from the septic tank, only to discover that the septic pipes mysteriously disappeared a short distance away. I was standing waist high in muck when my neighbor from across the street, Jack French, approached with a look of amusement on his face. "You've got a problem there," he said. "But nothing money won't solve." As usual, he had the ability to make me laugh in the worst of circumstances, and I threw down the shovel to take a coffee break with him.

When I first met Jack, he was like a breath of fresh air. He was a short and stocky man with a huge voice and roaring laugh. Most importantly, he was *not* one of Jehovah's Witnesses. Although his own family was of the Christian Evangelical persuasion, he considered himself an agnostic. I was instantly intrigued by him. It had been so long since I had met a non-believer that I was curious to know why he held the views he did. Jack and I subsequently had many long and interesting discussions about religion. He frequently challenged my beliefs as one of Jehovah's Witnesses, and I welcomed those challenges. As open and frank discussion about faith was simply not tolerated in the Witness community, I was anxious to put my faith, such as it was, to the test. With Jack, I felt engaged in a genuine and unconfrontational spiritual dialogue for the first time.

While Jack didn't exactly convert me to agnostic Darwinism, he did modify many of the rigid religious beliefs that I had been taught and was now beginning to doubt. Jack had spent much of his life as a fisherman off the British Columbia coast, and it was through his experiences and descriptions of natural life that he was able to persuade me that the world was not as static as I had been led to believe. He viewed creation—living beings and their environments—as being constantly in flux, and this idea appealed to me. What most impressed me was that his beliefs stemmed from his own experiences rather than the wordy expressions of religious authorities. In direct opposition to Witness doctrine, Jack taught me that it was not the Truth that mattered, but the ability to think for oneself—something I had not done much of up to that point and knew that I would need to do more of in order to become a mature adult.

On the May long weekend, in the spirit of "taking separate vacations," I took Juri on a special trip to Lytton, a quaint little town in the upper Fraser Canyon where warm winds funnel up from the coast. It's where the Thompson and Fraser rivers meet in a confluence of jade and muddy-colored water. I will never forget the joy we shared during that time as we watched a little ferry crossing the river. We also picked wild asparagus that grew in the sandy hills, and brought it home to Kim. She was there with Lindsay when we arrived—happy to see us again.

Once home, I needed to talk about all the questions and yearnings that were swimming in my mind. While I knew it was useless to talk to Kim about religion, I did talk to her about my job dissatisfaction. I told her that I was bored with cleaning buildings for a living and wanted to do something more rewarding with my life. She reacted to this with alarm, pointing out that I was making a reasonably prosperous living as a janitorial contractor and that it was too much of a risk to change occupations. Besides, a career change would also mean a move, and she was happy where she was.

In that moment I realized that my only value to Kim was as a provider. I also realized that I would have ended our marriage then and there had it not been for Juri and Lindsay. My children were my life, my rudder, and I could not imagine being without them. At the same time, I felt strangely unworthy of them. I often felt that they were with me only by some strange stroke of luck, and began to feel an irrational fear of losing them. A nameless anxiety would draw me to their bedroom in the middle of the night, when I would listen to their breathing, or cover a bare foot with a blanket, as though I needed to reassure myself that they were still there.

In retrospect, my fears were not unfounded. The religious gulf between Kim and I was widening daily and soon became an ocean. More and more Witnesses, people I knew and cared about, were being routinely disfellowshipped from the Society in an attempt to keep the organization "clean." In the mid-1970s, both my father and Kim's father were disfellowshipped, my father for disagreeing with the local elders over an obscure Biblical text, and Ken for (of all things) cigarette smoking. My father was not bothered by this development, as he had long been in disagreement with the Society, but Ken was deeply hurt, and to my knowledge was never reinstated as a Witness.

Then the Society began disfellowshipping Witnesses for even associating with those who had been disfellowshipped or had left the faith of their own free will, a practice that cruelly tore families and friendships apart. Wives could not talk to husbands, and children could not talk to parents. My sister Jeanette, who had become a Witness in 1974, stopped associating with my father, and Kim obediently distanced herself from her own father.

Kim and I argued bitterly over these and other matters, and on a couple of occasions our anger turned potentially violent. I remember Kim and I being on the floor once, with my hands around her neck in a bizarre kind of pantomime, meant to say: "Look how angry you make me." I did not apply any pressure to her neck and she was not hurt in any way, but I was deeply ashamed of the incident and it frightened us both. On another occasion, Kim punched me in the back with her clenched fist as I turned from her in the middle of an argument. Neither of these incidents were repeated, and Kim and I never discussed them afterwards, but they changed our relationship irrevocably.

Summer came and went, and Kim and I got into another argument. I forget what it was about, but it was bad enough that she put her jacket on and left the house without saying where she was going. She didn't close the door, nor did she look back. It was dark outside. She faced the wind and broke a trail through freshly fallen snow.

I sat on the doorstep with the light on, knowing that I shouldn't go after Kim because I would be leaving two sleeping children. I fretted and hoped she wouldn't be too long.

The air thickened with snowfall as I watched and waited. Twenty minutes later, she returned through the darkness and paused for a moment when she saw me, just outside the halo of the porch light. Tentatively, she came forward and sat on the step next to me. She looked hurt and buried her face in her hands in a gesture of utter frustration and futility. I felt sympathy for her and said, "Sorry, I don't know why I say the things I do. I don't know why I act this way." Snow-flakes continued falling like so much confusion, striking our hair, skin, and clothing and seemed to whisper as they touched the ground.

We both continued to hold on for the sake of the children, but my anxiety increased daily. One bright spring morning in April 1978, I was waiting in the car for Kim and the children. It had just stopped raining, and the kids were on the porch as Kim locked the door of the house. Lindsay was a toddler by now, with fair skin and wisps of fine, blonde hair, and Juri was a handsome boy of almost four. As the sun came out from behind the clouds, it reflected the children's blue eyes, and as Kim squinted into the light I thought I could detect a smile. At that moment, the sunlight and rain created a glittering, bleached picture that is etched into my mind forever. Also indelible was the desperate, panicky thought that entered my mind at that moment and remained with me for the rest of the day: as lovely as they were, I knew I was going to lose them.

A few months later, Kim asserted that I didn't love her anymore, and accused me of having an affair with another woman. As ridiculous as the latter accusation was, I couldn't deny the truth of the first. Nonetheless, I was stunned by her words. That feeling turned to disbelief when she made a startling announce-ment a few days later: "I don't love you anymore either, Jim. I'm leaving for the coast and taking the kids. You can come along or stay behind. I don't care what you do."

Her voice was calm and deliberate. Kim's decision to discard me as a husband was as logical and business-like as her agreement to marry me six years earlier. And, unhappy as our marriage had been, I was crushed and devastated.

5

ALTHOUGH THAT PAINFUL spring day marked the beginning of the end of our marriage, Kim and I did not actually separate for another four months. In extreme emotional denial, I made desperate attempts to keep my family together, soliciting the assistance of family, friends, and marriage counselors. Anxious to do anything that would make Kim happy, I agreed to move back to the west coast ahead of her and the children to make arrangements.

I stayed with Kim's mother and stepfather in North Burnaby, and within two weeks found a new job and an attractive two-bedroom apartment in nearby Capitol Hill. Jackie and Norman Cole were hospitable and supportive during my stay, though a strain developed between Jackie and me after she drew me into a conversation about my relationship with Kim that ended badly on the subject of my religious views. Needing to talk to someone, I described the problems in our marriage at length, including Kim's sexual coldness. Jackie seemed sympathetic, and nodded gravely. "I had that feeling," she said. "She's gone dead, hasn't she?" I realized then that she probably knew much more about her daughter's emotional and psychological problems than I did.

I also confessed that I was experiencing serious doubts about the Witness faith, and that this had contributed to the distance in our relationship. Responding to Jackie's initial sympathy, I spoke honestly and frankly, criticizing the organization and its doctrines at length. However, Jackie soon made it clear that her sympathy did not extend to my questioning her faith.

The Coles' house was small, so I stayed in their camper trailer during my two weeks in Burnaby. On the Sunday morning following my conversation with Jackie, I was in my trailer reading when I was surprised by a knock on the door. When I stepped out of the trailer, I encountered Mervin Lay, a serious and ambitious young man who had been working his way up within the power structure of the local Witness congregation. I invited him in, but soon discovered that he was not there to pay me a friendly social call. He chastised me for not attending meetings at the local Kingdom Hall, for indulging in "wrong thoughts" and discussing those thoughts with others. He reminded me that as a former Witness pioneer, my comments could do damage to the organization, and advised me in very serious tones that my subversive behavior would not be tolerated.

Although somewhat hurt by Jackie's betrayal and Mervin's hostile and impersonal attitude towards me, it was hard to view his visit as anything but ludicrous. I told him that it was not my intention to harm anyone, and could not understand how someone as small and insignificant as me could be a serious threat to an organization comprising millions of people. All I had done was express some doubts to a family member—didn't Christian saints have doubts from time to time?

Kim and I had not lived in a large, urban area for many years, and were a little out of touch with recent developments in the Jehovah's Witness organization. While I knew there had been a serious crackdown on dissension in recent times, I had no idea that there was such an atmosphere of fear and paranoia. I began to realize that I'd better tread carefully if I wanted to keep my family together.

After Kim and the children moved to North Burnaby on the Canada Day weekend, I made a concerted effort to keep up appearances in the Witness community. I attended a few meetings at the local Kingdom Hall with Kim and the children, where I was treated cordially by all. I even attended a large, week-long assembly of Jehovah's Witnesses held in Vancouver's Empire Stadium later that summer. These assemblies are annual events that Witnesses look forward to for months and participate in with great enthusiasm. Although I had never particularly enjoyed these gatherings, I found the August 1978 assembly almost unbearable. The atmosphere in the stadium made me think of a huge vacuum from which the ordinary, everyday cares of people's lives had been temporarily sucked out and would soon come rushing in again. I felt completely out of place, and found it difficult to participate in the celebration, for I always felt uncomfortable in crowds.

Of course, Kim knew my façade was a sham and was not impressed with my efforts in attending that assembly, or any others. I had convinced myself that things had improved between us after the move to Burnaby because we were no longer arguing and bickering as we had been. However, I soon realized that Kim's tolerance of me was in fact complete indifference. She had already decided our marriage was over and was now living in her own separate little bubble, happy to be near her family, friends, and congregation again. I began to feel that she didn't care what I did, as long as I continued to bring home a pay check.

But I wasn't about to give up just yet.

At the assembly, one of the younger elders from our North Burnaby congregation said hello to me. I didn't know any of the elders from that congregation more than superficially, but this man was warm and friendly, and he had a gentle voice. I liked him immediately.

Later, I asked this same elder if he would visit Kim and me at our home to discuss our marital problems. I asked Kim in advance if this particular elder's intervention was all right with her and she said, reluctantly, that although she wasn't pleased, I had her consent. When the elder arrived, accompanied by another, older man, Kim was sitting in an easy chair, knitting. He opened the discussion by saying that when Kim and I began our courtship, we must have seen some positive things in one another, or we wouldn't have married. All we needed to do now was to remember those things, cherish them, and continue to build our relationship on that foundation. I liked what the elder said and looked hopefully at Kim for any sign of approval. But by then it was evident to me—and I think to the elders as well—that she had no intention of salvaging our marriage. Kim was walking a fine line. She didn't want to provoke the elders' disapproval for her lack of cooperation. Apparently, that was why she had permitted the discussion in the first place. Nor could she afford to give the elders the impression she no longer cared about our marriage, for that would have been unchristian of her. Seeing how uninspired Kim was, the elder asked if she understood how difficult it would be to raise two children alone, without the benefit of a father. "Yes," she said with a coy little smile, continuing with her knitting, but said no more. She didn't argue or resist, other than passively, but neither did she take the elders seriously. It was a no-win situation for everyone concerned, especially for the children, and after that meeting with the elders, I felt demoralized. I never asked for another intervention from the elders again.

I was to become wildly indecisive about our relationship, not just from day to day, but from minute to minute. Kim's attitude towards me and our relationship was humiliating, and I wanted nothing more than to escape, but my children were the elastic that always pulled me back to Kim in the hope that we could still make it work.

I spent as much time as possible with Juri and Lindsay, and took great pleasure in watching them grow into unique personalities. Though I was not particularly happy to be living in a smog-filled concrete jungle again, the kids loved exploring and experiencing all that the city had to offer. I would often take them to Confederation Park, where Lindsay would shriek with delight when I obeyed her demands to push her higher and higher on the swings. Juri was fascinated with the city's landscape, and would spend many hours at the kitchen table making elaborate drawings of skyscrapers. His pictures were very accomplished for his age, and I could see him becoming an architect or artist one day.

Lindsay would spend many contented afternoons playing in the back garden by herself, creating worlds of her own imagination. I remember looking out the back window for her one day and feeling a momentary sense of panic when I could not see her. When I went out to look, I found her dwarfed among the tall weeds, her face smudged with dirt, looking like a mischievous nature sprite. She spotted me, gave out a happy cry and ran into my arms. I grabbed her up and squeezed her little body as hard as I could, reluctant to return her to the mysterious world of her play.

Incredibly, I hadn't completely thrown in the towel on our marriage. After breakfast one morning I mentioned to Kim that the offices of Family Services were located just down the street from where we lived. I asked if we could make an appointment with them to speak with a professional marriage counselor. She looked at me with astonishment. "What for?" she demanded. "I'm sorry I marr-ied you in the first place. Look Jim, you can go on living here with us. I won't stop you. You don't seem happy, but that's your problem. I don't care *how* you feel. I'm going to be happy regardless of what you do."

The way she spoke was hard to take.

"Why do you keep trying to save this marriage?" she continued, attempting a more reasonable tone of voice. "Can't you see it's no use?"

After a moment of silence, I asked, "Isn't there anything you find good about me?"

"Yes," she said. "As a matter of fact, you are a good breadwinner."

To make matters worse, I, as well, was becoming blunt and less civil. The following day, I said to her in exasperation, "Some day you're going to wake up and see what a crazy religion you're involved in."

Our marriage was dead; I just didn't know it yet. Eventually, though, I had no choice but to accept her words at face value. After all, what I expected of her was unrealistic. *You can't make a person love you.* And even if I had returned wholeheartedly to the Witness fold like the prodigal son of Jesus' parable, it probably wouldn't have made much of a difference to Kim. Such maneuvers would have seemed insincere to her.

I remained on friendly terms with Kim's family, but her friends were some-times openly hostile to me. One afternoon, her friend Jo-Ann told me that she wanted to discuss my "marriage troubles." Thinking she wanted to help, I told her about my conflicted feelings about Kim, but as soon as I mentioned my fear of losing the children, she suddenly became confrontational. "If you're thinking of leaving," she said, "you'd better not try to get custody of the children.

Jehovah's Witnesses have good lawyers and money to pay for them, and we will fight you every step of the way. Jehovah always protects his own." Her words hit hard. It had never entered my mind to take the children away from their mother, and now I began to wonder if I could even hope for access to them if Kim and I were to separate.

In early October of 1978, I paid a visit to my Uncle Jim, my mother's younger brother who had never been one of Jehovah's Witnesses. I had always been fond of Jim and visited him in Vancouver whenever I could. Tall, sophisticated and witty, he had a healthy skepticism about people and institutions, and could always make me laugh. I was also impressed with the fact that he had been married to the same woman for over thirty years, and had successfully established himself in the real estate business.

We sat drinking coffee at his kitchen table as usual while he chain-smoked and did most of the talking. I knew that Jehovah's Witnesses were a sore spot for him ever since his parents—my grandparents—had converted to the faith just before the Second World War. He once told me that he had been particularly disgusted by the number of draftees who had cynically jumped on the Witness bandwagon in order to qualify as conscientious objectors and avoid war duty. However, he had always been tolerant and respectful towards his Witness relatives, and that is probably why I sought him out that particular day.

As Jim talked, my thoughts frequently wandered to the various matters weighing on my mind. Then, seemingly out of the blue, I heard myself blurt out the decision that suddenly floated to my mind. Leaning across the table, I said, "Jim, I've decided to leave Jehovah's Witnesses."

My uncle sat back in amazement. "What? When did this happen?"

"Just now," I said, feeling just as surprised.

Jim's face broke into an enthusiastic smile. Then he brought his hand down hard on the table, and practically shouted his approval: "Well, hallelujah—that's great news! One more person saved!"

We both laughed like schoolboys, and I felt lighter than air. Now that I had finally said it aloud, I experienced great relief and happiness. After seventeen years, I was finally free to be the person I wanted to be. I wondered why I hadn't made the same decision years ago, and talked to my uncle with great enthusiasm until almost suppertime.

However, my giddy elation was short-lived, as I knew that I would now have to confront what my decision meant in terms of my marriage and children. After leaving my uncle's home, I ate out at a local restaurant in order to delay going home. Then I stopped at a tavern for a couple of beers, a habit that had become more and more frequent of late. When I finally arrived home after midnight and climbed into bed next to Kim, she kept her back to me as usual. When she refused to respond to my attempts at light conversation, I finally said the inevitable: "Kim, what if I was to leave you for good?"

She turned to face me and answered my question slowly and thoughtfully. "I'd say... that wasn't such a bad idea..." Then she paused and looked at me quizzically. "What finally brought this on?"

I told her that I was tired and fed up, worn out from being pulled between two unbearable prospects: a rancid marriage on the one hand, and a life without my children on the other. I talked about all the other times in my life I'd felt between a rock and a hard place, and how I always ended up making the wrong decision. I told her that this time, I was determined to get out from under, no matter what the consequences. At that point, I wasn't really certain about a separation; I was merely venting my frustration with months of Kim's icy silence and indifference towards me.

Kim's thoughts were elsewhere, and she barely listened to what I was saying. "You'll have to make child support payments, of course... and then there's the question of visitation rights..."

Her cold words quickly turned my "what if" into hard, irreversible reality, and I experienced a dizzying wave of nausea. "But what about the children?" I said on second thought. "How will they do without a father to support and guide them every day?"

"Yes, but do you think it's good for them to see us carry on like we do day after day?" she asked. "The atmosphere around here is poisoned."

I listened to her in silence, knowing she was right.

"When do you want to separate?" she went on. "Do you want to carry on like this until we're fifty?"

I kept listening.

"Look, Jim. Do you love me?"

She had me there, and I couldn't say in all honesty that I did.

"There you have it," she continued. "Zero plus zero leaves nothing."

I was determined not to cry, for I didn't want to suffer any further humiliation in front of Kim, but my body betrayed my emotions, and I began to sweat and shake uncontrollably. "I never thought it would turn out this way," I whispered. "Never."

To my surprise, Kim put her arm around my waist and held me tight for a long time. After a while, she said, "Jim, I hope you find somebody nice one day." At that moment, I thought it was kindness that had prevented Kim from leaving me first, that she had wanted me to make the final decision in order to minimize my pain. I would later realize how wrong I was, and to what extent I had played directly into Kim's hands and agenda.

The next morning was a Saturday. We had breakfast as usual. The children were cheerful, innocent, and unsuspecting. But Kim's intention was to move as quickly as possible before I had time to change my mind. After breakfast, she piled the dishes in the sink and packed some of my things in a trunk, which I carried out to the car. As I drove away from the house, I felt a dizzying kaleidoscope of emotions: excitement and elation at the prospect of a new life, deep sadness and loss, and extreme guilt and shame for the conspiracy that Kim and I were perpetrating against our children.

I knew that ending our marriage was the best thing possible for Kim and me as individuals. After all, it was 1978, the era of the Me Generation, and the individual was all that mattered. But what about the children? Weren't they individuals, too? Shouldn't they have had a say in what was happening to them? In the 1970s, social scientists were very optimistic about the positive aspects of divorce and family diversity. Deep down, though, I knew that the step I was taking would bring my children deep pain and unhappiness.

I immediately moved into the basement apartment of my Uncle Jim's house, where I was treated as one of the family. My Aunt Doris was a godsend to me at that difficult time, and generously gave me the emotional and moral support I so badly needed. We had many long and soulful talks during those first weeks, and she always encouraged me to leave the past behind and look towards the future. "Now is your chance to be and do whatever you want," she would say. "So go out and do it."

About a week later, Kim phoned to tell me that she and the children had moved into a townhouse not far from our old apartment. She explained that the children had been told about our separation, but she did not tell me how they were dealing with it. I missed them terribly, and when she invited me to come over, I jumped at the chance.

The children and I were happy to see each other after our week-long separation. I had expected to take them out on one of our outings, but Kim had other plans. She explained that she had already met a Family Court counselor, who told her that under the Family Relations Act we could arrange a separation agreement without the hassle and expense of lawyers. Kim had taken the liberty of making an appointment for us and wanted to know if I was prepared to cooperate. When I agreed, she quickly smiled and said, "Let's you and me be friends, Jim." I wondered whether such a thing would be possible, but saw no reason to create unnecessary animosity between us.

Kim even tried to make light of the situation with a little black humor. "We'd better cancel those life insurance policies," she laughed. "After all, you might decide to kill me, or I might think about doing you in." Within a few days, we cancelled the policies, both of which had a face value of $50,000.

The following day, we met with a Family Court counselor, whose office was located only a few blocks from Kim's new home. She was a pleasant woman who had obviously developed a friendly relationship with Kim. We had spoken on the phone before my appointment, and when I saw her, she asked me for a copy of the income and expense report she had asked me to prepare. To my surprise, she gave it a cursory glance and said, "That looks all right. You have about $250 per month left over for child support. Can you manage that?" I quickly agreed, and the separation agreement was typed up in a matter of minutes.

When she read the agreement aloud to us, I wondered about the last clause, which stipulated that Kim would have custody of the children and I would have "reasonable access on reasonable notice." My child support obligations under the agreement were precise with regard to payment amounts and schedules, but I thought Kim's obligation to give me access to the children was rather vaguely worded. When I asked the counselor about my options in the event that Kim failed to honor that obligation, she shrugged and said that Kim was legally bound by the agreement and could face police intervention if she did not comply. She also stressed that I could face garnisheed wages or even prison if I reneged on my child support payments.

I signed the agreement along with Kim, and afterwards the counselor beamed at us with approval. "You two are a model of civilized behavior," she said. "The couples who come in here are usually at each other's throats and can't agree on the smallest details. You're an example of how simple and congenial it can be." I didn't explain to her that Kim and I could afford to be reasonable because we both wanted out of our marriage as quickly and cleanly as possible. Nor did I tell her that I saw nothing to celebrate in the situation.

Within two weeks of meeting with the counselor, I took the children to Confederation Park, where we pursued our usual activities. The children enjoyed themselves, but soon started asking the questions I was dreading. Lindsay (now two years old) wanted to know where "my house" was, whether I would take her there and if she could stay with me for a while. I was surprised how quickly she had grasped and accepted the idea that her mommy and daddy were living in separate places. When I explained that she could indeed visit me at my house, and very soon, she did not seem angry or upset in any way.

However, that was not the case with Juri, who was now five years old and seemed to have a fuller understanding of the situation. When we were out of Lindsay's earshot, he whispered to me that he didn't want to live with his mother and wanted to come and live with me instead. I held him tight, deeply touched by his affection and overcome with sadness for him, for though I wanted nothing more than for Juri and Lindsay to live with me, I knew that could never be possible, even on a temporary basis. I remembered only too well Jo-Ann's warning to me: Jehovah's Witnesses believed that their children would be better off dead than raised by an unbelieving parent. I also knew that the justice system would favor Kim in a custody battle, no matter what the circumstances.

I remember thinking that the only way I would be able to acquire custody of my children would be in the event of Kim's death. I also remember giving serious consideration to the only other option available to me—to kidnap Juri and take him to my parents' farm in Manitoba. Even in my most desperate moments, I never considered taking both of Kim's children away from her; that would have been too cruel.

I felt as rash, impulsive, and reckless as anyone would in my situation, and I almost followed through on my plan to abduct my son, but I lacked the necessary ruthlessness. I knew Juri would be permanently and irreversibly separated from his mother and sister, and I could not bear the thought of him crying out in loneliness for them. In the end, I realized that there was absolutely nothing I could do to spare my children the inevitable emotional pain, and instead vowed that I would do everything within my power to remain a part of their lives.

6

KIM AND JAMES KOSTELNIUK formally separated in October 1978. From all reports, the separation was amicable and the details agreed to by both parties. The couple had been married for six years, with no history of domestic abuse, alcoholism, or infidelity. It appears that the main reasons for the separation were incompatibility and religious differences.

Kim had been born into a family of the Jehovah's Witness faith, and like many people of specific religions, cultural, and social backgrounds, was expected to marry one of her own. When she met James Kostelniuk in 1972, she was actively seeking a husband and considered him a suitable Witness mate. She quickly became disillusioned after their marriage in 1973, as Jim did not live up to her image of a strong, dominant household leader. She considered him to be a soft disciplinarian (he refused to use corporal punishment on their children, for instance), and was alarmed by his increasing doubts about the Witness faith. She no longer felt that he was a husband she could be proud of in the Jehovah's Witness community.

After her separation from Jim, Kim expressed the desire to find a new father and spiritual role model for her children, one who could give her the ideal family life that she had always wanted. She sought a speedy divorce so that she could remarry. She also sought to reduce Jim's unsupervised contact with the children, as she was concerned that he might try to abduct one or both of them.

BY FEBRUARY 1979, I had settled in comfortably at my Uncle Jim's. My basement apartment was private and self-contained, but I frequently spent time with him and Doris during my time off, playing cribbage, shooting billiards, and watching our favorite television shows. It was quite different from the structured life of a Witness family, and I began to enjoy the new lifestyle. After a few months, however, Uncle Jim told me in no uncertain terms that it was time for me to stop hanging around with him and Doris. I should go out and meet some people my own age. "I know it won't be easy after being married for so long," he said. "But you've got to start dating again."

I knew he was right and finally got up the nerve to attend a single parents' dance in New Westminster. I spent the whole day picking out some fashionable new clothes, but still felt awkward and out of place. However, I eventually began talking with an attractive, petite woman with freckles and auburn hair named Linda. She had a lilting Scottish accent that betrayed a teasing, playful charm beneath her dignified appearance, and I liked her right away. I eventually asked her to dance, and we spent a very enjoyable evening together.

I later visited her apartment in Coquitlam, where she talked about her grown son and her recent divorce from an alcoholic husband. She explained that she was not looking for a serious relationship, just a companion to dance and have a good time with. She also warned me that she was not as young as she looked, that I was getting involved with an older woman, but that didn't bother me in the least. In fact, I was rather attracted to her womanly maturity.

It wasn't long before I found myself in Linda's arms and in her bed. Our sexual relationship was natural and effortless, and it was with her that I finally found the physical passion that I had missed for so long. With great relief, I discovered that I was a normal, red-blooded man who had no problem relating with a woman both physically and emotionally. Linda provided me with a sexual healing that I will always be grateful for.

Despite Linda's companionship, I missed the children terribly. I was allowed to see them every other Saturday afternoon, but the pattern of our father-child relationship was changing. I started to feel more like a distant relative than a parent who was there for them whenever they needed me. I quickly became a weekend father, or what Judith Wallerstein, one of the world's foremost authorities on the effects of divorce, calls "a parent without a portfolio." Our strictly scheduled visits meant that I was out of touch with the rhythms of their everyday lives, and I was losing my place as someone who really mattered to them. I felt disconnected and adrift.

The clock was always ticking during our visits, and our activities would become more hurried and frantic as the precious time slipped away. When I brought the children home to Kim, Juri would wrap his arms around my knees and cry, begging me to stay. I would try to persuade Kim to let me comfort him until he calmed down, but she viewed his behavior as manipulative and theatrical, and didn't want to encourage it. She always complained that my visits caused her and the children too much disruption and that it always took days to get the children—particularly Juri—back to their regular routines.

Lindsay was usually calm when I dropped her off, but always expressed an intense curiosity about my new life. She would often comment on things she found different about me, like my clothes or hairstyle (I grew my hair longer and lost some weight). One day when I picked up Lindsay to hug her, she reached for the new gold chain pendant around my neck. "What is that?" she asked, fascinated by the glittering image of a lion. I explained that it was my astrological sign, and as her eyes widened with delight, I had the urge to give it to her as a memento. However, I knew that Kim would consider it a sacrilegious object and throw it away, so I just let her play with it for a while, then squeezed her tight and kissed her goodbye.

One afternoon in the spring of 1979, Kim invited me to stay for supper—which meant she wanted to discuss something. After dinner, she sent the children to their room to play, then sat back and smiled at me. "You look different," she said. "Something tells me you've got a girlfriend. Am I right?"

I had not intended to tell Kim about Linda, because at that time I was in no hurry to grant Kim a divorce and had no desire to give her grounds for one. Then a strange thing happened. It was as though the mask of Kim's smile slipped away and I could see what was behind it: a lonely, disappointed woman with broken dreams, anxious to pursue new ones. In that moment, I felt sorry for her and didn't have the heart to deny her what she wanted.

When I told Kim about my relationship with Linda, she didn't say much at first, but when I later mentioned that my uncle and aunt were going away for the weekend, she began to ask questions. "Are you going to look after the house while they're gone? Will you be walking the dog? Will Linda be staying with you?"

I thought her questions were nothing more than idle curiosity, but the following Saturday evening, I spotted Kim and a friend nearby when Linda and I were out walking the dog around the block. On my next visit with the children, Kim told me that she would be seeking a divorce on the grounds of adultery. She explained that her friend would act as a witness and Linda would be served as a co-respondent, but would not have to appear in court. All I had to do was sign the necessary papers.

Offended by her deviousness, I almost told her to forget it. However, I also feared that things could get ugly if I did not cooperate. Once again, there was no escaping Kim's agenda. If I didn't agree to a divorce based on adultery, our marriage would have dissolved automatically within three years, but for Kim, that was unthinkable. Without being able to demonstrate adultery on my part, she would not be allowed to remarry in the eyes of Jehovah's Witnesses. Knowing how important her Witness faith was to her, and how anxious she was to re-marry, I reluctantly agreed and signed the papers.

It seemed Kim was not content with that. She also wanted a legitimate reason, in the eyes of Jehovah's Witnesses, to limit my access to the children. After my next visit, she took me aside and spoke in low, serious tones: "I thought you should know that the elders of the congregation have heard a rumor that you've been seeing another woman." Though Kim assured me that the information had not come from her, I knew better. She went on to say that the elders were going to hold a meeting about my transgression and were considering severe sanctions, if not disfellowshipment. When I shrugged my shoulders, non-plussed, she urged me to attend the meeting to defend myself, to protect my reputation in the community for the sake of the children. I finally agreed, but later discovered that it was not my reputation she wanted me to protect.

The next day, I stood before three Witness elders who were to be my judge, jury, and prosecutor. They demanded to know if I had been with another woman, and I replied in the affirmative. Then they asked if Kim had done anything "unchristian" in our marriage to cause me to break my marriage vows. I knew immediately where that question was leading, and refused to take the bait. I knew the elders were convinced that Kim must be to blame for my sins and the break-up of our marriage, since she had a reputation for being a woman who was not good at accepting commands, either from her husband or congreg-ation elders. Disappointed with my refusal to incriminate Kim, they continued to press the issue. Had she performed her duties as a wife? Did she withhold marital relations? Did she refuse to submit to my leadership as a husband? I could have answered "Yes"—truthfully—to all of those questions, but it was Kim who was desperate to remain a Witness in good standing, not I, so there was no reason to cooperate with them.

I told them that Kim had been an ideal wife and took full responsibility for my sins. When they asked if I wished to repent and mend my ways, I remained silent. Then the elders told me that they had no choice but to disfellowship me, and I accepted their decision. No effort would be made to restore my faith and return me to the Witness brotherhood. From that point forward, I was as good as dead in their eyes.

As I walked away from the same Kingdom Hall where Kim and I had marr-ied six years earlier, I reflected on the seventeen years I had wasted on this crazy religion. And as I got into my car and drove away, I felt years of pain, misery, and boredom ebbing away at last.

When I got home, I told my Aunt Doris—a shrewd judge of character—about what had just happened. When she heard that Kim had probably shared incriminating details about another woman in my life with the elders, she nodded knowingly and said, "Kim didn't want you, but she didn't want anyone else to have you either." Doris's words surprised me, and despite myself, I had to laugh, realizing what there was to learn about human nature.

Soon there was little to keep me in British Columbia. Kim used one excuse after another to cancel or postpone my visits with the children, and I began to see less and less of them. Linda and I gradually drifted apart, and by September 1979, I found myself without a job. Feeling empty and low, I became homesick for Manitoba and decided to move back to my parents' farm to start fresh.

In October 1979, I visited the children to say goodbye, knowing I would not see them again for a very long time. Kim seemed happy about my decision to move away, and embraced me cheerfully like an old friend. Everything I had was packed in the back of my little Ford Pinto, and I immediately headed east on the Trans-Canada Highway. When I reached the Port Mann Bridge, however, I felt an irresistible urge to go back, and it was only sheer will power that kept me driving forward. The long, lonely trip across the mountains and prairies was like a slow death.

7

Kim Kostelniuk felt relieved when her estranged husband moved to Manitoba in the fall of 1979. His visits with the children had become increasingly stressful and disruptive, and she was always left to deal with the aftermath. Juri would act out for days afterwards and Lindsay would pester her with endless questions. She told her husband that she thought the move was a good idea, and that it was best for him to make a clean break from the children.

Kim's life as a single mother was more difficult than she had expected. Though she received $250 a month from her husband in child support, she had been too proud to ask for alimony payments as well. Her parents helped out whenever they could, but she eventually had to accept welfare in order to keep the children fed and clothed. She frequently felt deeply lonely and depressed, and once told a friend that she didn't know how she could continue to raise the children alone.

Kim knew it was imperative that she find a new husband, but there were few single men in her Witness community her own age who appealed to her. In November, her friend Alma talked about taking a trip to Maui in the spring, and invited Kim to join her. During the last assembly in Vancouver, she had met a Witness brother who ran a bed-and-breakfast there, catering specifically to Jehovah's Witnesses. She told Kim that he offered very inexpensive rates and cheap flights were available.

Kim protested that she couldn't afford a vacation and didn't want to leave the children, but when her mother offered to look after the children, Kim told Alma to go ahead and make the arrangements. She told herself that she was still young and attractive, and simply needed the opportunity to meet the right person. She began to look forward to the trip with the expectation of meeting a prospective husband.

When I arrived at my parents' farm near Clandeboye, the harvest had just finished. The fields were bare, and the prairie looked like a vast, empty desert. My parents welcomed me with open arms, but I didn't find the comfort I was looking for. The homesickness I was feeling for the home I had lost—my home with Kim and the children—was something I thought would magically turn up in the environment of my childhood. But nothing about the place felt the same. Most of the people I had known had moved away, died, or become strangers.

I did try to make a go of it. I got a job as a bus driver for Winnipeg Transit, commuting thirty miles to and from work. The shifts for new drivers were awful, starting at three in the afternoon and finishing in the early hours of the morning, often in seven-day stretches. The first few months were exhausting, but I soon settled into the routine.

My parents enjoyed having me home. My mother cooked, cleaned, and fussed over me, and my father and I enjoyed many long talks. He was semi-retired now, with a lot of free time, and seemed to want to spend most of it with me. Impressed with big machines, he wanted to know all the details of my bus-driving job at the end of the day. He still played fiddle with a local band—more for pleasure than money—and loved to tell me about the dances, weddings, and bars where he played. I would sit in a big easy chair and often fall asleep exhausted as I listened to his stories.

More than once, the conversation turned to the breakup of my family back in British Columbia. I speculated that the main reason for my separation with Kim was religious differences. He didn't agree. "That's just an excuse," he said. "The real reason you broke up with Kim was that she no longer wanted you." What seemed obvious to others wasn't so obvious to me. Perhaps he was right; if a person truly wants you, they'll say anything, suffer anything, sacrifice almost anything to keep you.

My father sometimes tried to inject a little levity into that sad topic of conversation. "My poor Jim," he would laugh good-naturedly. "You're like that little boy I remember—lost in the woods." He was referring, of course, to when I had wandered away from the yard when I was little, and he had to send out a search party for me.

By the spring of 1980, I had been separated from my children for almost six months and could not bear to be apart from them any longer. We had exchanged letters and cassette tapes throughout the winter months, and I regularly received fat manila envelopes stuffed with drawings—but it wasn't the same as seeing and touching their dear faces. I wrote Kim a brief letter announcing my intention to return to British Columbia, then told my parents about my decision. I tried to explain to them that I had had no idea how much I would miss my children when I first moved back to Manitoba, that my longing for them was so intense that it made me physically ill.

My father sympathized but tried hard to dissuade me, telling me what a good life I had with him and my mother. He reminded me about my good-paying job, and the future it offered me. I had to realize, he insisted, that my life with Kim and the children was gone. My mother was not happy about my decision, but accepted it. My father was deeply hurt when I left Manitoba a month later. He had grown used to my companionship, and would be without it again. I felt the pull of a son towards a father, but the pull towards my own children was stronger.

IN APRIL 1980, Kim received official notification of her divorce from James Kostelniuk. She immediately sent her ex-husband a copy of the Decree Absolute, telling him he would need it if he ever decided to remarry.

In early May, she said goodbye to her children, whom she left with her mother Jackie, and set off with Alma on a week-long vacation to Maui. She was very excited about the trip and had bought some attractive new outfits for the occasion. When they arrived on the island, they were welcomed by a Witness brother named Earl and were taken to his small bed-and-breakfast establishment where several other Jehovah's Witnesses were staying.

The next day, Kim and Alma were approached by a young Witness man who introduced himself as Jeff Anderson. He was a large blond man with a southern American accent, and Kim found him rather handsome. They chatted together at the breakfast table, where Kim learned that Anderson was originally from Texas and had been living in Maui for some time. He suggested they spend some time together and she agreed.

Alma and Earl acted as chaperones while Kim and Jeff toured the island of Maui over the next few days. At first, their conversations remained serious and polite. She talked about her children and recent divorce, and what it was like being a single mother. He talked about his job as a disk jockey at a local radio station, and how much he wanted to meet a good Christian woman to share his life with. His conversation was generously peppered with the words and phrases that a dedicated Jehovah's Witness would use, and he impressed Kim as a man who was very serious about his faith.

Anderson later revealed that he was six years younger than Kim, and teasingly suggested that she should "try a younger guy." Soon Kim started to become quite relaxed and comfortable with him—and even became a little flirtatious, flattered by his glowing compliments about her "country girl" beauty. Perhaps she found his transparency disarming.

On the night before Kim and Alma were scheduled to leave, a group of Jehovah's Witnesses went to a family restaurant called the Maui Lu, where there was a band and dance floor. At one point in the evening, Alma leaned over and told Anderson, "This is your last chance. If you don't ask Kim to dance, you'll lose her." During their dance, he told her that he was really going to miss her when she left.

Later that night, Anderson sat next to Kim on the sofa and declared his love for her. When asked for a response, she smiled nervously and said, "I don't know. I feel scared, like I want to run away." He told her that he would like to move closer to her—to Canada—to continue their relationship and get to know her. She said she would like that.

The following morning, Anderson placed a lei around Kim's neck at the airport, and assured her that he would be coming to Canada within a few months, as soon as he saved enough money. She laughed and said, "We'll see. I believe things when I see them." Then she kissed him on the cheek and waved goodbye.

When Kim returned home to Burnaby, she was dismayed to read her ex-husband's letter telling her he was returning to British Columbia to be near the children. It was not something she had anticipated, and she was determined that he would not interfere with the new life she was planning for herself and the children.

WHEN I ARRIVED IN BURNABY, I met Kim at a McDonald's restaurant near her apartment. There was something quite different about her. She had a bit of a tan and a sparkle in her eye, and at first appeared cheerful and friendly. However, when I asked when I would be able to see Juri and Lindsay, she became difficult and unmoved. She stated that she wanted to limit my visits to national holidays only, as they were simply too disruptive for her and the children. I was told that I could see them on Victoria Day (May 25) and Canada Day (July 1), and that we would just have to see after that.

I was stunned. "That's over a month between visits," I said. "Do you think I came all this way to look at the scenery?"

She was unsympathetic. "I warned you not to come back, Jim. The kids and I could leave here anytime. You should know that I just met an American man in Maui who wants to marry me. I also recently met someone from New Zealand who says he's crazy about me. We could move anywhere—who knows? You can't follow us all over the world."

At the time, I didn't know whether the men she mentioned even existed, but I knew she didn't have the right to prevent me from seeing my children.

I was determined to prevent Kim from violating my parental rights. The only job I was able to find since my return to Burnaby was as a manager/trainee at a Wendy's restaurant, so I couldn't afford to pay for a lawyer. However, I made an application for legal aid and got it. The young legal counselor who met with me told me that the only thing I could do was file an order preventing Kim from leaving the province with the children; if she were to leave the country, she would then be outside the jurisdiction of Canadian law. The situation seemed hopeless, and all I could do was count the days until the next national holiday.

When I saw the children on Victoria Day, it had been seven months since I had seen them. Lindsay was now three years old and a little taller, with a full-moon face and a generous smile that was as accepting as ever. Juri was almost six, taller and lankier, with the same thoughtful disposition that I remembered. I delighted in seeing, hearing, smelling, and touching them again, and they seemed their same sweet selves.

It soon became clear, though, that Juri had not adapted well to our separation. At one point during our visit, he suddenly told me that he knew that he was to blame for our divorce, that he had caused Kim and me to fight, and that everything was his fault. I was shocked and dismayed. Though I hugged him hard and tried to tell him otherwise, he would not be persuaded or comforted. I could not remove that heavy load from his fragile little shoulders.

Though I was allowed to see the children again two months later, on Canada Day, I began to feel frustrated and foolish about moving all the way back to Burnaby for nothing. Then I received some shocking news that would abruptly change my direction. On the evening of July 17, I received a telephone call from a relative telling me that my father had died. He had suffered a heart attach while defending his chickens from a neighbor's dog.

His death was cruel and untimely in view of the way we had parted company when I left Manitoba. Although I had spoken to my father on the phone since, something between us had been left unsaid. After the funeral, my mother told me that my father had been sad and out of sorts ever since I left. "It was as though he'd lost his purpose in life," she said. "He went about the farm, doing his chores. But he quit playing with the band, which was so unusual for him." She speculated that he had started to get sick about then, but she of course had no way of knowing he had heart disease, because he avoided doctors like the plague.

After my father's funeral, I moved my things back to Manitoba in order to be with my mother when she needed me. I realized that I could no longer structure my life around Kim's whims and broken promises. However, I made a solemn vow that I would continue to see my children and would never, ever lose touch with them entirely.

8

OVER THE SPRING and summer of 1980, Jeff Anderson made a number of long-distance phone calls to Kim Kostelniuk, and they exchanged many letters. She told him that she missed him, and in one letter told him that he had "rattled her chains."

In August 1980, Anderson left Maui to live near Tacoma, Washington, where he told Kim he had obtained a job "in business." On weekends, he would cross the border into Canada to spend time with her. When in Burnaby, he stayed in Norman and Jackie Cole's camper trailer, near Kim's Beta Avenue apartment.

However, in January 1981, Anderson suddenly decided to move back to Maui. He told Kim that he wanted to save enough money to marry her, and would earn a much better salary at his old radio job in Maui than he would on the mainland. He promised to phone and write to her regularly, and return as soon as he could.

WHEN I RETURNED TO MANITOBA, I was fortunate to get my old job back at Winnipeg Transit. The small parcel of land that my father had left to my mother was rented to a neighbor on a sharecrop basis, and I helped my mother care for the small flock of chickens that was left.

In December 1980, I flew to Vancouver over a long weekend to see my children. My mother and niece—Jeanette's ten-year-old daughter Sherry—came along, and the five of us stayed in a suite at the Holiday Inn. Although it rained almost the entire time, the children had great fun playing in the indoor pool. I, of course, was happy to be with Juri and Lindsay under any circumstances.

In early 1981, my life took a sudden turn for the better, when I had the good fortune of meeting Marge Erhart Romanyshyn, the woman who would become the love and rock of my life. Marge reminded me of a 1930s movie star—a smart, sharply dressed, and sophisticated woman who knew something about the seedier side of life. She was pretty and petite, with neatly coiffed brown curly hair and beautiful eyes that bore a trace of sadness. Her voice was deep-toned, and when she spoke her words were direct, honest, and unadorned. I fell for her immediately.

Marge was divorced, like me, and had grown up in the ethnic, working-class north end of Winnipeg. Though very sociable and fun-loving, she was also a hard worker with abundant amounts of energy. When we first met, she worked full-time at a beauty supply agency in downtown Winnipeg and also held two part-time jobs. But she was no miser. She believed in enjoying her hard-earned money, and did it with panache. Marge widened my horizons, introducing me to her wide circle of friends and taking me to small, glittering dinner parties and the occasional cultural event. She had an abundance of the *joi de vivre* that had been so lacking in my life, and it was through her that I really began to loosen up and enjoy myself.

Our relationship moved quickly, and we were soon living together in her apartment in Winnipeg. However, we both had the experience of rushing into relationships too quickly, and in March 1981, we decided to take a break and reassess our feelings before making any long-term commitments. I moved out and looked after the farm while my mother visited with her older brother Clare in Florida.

In April 1981, I took a two-week vacation from my job and flew to Burnaby to see my children. When I arrived at Kim's apartment to pick them up, Lindsay was waiting for me under a cherry blossom tree, her face flushed with the gentle, spring sunlight. And Juri—who had grown even taller and lankier since I'd seen him last—stood beside her, wearing a t-shirt that read "Here Today, Gone to Maui."

The children seemed subdued during our visit. At one point, they asked me in the most urgent tones to move back in with them and their mother; they spoke so seriously and specifically that for a split second I thought this might be a feeler from Kim. I quickly dismissed the notion, and spent a long while trying to uncover the reason for their unexpected request. All they would tell me was that they missed me and wanted me to be their daddy again.

When I returned the children to the apartment, Kim invited me to stay for a while. In her typically direct way, she asked if I was seeing anyone, and I told her about Marge and our temporary separation. Kim smiled knowingly and said, "She sounds perfect for you, Jim. This time, don't let her get away."

Suspecting that she had broached the subject for a specific reason, I asked if there was anyone new in *her* life. She told me that she'd been seeing the man she mentioned on one of my earlier visits to Vancouver—the Texan she'd met in Maui. When I asked if the relationship was serious, she appeared uncertain. "What's the matter?" I asked jokingly. "Can't stand the heat?" I was referring to both the heat of romance and Kim's well-known dislike for hot weather. She laughed at my little joke, but I could also sense concern and unease through her smile.

I thought about how difficult it would be for Kim to find someone who would measure up to her unrealistic expectations and standards, and doubted whether she was ready to make a commitment to a new relationship. I also considered how difficult life must be for her as a single mother, and felt a renewed sense of regret about our past relationship. "You know, Kim," I said, "if I had known then what I know now, I would have treated you differently. I would have tried to be more patient, more kind." She seemed to appreciate the sentiment, and our visit ended on a friendly note.

Marge and I happily resumed our relationship on my return to Winnipeg. Our separation had only deepened our feelings for each other, and we decided that we wanted to spend the rest of our lives together. We were married on June 13, 1981 in a United Church ceremony, in an old stone church on the banks of the Red River, near St. Andrews, Manitoba. I had only recently returned to the United Church, the church I had grown up in, and still held out hope that God could be found outside the extremism of the Jehovah's Witnesses.

IN JUNE 1981, Jeff Anderson proposed to Kim Kostelniuk on the telephone and she accepted. They planned to wed and live in Maui, and Kim started to sell off her furniture in anticipation of a move within two or three months. Anderson told Kim he had saved enough money for a nice wedding and had already rented and furnished a three-bedroom house for her and the children.

The wedding date was set for mid-August 1981. Anderson told Kim that he had booked a Witness Kingdom Hall on the island for the ceremony. As the wedding day approached, he suddenly telephoned her to tell her that the wedding location had been changed to Houston, Texas, so that his family could attend.

IN JULY 1981, I phoned Kim to tell her of my recent marriage. She gave me her hearty congratulations and then announced that she herself had become engaged to Jeff Anderson. I felt genuinely pleased for her and asked where they planned to live. At that point, her voice became uncertain. "I don't know... I think Maui, or maybe Houston, Texas." Then she quickly reassured me: "Don't worry, Jim, I'll let you know as soon as we get there." When I expressed my disappointment that the children would be living so far away, she suggested that Marge and I combine a visit with a vacation. I told her that we would seriously consider that, as soon as we knew where she and her new husband were settled.

When I got off the phone, I told Marge about Kim's plans and expressed my surprise. "She's been undecided about him since April, and I'm surprised she's going through with it." Nonetheless, I hoped that it would all work out for her.

JEFF ANDERSON FLEW to Seattle in early August, where he was joined by Kim, Juri, and Lindsay. From there, they flew to Houston, where they met up with Jeff's mother, brother, and sister-in-law, as well as two of Kim's girlfriends who had also come down from Vancouver.

Jeff Anderson and Kim Kostelniuk were married the next day at a Houston Kingdom Hall. The day was hot and muggy, and things went awry from the very beginning. Anderson arrived late, and the ceremony was rushed. The wedding rings went missing, and Kim had to use Anderson's mother's ring as a substitute. That ring was later lost, and Kim would eventually revert to using the wedding ring from her first marriage.

Kim cried after the wedding—but not with tears of joy. She had expressed doubts about marrying Anderson and had wanted to back out of the wedding, but as a Jehovah's Witness, she had entered into a binding contract when she agreed to become engaged. To break that contract unilaterally would bring severe sanctions from the Witness community, and she felt that she had no choice but to go through with it.

For the first week of their marriage, Kim and Jeff Anderson lived in his mother's home, along with Kim's two children. The following week, they moved into a small, unfurnished apartment in Houston.

IN SEPTEMBER 1981, I received a change-of-address card from Kim, instructing me to send my child support checks to her mother-in-law's address in Houston until she and her new husband had a permanent address of their own. Two months later, in November 1981, I received another change-of-address card from Kim, this time indicating that she had left Houston and moved to Calgary, Alberta.

I was surprised to hear that she and her husband had moved to Canada, as it was my impression that Kim had wanted to move the children as far away from me as possible. I also wondered why they chose Calgary as their new home, rather than British Columbia, where Kim could be near her family.

KIM KNEW SHE WAS MAKING a mistake before she married Jeff Anderson, but did not find out until after the wedding how serious a mistake it was.

She quickly discovered that Anderson had deliberately misrepresented himself to her, in hopes of winning her love. He was forced to confess that he had lied to her from the moment they met. He had led her to believe that he had an established life in Maui, when in fact he had arrived there only a few days before she had; his so-called career in radio was a casual, part-time job at a local station that paid next to nothing, and when he moved to Tacoma, Washington to be near her, he was reduced to selling vacuum cleaners door-to-door during the day and sleeping in his car at night. Although he did get his old radio job back when he returned to Maui in January, the pay was so poor that he had not managed to save enough money for the wedding, much less rent and the furnishing of a three-bedroom house as he had claimed. He explained that he had changed the locale of the wedding so that she wouldn't discover his dishonesty and break their engagement.

He also revealed that he had no money to cover her airfare from Canada, as promised, nor any money to cover the rent and security deposit on their new apartment. Though he eventually started earning a small income as a machinist in his brother's shop, it was not nearly enough to sustain two children and two adults. Kim had to draw from her own meager savings to keep the family going, and eventually had to dip into the children's savings accounts to pay for basic necessities. She was completely unprepared for these financial problems, as she had never had to worry about money in her previous marriage and had assumed that Anderson would be able to support her and the children.

Kim became frightened by their financial situation and Anderson's increasingly bizarre behavior. He insisted on controlling everything the family did: the shopping, the cleaning, what the children wore, where they went, and what Kim did with her time. Kim still felt the same revulsion towards sex that she had in her previous marriage, which was now exacerbated by her growing anger at and fear of Anderson. When she refused to fulfill her duty as a wife, he threatened violence and the intervention of Witness elders.

Within weeks of their marriage, Anderson fell into a deep depression. He began to eat obsessively, regaining most of the forty-five pounds he'd lost before he met Kim. He also stopped going to Kingdom Hall meetings and frequently missed work. One day, he got caught shoplifting at a local grocery store and had to spend the night in jail. His brother Luke paid the $100 to bail him out.

Anderson would not speak to the elders who Kim brought home to talk to him, and refused to seek outside professional help. He became increasingly physically abusive, often grabbing Kim and pinning her down when angry. Then, during a particularly heated argument in front of the children, he viciously bit her on the shoulder, drawing blood.

A week later, Kim packed her belongings and moved herself and the children into her brother-in-law's house. Within three days, Luke bought Juri and Lindsay new winter coats and gave Kim a couple of thousand dollars so that they could relocate to Canada. He then drove the three of them to the airport without informing Anderson of the time of their departure or their destination.

Kim and the children flew to Calgary, Alberta to stay with her friend Jo-Ann Lay. Terrified that her ex-husband would find out about their domestic situation and try to get custody of the children, she did not tell her own family about her problems with Jeff Anderson. Even worse, she was deeply ashamed that she had failed in her second marriage—and so quickly. Her mother would not find out about Kim's move to Calgary until several months later.

PUZZLED AS TO WHY Kim had moved to Calgary so soon after arriving in Houston, I decided to telephone her at the number on her address card. When Kim answered the phone, she told me there was no reason to be alarmed. She explained that she and her new husband had decided to move to Canada, and that he would be joining them soon to find an apartment and a job in Calgary. When I asked what her husband did for a living, she told me that he was in business with his brother in Houston. She did not specify the nature of that business.

When I told Kim that Marge and I wanted to come and visit the children in the spring, she vehemently objected. She bluntly stated that what she had promised me in July—a visit with the children combined with our vacation—was no longer possible. When I asked why, she told me that a September 1981 *Watchtower* had announced a stronger policy regarding disfellowshipment. All of Jehovah's Witnesses would also risk disfellowshipment if they associated with a disfellowshipped or lapsed Witness in any way. She explained that she intended to follow that policy to the letter, especially with regards to the children.

Although outraged by Kim's announcement, I was not surprised. I was already aware of the Society's crackdown on association and had experienced its effects firsthand. My sister Jeanette's family had attended our wedding in June and visited with us in our home in August. However, after the *Watchtower* edict, she immediately terminated her relationship with me. My mother tried to follow suit, but gave up after two weeks, telling me that she wouldn't be separated from her only son just because some religious magazine told her to do so. The situation was very upsetting to Marge, who, through no fault of her own, was shunned by my family along with me.

When I told Kim about the havoc this Witness policy was creating for my family, she was unsympathetic. "Let your family go, Jim. It will be easier for everyone concerned if you don't struggle against Jehovah's will."

"But Juri and Lindsay are so young," I protested. "They're not old enough to make that kind of decision about their own father."

Kim replied slowly and thoughtfully. "They probably don't want to make that decision, but they do want to please Jehovah." She ended the conversation by telling me that she would see how the children felt about a visit come spring.

When I told Marge about my conversation with Kim, she immediately expressed suspicion and alarm. Always a shrewd judge of character and behavior, she spoke bluntly. "Something's not right, Jim. Kim didn't move all the way from Burnaby to Houston and then to Calgary in three months time just on a whim. Something serious has happened—something she's not telling you about."

AFTER KIM LEFT JEFF ANDERSON in October 1981, he stayed in Houston and continued to work at his brother's machine shop. He also started to attend Witness meetings again, and soon became obsessed with the idea of getting back together with Kim. Over the next two months, he called her at least once a week, and sent her and the children numerous letters and gifts. Kim was not receptive to his overtures, but did not firmly close the door on a potential reconciliation. She suggested she might consider taking him back in a year or two, when he had demonstrated more financial responsibility and spiritual growth. Anderson obsessively hung on to that remote hope.

Kim would have felt that she could not return to her Witness community and family in Burnaby without her new husband, and may have genuinely hoped that Anderson would be able to get it together enough to allow her to return with honor—in other words, without having to face shame and chastisement for having abandoned her marriage so quickly. She also may have wanted to punish Anderson for the pain he had caused her.

However, it wasn't long before Anderson got tired of waiting for Kim to accept him back. In January 1982, he quit his job at the machine shop, moved out of his apartment, and spent the last of his money on a one-way bus ticket to Calgary. He was confident that he would be able to persuade Kim to take him back and that they would live happily ever after in Calgary.

Kim was alarmed by Anderson's unannounced arrival and gave him a cold reception. She refused to let him stay in the new apartment she had rented, and he was forced to accept the hospitality of some Witness brothers who lived down the hall from her. Angered and humiliated by her rejection, he sought the assist-

ance of Witness elders from her local congregation. They subsequently met with Kim and forced her to concede that she was scripturally obligated to accept Anderson back as her rightful husband in the eyes of Jehovah. They also told Anderson that he was obligated to become an adequate breadwinner and provider before she did so. Only a month after arriving in Calgary, Anderson was forced to return to Houston to get his affairs in order.

His brother gave him the money to fly back to Houston, where he moved back in with his mother and began a cycle of low-paying jobs and unemployment. He grew increasingly depressed and overweight, and even more obsessed with Kim than he had been before. As soon as he returned to Houston, he renewed his campaign to get her back, telephoning her once a week and writing letters to her on an almost daily basis. She gave him little encouragement, but never stated that reconciliation was out of the question.

Kim was now walking a fine line in the Witness community. The elders knew that she already had one failed marriage and a reputation for being a head-strong woman who resisted leadership from men. If she cut the ties with Anderson, she would be shunned and possibly disfellowshipped for leaving her marriage without cause. So she was forced to play a waiting game, probably outwardly hoping Anderson would become the provider she and the children needed, but inwardly praying that he would not. For if that happened, she would have no choice but to take him back.

IN MAY 1982, Kim finally agreed to let me see Lindsay, but she said a visit with Juri was out of the question. At the mature age of seven, he had decided that he would rather obey the wishes of Jehovah than associate with his father.

Marge and I moved quickly, before Kim had a chance to change her mind. We drove from Winnipeg to Calgary in less than sixteen hours and checked into our hotel room in the late afternoon. When we picked Lindsay up at Kim's apartment on Holmwood Avenue, I was startled by her changed appearance. She had, of course, grown, but she also appeared rather pale and thin. Kim told us that she had a mild case of bronchitis, but felt she was healthy enough to stay overnight with us at the hotel. Juri was nowhere in sight. When I asked Kim if we would have the opportunity to meet her new husband, she said he was at work.

As soon as we left the apartment, Marge privately expressed concern about Lindsay's ragamuffin clothes and rubber boots, which were very worn. We immediately took her to a nearby mall, where we bought her a brand new, purple and white gingham dress, with matching striped socks and a pair of white sandals. She proudly wore her new outfit to the local movie theatre, where we all enjoyed a Disney film. When we left the theatre, we noticed that her breathing had started to become raspy, so we took her back to the hotel and put her to bed early.

Lindsay was much improved in the morning and decided to entertain us with a little dance on her bed. Marge and I applauded her performance and encouraged her to dance some more, but she suddenly became very serious. "Daddy," she said, "why don't you love Jehovah anymore?" I gently explained that I still loved Jehovah very much, but didn't call him by that name anymore. She seemed troubled and unsatisfied by my answer, so I quickly changed the subject.

I cheerfully asked how she liked her new stepfather, Jeff. To my surprise, Lindsay solemnly shook her head in reply, and stated that Jeff no longer lived with them. When I asked why, she told me there had been "a terrible fight." She then went on to describe how Jeff had pinned her mother down on the bed, "yelling very loud," and how Kim had cried out for help.

Lindsay looked at me with terror in her eyes. An instinctive fear raced through my veins and raised the hair on the back of my neck. I quickly grasped both of her hands in mine.

"There was blood on their faces, Daddy. I was so scared..."

9

LINDSAY'S STORY LEFT ME feeling very alarmed and fearful for the safety of my children. Unable to bear the thought of my daughter being exposed to such a scene, I wondered if she had possibly fabricated the story or exaggerated a relatively harmless incident. But the emotion in Lindsay's voice and in her eyes was unmistakable, and Marge had no doubt that she was telling the truth. "Children don't lie about something like that," she said.

The next day, we took Lindsay to the Calgary Zoo before taking her back home. When Kim met us at the door, I told her we had something important to discuss with her. She was reluctant to let us into the apartment, but eventually led us into the living room and asked us to sit down. Marge and I were immediately struck by the dreary shabbiness of her home: gone were the beautiful new sofa and kitchen set that I had bought before I left Kim. And the large color television set had been replaced by a smaller, black-and-white model. Kim herself seemed tense and drawn, and displayed none of the joyful optimism that I had observed at our last meeting.

Before we could begin our conversation, Juri suddenly ran out of his room and slid into the living room in his stocking feet. My first reaction was joy at seeing him, and I smiled widely. That feeling soon turned to hurt and dismay as Juri ran toward me—not for the hug I expected, but to violently slam his little body against mine with obvious anger. As Kim attempted to restrain him, he tried to bite my arm right through my leather jacket and then continued to run around the apartment, hyperactively sliding around on the hardwood floors.

Needless to say, I was shocked and very concerned; he had always been such a gentle and thoughtful child. Later, I learned that the aggressive behavior he displayed is not uncommon in boys his age who live with a divorced parent. I also realized later that he was intensely angry that I had abandoned him, and that his refusal to see me probably had less to do with pleasing Kim and Jehovah than it did a need to punish me.

When things calmed down and the children finally settled in their bedroom to play, Marge and I sat down in the living room to talk to Kim. I asked about Juri's behavior and whether it was a common occurrence. Kim just shrugged and said he'd been "a little hyper" lately. Upset by her seeming lack of concern for our son, I began to speak to her with escalating anger. I told her how deeply disappointed I was that Juri had not been included in our visit. I demanded to know how she could be so unfeeling, and asked how she would feel in my position.

Kim responded to my anger with icy silence, which made me feel ready to explode. At that point, my levelheaded wife calmly pointed out to me that Kim could not be expected to sympathize with my feelings—her primary concern could only be for herself and the children. Her astute and carefully chosen words diffused the situation and averted a potentially explosive and unproductive argument.

Composing myself, I calmly relayed the story Lindsay had told us and asked Kim to explain it. I told her that I was especially concerned that bloodshed appeared to have been involved. Kim immediately smiled and waved her hand dismissively. She explained that there hadn't been a fight; she and Jeff had simply bumped heads as they bent over to unpack the same box, resulting in a nosebleed. When I asked why Lindsay would tell such a monstrous story, she again shrugged off my concern. "Oh, she's at the age where she likes to dramatize things...."

Kim then quickly changed the subject, telling us that it was too bad we had not been there a few days earlier to meet Jeff, who was now again "away on business." She also told us how much he had wanted to meet us. As she spoke, Marge and I were both privately speculating as to why a newly married man would be away from home so much of the time, and wondering whether she was telling the truth. But we also noticed a large photograph of a fair-haired young man hanging on the wall whom I correctly assumed was Jeff Anderson. The picture somehow reassured me and I tried to put my concerns out of my mind.

When we left, the children came out of their bedroom to say goodbye. Lindsay gave me a strong, lingering hug and a kiss on the cheek. Juri shook my hand with great seriousness, and then pointed to a watch on his wrist. "Do you know who gave me this?" he asked.

"Of course," I said, rubbing his head. "I gave it to you last year."

He then smiled at me for the first time, with a familiar, affectionate grin that broke my heart.

When I looked up at Kim, I realized by the look on her face that she meant this to be my last visit with the children. Feeling helpless against her willful stubbornness, I vowed inwardly that I would see them again, no matter what. That was not to be the case. I would see my daughter one more time, a year later in May 1983, but I would never again see my son alive.

On the way home, Marge said that it was "obvious" Kim was lying about the incident between her and Jeff, as well as his whereabouts, but I was unconvinced. For all her faults, I had always known Kim to be an honest person and did not think her capable of lying with such ease. "I've never known her to lie to me before," I protested.

"Nonsense," said Marge. "Everybody lies when they have to. Believe me, Kim is keeping the truth from you because something has happened and she's afraid of losing the children."

I knew Marge to be an astute judge of character and human nature, and could not argue with what she was saying, so we began to talk about the options that were available to us. We discussed the possibility of my seeking custody of the children, but we both knew that such an attempt would likely be an exercise in futility. In desperation, I asserted that we had no choice but to go back and forcibly abduct the children. Marge looked at me grimly. "Yes, and if we do, the RCMP will be waiting in our driveway when we get home."

The next day, I told my mother about our concerns, and she tried to reassure me. "Kim is such a faithful Witness," she said. "You know she would never lie."

I was almost convinced by my mother's words. I also remembered, though, that Jehovah's Witnesses were taught to think of themselves as "sheep among wolves," who needed to be "as cautious as serpents and yet innocent as doves." A 1960 issue of the *Watchtower* stated, "We must tell the truth to one who is entitled to know, but if one is not so entitled we may be evasive..." I realized that in Kim's eyes, I had become someone "not so entitled," and she would not hesitate to lie to me in the name of Jehovah himself if she felt justified in doing so.

Marge and I tried to see the children many times after our trip to Calgary in May of 1982, but were always denied access. The only news we received about Kim and the children was through my mother, who, as a fellow Witness, was occasionally in contact with Kim's mother. Jackie told my mother that she was concerned about Kim and was trying hard to persuade her to return to Burnaby. We hung on to the hope that she would succeed.

IN THE FALL OF 1982, Anderson received a note from Kim telling him that she and the children had moved back to Burnaby to be near her family. When she refused his request for a visit, he immediately contacted the local elders for their assistance, who chastised Kim for her unchristian attitude towards her husband. Encouraged by this support, Anderson began saving for the trip to Burnaby, convinced the elders would make Kim take him back when he arrived.

Kim knew it was only a matter of time before Anderson would show up on her doorstep again, and realized that she would have to demonstrate—at least outwardly—a willingness to work things out with him in order to avoid being sanctioned by the Witness community. However, she took comfort in knowing that Anderson would now be the one in foreign territory, and that he would risk the censure of her family, friends, and congregation if he did not stay in line and fulfill his obligations as a husband.

IN APRIL 1983, I asked Kim if Marge and I could come to Burnaby the following month to see the children during our vacation. Kim bluntly replied that neither Juri nor Lindsay had any wish to see me and that she could not force them to do so. According to Kim, six-year-old Lindsay had now also made the mature decision to follow Witness teaching and not associate with her father.

I finally consulted a lawyer in order to find out how I might enforce my visitation rights with the children. When he asked whether Kim received financial support from anyone other than me, I told him that she had remarried and probably received support from her husband as well. When he asked if I was sure about that, I told him that we did have reason to believe that she might have left her husband.

The lawyer raised his eyebrows. "Well, if that's the case, she's probably back on welfare. My advice is to delay sending your child support payments for a couple of weeks." He went on to explain this was not meant to cause her and the children financial hardship, but to find out whether she had any other means of support.

"Believe me," he said, "if she's living on nothing but welfare and child support checks from you, she'll quickly see your point of view with regard to the children."

I had always promptly honored my child support obligations under our divorce agreement, and was reluctant to look like a deadbeat father, but I decided to take the lawyer's advice and see what would happen. Sure enough, it didn't take long before I received a phone call from Kim.

Her voice was hard and businesslike: "What do you want, Jim?"

"To see my children," I replied.

"I'll see what I can do and get back to you."

Within three days, Kim telephoned again, telling me that Lindsay had changed her mind about seeing me. However, she was unable to persuade Juri to "disobey Jehovah." I did not push the issue further, for I felt that Juri was already under enough strain without further pressure from me. I quickly agreed to a four-day visit with Lindsay in Burnaby before Kim had a chance to change her mind. When Kim asked when she would receive the overdue check, I told her I would mail it that day.

Marge and I drove to Burnaby in less than three days. When we arrived at her rented house on Union Street, Kim seemed much friendlier than when we had seen her last. She invited us inside, and chatted amiably with Marge while Lindsay got ready to go. While they talked, I looked around the room and peered into the hallway leading to the children's bedroom, hoping to catch a glimpse of Juri, but he did not appear to be in the house. Lindsay suddenly came bounding into the room, wearing a colorful outfit and yellow-rimmed sunglasses.

"Why, you look like Hollywood," I teased.

Kim smiled and agreed. "Yes, she's cool, isn't she?"

Lindsay was clearly pleased to be the center of attention, and excited to be spending a whole four days with Marge and me. She was now six years old and a little taller and more self-confident than when we'd seen her last. I also noticed that she had begun to develop a striking resemblance to her mother—both physically and in her clever manner of speaking.

We spent the next four days at a pleasant motel on the southern edge of Lake Harrison, where Lindsay had a bedroom all to herself—something she had never had at home. In the mornings, we took dips in the resort's heated indoor swimming pool, where Lindsay would show off her swimming skills. She would stand a few feet away from me in the water, dive in, and do a few clumsy strokes before grabbing hold of my supportive arms. I remember how happy and alive she seemed, practicing her swimming again and again, until her skin was flushed from the heat and exertion. "Take her out of the water, Jim," Marge would insist. "She's starting to look like a lobster." If it hadn't been for Marge, Lindsay and I would have stayed in that mineral-heated pool all day.

In the afternoons, we cruised the mountain roads on the east side of the lake and visited a provincially-operated dairy farm in the nearby town of Agassiz. Lindsay loved to see the Holstein cows lined up at their milking stations and watch the chalk-white milk being pumped into glass containers. One morning, she was lucky enough to see a newly-born black and white calf.

During most of our visit, Lindsay seemed like a normal, happy kid. At times she was even refreshingly assertive. One afternoon, after a vigorous swim in the pool, I suggested we all take a nap. "Only babies take naps," she said. "I'm not a baby. *Nighttime* is for sleeping."

Lindsay loved to tussle with Marge on her motel bed, indulging in mock fights. One morning, however, Marge got the better of her and playfully pinned her down on the bed. To our surprise, Lindsay suddenly became very upset, struggling fiercely against Marge.

"Let go of me—let me up!" she yelled.

Marge immediately released her, and Lindsay quickly returned to her playful self, but it was a disturbing incident.

Towards the end of our visit, I tentatively asked about her stepfather. "Jeff doesn't live with us anymore," she said matter-of-factly. "He and Mom are separated." She did not seem to want to discuss the subject—or perhaps had been told not to discuss it—and so I did not press her further, but I felt immensely relieved to know that the children were no longer in a violent environment.

As we prepared to take Lindsay back home again, she began to talk excitedly about Juri and asked if we could buy a present for him. I had the impression that she felt badly that Juri had not come with us on the visit and wanted to do something to make him feel better. We stopped at a Burnaby mall where she picked out two metallic-colored, heart-shaped balloons.

As we drove over the crest of Capitol Hill in North Burnaby, we stopped at the house where Kim and I and the children used to live. Lindsay showed no interest in it; she had only been a toddler at the time and could not remember living there. But out of the blue, she said, "I know why you divorced Mommy. It was because of another woman!" Taken aback by her sudden declaration, I tried to explain that Kim and I had separated long before I met anyone else. However, she refused to believe me and I let the subject drop.

When we arrived at Kim's home in North Burnaby, she was sitting on the doorstep, surveying her front yard with a lawn mower sitting nearby. She was now twenty-nine years old, and looked older than the last time I had seen her— more mature, healthy, and self-assured. I remember noticing that her long hair was plaited in a braid, a style I'd never seen her wear before.

As we got out of the car, Kim came forward to tell us that we could not come in because Juri was in the house. At the sound of her brother's name, Lindsay jumped out of the car, crying "Juri, Juri, look what we brought you!" With fondness and amusement, I watched Lindsay run into the house, trailing two bright, heart-shaped balloons behind her. I did not realize that it would be my last glimpse of her.

Marge and I spent a few minutes telling Kim about our visit—how much Lindsay had enjoyed the swimming pool, the milk cows, and the newborn calf—

and she seemed pleased Lindsay had had a good time. As Marge got back into the car, I lingered a little longer, hoping Lindsay—and Juri—would come out of the house for one last goodbye. But they did not appear.

As Kim wished us a safe journey home, I sensed a calm sense of expectation about her. She started to mow the lawn as we drove away, which is the final image I have of her: pushing that lawnmower across the yard, her cheeks reddened by the spring sunlight, and her jaw set in quiet determination.

WHEN ANDERSON ARRIVED in Burnaby in the summer of 1983, he was encouraged by Kim's agreement to meet with the local elders to discuss the future of their marriage. The elders supported his desire to effect reconciliation with Kim, and agreed she had a scriptural obligation to contribute to that process. However, much to Anderson's surprise—and anger—they also said he should return to Houston until such time as he had demonstrated the financial security to move Kim and the children there and properly provide for them. They also advised him to attend Witness meetings more frequently and to work on improving himself spiritually.

Anderson returned to Houston humiliated. He felt betrayed by the elders and angry that Kim had won. He soon obtained a job as a security guard, but was unable to save much money from his low income. He attended Witness meetings to please the elders, but found he was no longer very enthusiastic in the Witness faith. His one and only preoccupation was Kim and his obsessive need to reunite with her.

IN AUGUST 1983, my mother Nellie visited her brother Clare at his new home in Surrey, British Columbia. While there, she took the opportunity to telephone Kim, who lived across the Fraser River in Burnaby, to see if she could visit her grandchildren. Though my mother had not obeyed the Witness edict to shun me as a disfellowshipped person, she was in all other ways a devoted Jehovah's Witness and Kim had no reason to refuse her. However, Kim made it clear that she did not want my mother to visit her, and instead offered to bring the children to Surrey.

My mother later reported that she spent a lovely time with Kim and the children on that gorgeous summer morning and afternoon. She was delighted to see Juri and Lindsay after so long a time, and the children were equally happy to see her. The four of them spent the morning chatting over cookies and milk. Later, they took a tour of the local Jehovah's Witness Assembly Hall. My mother was very impressed with the large building, the walls of which were decorated with colorful drawings illustrating Biblical stories and themes. Lindsay pointed out each picture to my mother, starting with the Garden of Eden, and was able to describe in detail the story behind each scene.

From the Assembly Hall, they drove to a large, vacant lot where wild raspberries and blackberries grew. Kim picked a large bowl of berries while the children played nearby, and then they all returned to Clare's house for lunch. At the kitchen table, my mother asked Kim to say the mealtime blessing. After lunch, she rested on the couch while Kim knitted and talked—"mainly of spiritual things." My mother reported that Kim was very kind to her during the visit, often expressing concern for her comfort and well-being.

When it came time for them to go, they all hugged my mother goodbye. She followed them to their car and stood on the curb, watching. At that moment, my mother had the strongest premonition that she would never see them again. The thought frightened her and she started to cry. Seeing her distress, Kim and the children got out of the car and returned, hugging her again for the longest time. "Then," Nellie said, "they drove away and disappeared from sight."

While in Surrey, my mother also contacted Kim's mother, Jackie. I had told her what Lindsay had reported during our last visit—that Kim and Jeff Anderson were separated—and she wanted to find out if it was really true. Jackie confirmed the report, telling my mother that Kim and Jeff had been separated for almost two years. She did not say anything about a possible reconciliation, nor did she express any opinion on Anderson or the separation.

When my mother reported this to me on her return trip to Manitoba, I immediately telephoned Kim. Her voice was flat and unemotional: "Yes, Jeff and I have been separated for some time." At that moment, I knew beyond a shadow of a doubt that all of Lindsay's stories had been true—including her report of a violent argument involving bloodshed. Marge's intuition had been right: Kim had been lying to me.

I told Kim that I was sorry to hear about her separation, for I had sincerely wanted Kim to succeed in her second marriage, not just for her, but for the stability and welfare of our children. Kim herself seemed strangely unemotional and philosophical about the situation. "That's the way it goes sometimes," she said. When I asked how she was coping financially, she told me she and the children were making do on my child support checks and welfare.

I was dismayed to see Kim trapped in a cycle of poverty, one that I had hoped she would avoid by getting married again. I also felt badly that her dream of the perfect Witness family was slipping further and further away. I wondered whether she was fooling herself, perhaps already dreaming up some other fantasy life for herself, and I worried how my children would fare in life with only one parent and so few resources.

On the other hand, I also felt relieved that Jeff Anderson was ancient history and no longer posed a threat to Juri and Lindsay.

IN SEPTEMBER 1983, Anderson took a vacation from his job, bought a motorcycle, and drove from Houston to Burnaby, determined to settle the issue of his marriage once and for all. He checked into a motel room near Kim's home and once again arranged a meeting with the local elders. To his surprise, Kim agreed that the time had come for reconciliation.

Kim made it clear that the reconciliation had to be on her terms. She refused to return with him to Houston, and insisted that he move to Burnaby and find a job. The elders also advised Anderson to sell his motorcycle in order to make an immediate financial contribution to the family, and said he should make every effort possible to financially support Kim and the children in the future.

Anderson had no choice but to agree. The next day, he and Kim went to the immigration office to apply for a move to Canada, and then he returned to Houston to wait for confirmation. While he waited, he fell into another cycle of depression and overeating, and lost his job as a security guard in late 1983. But his Canadian visa papers arrived just in time.

Anderson became elated about his new future. He arrived in Vancouver in March 1984, after a three-day bus ride from Houston, tired, but excited to see Kim again. When Kim's stepfather Norman picked him up at the bus station, he warned Anderson not to expect too much from Kim—it would be a difficult adjustment for her after being alone for over two years. When Kim met him at the house, she had a scared look in her eyes, but otherwise put on a brave face, giving him a quick kiss of the lips and a cavalier welcome: "Welcome to Canada, tall Texan." Then she quickly pulled away and began to tidy the house.

Undismayed by Kim's less-than-passionate welcome, Anderson was able to express his happiness and excitement with the children—especially Juri, who immediately dragged him into the bedroom to show off his toys and books. The two of them hung out together for the rest of the evening, playing, reading, and roughhousing. When Anderson and Kim were alone, he offered to sleep in a motel for the first week or so until she adjusted to him being back. She said that wasn't necessary and she allowed him to sleep on the couch. After about three days, he began to make sexual advances towards her, and by the fifth day she gave in, saying, "Oh, go ahead, you'll go crazy if you don't." To Anderson's great disappointment, she was as unresponsive to him as she had been in Houston over two years before.

However, unlike before, it was now Kim who controlled every detail of the family's life. Although she did not work, other than doing small housecleaning jobs, she kept the car for her own use while Anderson had to ride public transit to look for a job. The only time she allowed him to drive was when they attended Witness meetings, since she was very conscious of keeping up appearances in front of the congregation. When he tried to get the car's muffler fixed, she told him that she would take care of it. When he wanted to look after the family finances and bookkeeping, she told him that she didn't trust him with money. When he wanted to play a part in the children's religious instruction, she told him they would continue Bible studies with a local Witness elder. Frustrated by Kim having the upper hand in their relationship and her increasing indifference towards him, he went on frequent eating binges and became more and more overweight.

After two months, Anderson finally landed a part-time job with B.C. Transit, driving a wheelchair van for the handicapped. Though the job didn't become full-time until several months later, Kim was immediately informed that she would no longer receive welfare, now that Anderson was bringing home a paycheck. At the time, Anderson's part-time income was far less than Kim had been receiving from welfare and the situation made Kim feel angry and insecure. She had lost her financial stability the last time she had been with Anderson, and here it was happening all over again, like a bad dream.

Against Anderson's wishes, the family moved from Kim's small, rundown, two-bedroom rented house on Union Street to a nearby Beta Avenue apartment complex so Kim could be near several Witness friends living there. It didn't take long before they started to pop in and out of the apartment for coffee klatches and knitting sessions. Soon Kim's indifference towards Anderson turned into public anger and disdain. Feeling trapped in her marriage, she frequently belittled her husband in front of her family, friends, and other Witnesses—so much so that many people in the Witness community began to take his side in what was obviously a deeply unhappy marriage.

Anderson used the community's sympathy to his full advantage, getting Witness elders to come to their apartment for marriage counseling sessions, and even getting Kim's stepfather to give her a talk on how to keep her husband sexually happy. He also began to act out his anger towards her in increasingly disturbing ways. He would frequently take the children on outings without telling her, causing her panic and worry, sabotage her washing days by disconnecting electrical wires in the washing machine, and once caused serious water damage to the apartment by removing the plug from her waterbed. Anderson grew so desperate to gain some control in his relationship with Kim that at one point he even tried to romance her as he had when they first met in Maui, bringing her flowers, leaving little love notes around the apartment, and asking her out to dinner. Kim's response was utter disbelief. The very thought of him touching her made her skin crawl.

The arguments between them escalated to the point where the children became emotionally distraught, frequently crying or lashing out in anger for no reason. Unable to bear the situation any longer, Kim contacted the local elders and told them that she wished to discuss her marriage with Anderson, but only on condition that what she told them in the meeting would be kept strictly confidential. The elders agreed and, in July 1984, met with Kim and Jeff at the Kingdom Hall.

In that meeting, Kim made certain accusations against Anderson, confident that what she told the elders would convince them that a permanent separation was justified. Her confidence proved misplaced. After interviewing both parties separately, the elders came to the conclusion that Kim was the cause of the problems in her marriage. They gave her a long and severe chastisement in front of Anderson, ordering her to be a better and more supportive wife to her husband. Kim was reduced to tears, and went home feeling shocked and bewildered. For his part, Anderson could hardly contain his happiness at this vindication. The tables had turned, and now he would have the upper hand in the household.

That night, Kim sat in the park behind her apartment building, sobbing uncontrollably. When Anderson came out to join her, he asked what was wrong. "I'm mourning my former self," she said. "The one who has to become a robot tomorrow."

Thereafter, Kim indeed became a robot. At first she obeyed Jeff with deep sarcasm and indifference, but eventually withdrew into a silent shell, sinking into depression. At one point, she told a friend she thought it best to commit suicide, so "at least the kids would be taken care of." Her mother felt increasingly concerned about her daughter, and feared that she was on the verge of a nervous breakdown. She encouraged her daughter to seek help outside the Jehovah's Witness community.

On July 20, 1984, Kim met with a social worker at the Ministry of Human Resources, who advised her to leave Anderson immediately for the protection of the children. She took that advice, and on July 21, packed some clothes and provisions and moved in with a close friend in Coquitlam.

When Anderson discovered Kim had left him once again, he became frantic and enraged. When Kim's mother would not tell him where she was, he contacted the Witness elders, who ordered her to return to her husband. Kim refused, and was placed on "private reproof" and deprived of some of her congregational privileges. But she fought back, putting in more and more hours preaching from door-to-door—even though she was not technically allowed to preach anymore. Over the next few months, Kim succeeded in winning the approval of those in the congregation who had at first blamed her for her marriage problems, and—like her mother before her—her respectability was eventually restored.

In August 1984, Kim told Anderson that if he did not move out of the apartment, he could keep the lease on it and she would move into a new apartment. After a month or so, he was no longer able to afford the rent and he let Kim and the children move back in. At first, he moved to a rundown basement apartment about a mile away, but later found himself an apartment directly across the street from Kim, where he could keep a close eye on her and the children.

In early November 1984, Kim's file with Family Services was closed with the following notes: "Kim says she had talked to the school, given them pictures of Jeff, and instructed them that he has no legal rights re the children. At any rate he has not attempted to see them at school... There are no protection concerns at this time. Kim has agreed to call if she feels there is a need."

Meanwhile, Anderson, realizing he had again lost control of Kim, fell into his usual pattern of depression, self-pity, and overeating. For several months, he told anyone who would listen—Kim, Jackie, his mother, the elders—that he planned to commit suicide if Kim did not return to him. However, whatever support and sympathy he had had in the community had dried up, and the elders advised him to let Kim go and get on with his life.

Anderson's depression grew into anger and bitterness, finally focusing into hatred and rage: against Kim, the elders, and all of his fellow Witnesses. His obsessions grew pathological, and he began to weave revenge fantasies that grew increasingly elaborate and violent.

Like an out-of-control gambler who had lost everything, he was ready to go for broke.

10

AFTER OUR VISIT with Lindsay in May 1983, I periodically phoned Kim to request visits with the children, but was always given the same party line: the children wished to obey Jehovah and avoid association with those who had been disfellowshipped. She remained polite and pleasant—as though what she was saying was the most natural and reasonable thing in the world—but calmly explained I could not expect to see my children again unless I returned to the Witness fold.

As it was highly unlikely that I would ever become one of Jehovah's Witnesses again, I reluctantly came to accept that I would probably not have a relationship with either of my children until they were mature enough to make decisions for themselves. I could only hope that they would eventually develop discerning minds of their own and not blindly follow Witness teachings for the rest of their lives.

Over the next year, Marge and I worked very hard, managing two apartment buildings in Winnipeg in addition to demanding full-time jobs. In March 1985, we had finally saved enough money for the down payment on a house, and were able to move into our cozy nest on Scotland Avenue in Fort Rouge. Our marriage was stable and loving, and for the first time in my life I knew what it was like to be happy in a relationship.

However, in addition to missing my children, I continued to experience a kind of spiritual restlessness, and a yearning for a connection with God that went beyond the comfortable pew at our local United Church. Although I had left Jehovah's Witnesses far behind, I was still struggling with some of the damaging beliefs that had been instilled in me from an early age.

My children might have been physically separated from me, but they frequently appeared in my dreams, and I often experienced periods of intense sadness and loneliness for them. These feelings would come out of the blue, at the sight of a child when passing a playground or when watching a particular movie or television program. I also experienced intense feelings of guilt for having left my family in the hands of the Jehovah's Witness community. In many ways, I felt that I had achieved my personal happiness at the expense of my children, and expected God to punish me for my selfishness.

In May 1985, I noticed a dead animal on the street while driving my bus route. As I drove closer, I saw it was a freshly killed young robin. For some reason, the sight of the crushed body of that little bird upset me deeply and I could not get its image out of my mind. I told myself that I was being irrational, but I felt convinced that it was a bad omen that had something to do with my children, and for many days afterwards I felt worried and concerned about them.

Though the feeling eventually subsided, I continued to feel vaguely uneasy, and several times resisted the impulse to phone Kim in Burnaby to ask how the children were doing.

AFTER THEIR SEPARATION in the summer of 1984, Jeff Anderson continued to live in a basement apartment across the street from the Beta Avenue apartment complex where Kim and the children lived, and he also attended the same Witness congregation, even sitting together with them at meetings as though they were still a family. Eventually, though, Kim refused to answer his obsessively lengthy and frequent letters, and Juri and Lindsay eventually stopped acknowledging him in public.

Anderson was still manifesting his anger in disturbing ways. Kim had to change the locks on the doors and keep the windows locked at night after she found Anderson lurking around the apartment on more than one occasion. On hearing that she and the children were going on vacation, he punctured the tires on her car in order to prevent them from being able to go. He was also suspected of having punctured the tires of other Jehovah's Witness vehicles in the neighborhood. In July 1985, he lost his job as a driver for the handicapped for "borrowing" the company's vans on his off-time without permission. He continued to use the vans even after he was fired, and narrowly escaped being charged with auto theft.

Anderson's mother visited Burnaby in July 1985, hoping to talk him into coming home with her to Houston, but he was consumed with the idea of getting back together with Kim and the children, and refused to leave Burnaby without them. She begged him to forget all about Kim, but to no avail.

Anderson first began to think about buying a gun that spring of 1985, but was not familiar with Canadian gun laws. He answered an ad in the paper for a .357 Magnum handgun, the same model he had owned in Houston, but the *owner refused to sell it to him without a Firearms Acquisition Certificate. He subsequently succeeded in buying an illegal shotgun for $100. After buying a box of twenty-five shells, he sawed off much of the barrel of the gun, put three shells in the chamber, and stored the gun and ammunition under his bed. He also began to compose a letter to Jackie Cole.*

IN LATE JULY 1985, I experienced a frightening series of dreams, all in the same night. In the first dream, I was wandering the forest hills near 100 Mile House, the village where Kim and the children and I had lived in the 1970s. All of the trees in the area had been slashed and burned, and the village was now an empty ghost town. I anxiously searched for survivors, but could find no one. The landscape was utterly desolate.

In the second dream, I was able to see into a woman's womb, where I watched a single cell develop into a living fetus with a beating heart. When the fully formed infant was placed in my arms, I recognized it as my own son, and felt overwhelmed with intense feelings of nurturing and bonding.

In the final dream, I saw the same infant sinking into a pool of milk, with everything but the circle of his face submerged in liquid. Terrified, I realized that the baby was drowning, but didn't know how to save him. At that point, I awoke, drenched in sweat and shaking violently.

I was so distressed by this dream that I telephoned Kim as early as possible that morning to ask about the children. When she answered the phone, there was a cheerful tone in her voice that I had not heard in some time. She updated me on the children's progress in school, telling me that eight-year-old Lindsay had done especially well in her first two years of elementary school and was now looking forward to Grade Three, and that ten-year-old Juri had developed into a serious young man who loved mathematics and television programs about outer space. I had the distinct impression that Kim had finally found stability and happiness after her separation from Jeff Anderson and was now embarking on a new chapter in her life. The frightening dream of the previous night quickly vanished, along with my concerns.

It had been two years since I'd visited Lindsay, and three years since I'd seen Juri. I once again asked Kim if I could come to Burnaby to visit them, and she once again told me that they did not wish to disobey Jehovah. When I persisted, she offered to put the children on the phone so that they could tell me themselves. Remembering the last time I had tried to speak with Juri on the phone—a painful conversation in which he barely said a word—I declined her offer. Satisfied that the children were safe, I did not push the issue further.

Kim seemed pleased that I was being so cooperative, and continued to talk to me a little while longer about the children, once again letting me know that the children would probably be quite happy to visit with me should I again become one of Jehovah's Witnesses. At no time in our conversation did she mention Jeff Anderson.

It was the last time I would hear her voice.

IN EARLY AUGUST, Jeff Anderson left Burnaby for a three-week motorcycle tour of the southwestern United States. During his absence, his basement apartment at 250 Beta Avenue was accidentally flooded after a heavy rainstorm. The building's caretaker, one of the Jehovah's Witnesses, had to enter the apartment to remove his belongings. Discovering the gun and ammunition under Anderson's bed, the caretaker, understandably concerned, consulted with two local elders, who confronted Anderson when he returned. Knowing that he was depressed, they questioned what he was planning to do with the weapon. Anderson at first claimed that he needed the gun for self-defense, but then confessed that he had been thinking about taking his own life. He angrily demanded the return of his property, but the elders refused and handed the gun over to the RCMP on August 24, 1985.

The very same day, Anderson went out and bought a semi-automatic, twelve-gauge shotgun for $500, on a line of credit he had just obtained on his Visa card. Once again, he sawed off part of the gun barrel, bought a box of ammunition, and placed three shells in the chamber.

The next day, a Burnaby RCMP constable visited Anderson's apartment to question him about the seized weapon. Anderson produced a United States passport and told the officer that he was in Burnaby to reconcile with his estranged wife. He explained that he was familiar with firearms as a former security guard in Texas, and did not have the necessary Firearms Acquisition Certificate for the shotgun because he hadn't realized he needed one. When asked why he had sawed off the barrel of the gun, he said it was easier to handle that way. The constable advised Anderson that it was illegal to shorten a shotgun barrel, and that he would be making enquiries about him in Texas.

The constable did not receive any information about Anderson from Texas and as a result saw no need to follow up. At the time of his visit, he was unaware of the new shotgun that Anderson had bought the day before, which had been placed in a closet below the stairway, freshly oiled and filed, just as the officer knocked on Anderson's door.

On the morning of August 29, 1985—a Thursday—Anderson wrote the final portion of the suicide note that he had been composing since the early spring.

The note was addressed to Kim's mother and stepfather, Jackie and Norman Cole. In it, he expressed sorrow for "the terrible thing I've done," complaining about the "pain," "heartache," "rage," and "frustration" that Kim's "indifference" had caused him, and the fact that Kim seemed to be "enjoying her freedom" and "rubbing my face in it." He ended the letter with the assertion that he no longer deserved to live, "and wouldn't want to anyway without Kim."

After finishing the letter, he took a short motorcycle ride through Burnaby Mountain and other local areas. It was a beautiful, late-summer morning. When he returned to his apartment, he placed the sawed-off shotgun upright in a large, paper grocery bag and covered the barrel of the gun with a camera-tripod box. There were three shells in the barrel of the gun, and he put the remainder of the ammunition—twenty-two shells—in his jacket pockets. Shortly after 11:00 a.m., he telephoned Kim.

When Kim answered the phone, Anderson hung up without saying anything. Possibly thinking it might have been her mother calling, she immediately phoned Jackie Cole. After hanging up the phone, Anderson left the suicide letter in his apartment and walked the half-block to Kim's apartment at #107-205 Beta Avenue. When he arrived at the front door, he took the gun out of the bag and discovered that the door was unlocked. He entered the apartment, quietly closing the door behind him, then took two or three steps down the hall to the kitchen, where Kim's view of his entry was obstructed by a wall.

Anderson found Kim sitting at the kitchen table in her nightgown, talking to her mother on the phone. Holding the shotgun at waist level, he pointed it at her and waited for her to notice him. He then asked her to hang up the telephone and told her that he needed to talk. Kim stared at him for a moment, then calmly told her mother: "I have to go, there's a shotgun pointed at me. Call the police." She repeated the message a second time, to ensure that her mother did not think she was joking, then hung up the phone and stood up.

The telephone rang moments later, but neither of them moved to answer it. Standing in the doorway between the hall and the kitchen, Anderson asked Kim to go into the bedroom. Thinking he intended to force her to have sex with him, as he had done before, she stated that she would not—"That would be rape." Anderson explained that he only wanted to talk. He also warned her that she should take him seriously, and asked if she knew "what a sawed-off shotgun will do." She nodded in the affirmative, but when he moved closer to her, she confidently brushed past him, shoving the gun a little to one side, saying, "I don't know about you, but I am going to fix lunch for the kids." She then walked to the kitchen stove and began to prepare a meal.

Anderson went looking for Juri and Lindsay, and found them in their back bedroom standing together near a window, looking frightened. He stuck his head in the doorway and said, "Kids, don't worry, I am just here to talk, nobody is going to get hurt," then went back to the kitchen. Kim seemed more concerned now that Anderson had located the children. "Let them go," she said, "and you can have me." Anderson refused.

The telephone rang and Kim answered it. RCMP Constable Mel Trekofski told Kim that he was phoning in response to Jackie Cole's call about some trouble in Kim's apartment. Kim sighed with relief, and a four-minute telephone conversation followed, in which Trekofski spoke first with Kim and then with Anderson.

Kim: "Ah, will you please... My kids are... He's going in the bedroom with a shotgun on my kids. Hold on, please."

Trekofski: "Okay, who's there, who's there?"

Kim: "It's Jeff, my husband."

Trekofski: "Is he drunk?"

Kim: "No, he's very serious."

After a few further exchanges, Trekofski asked: "What do you think he's going to do?"

Kim replied, "I don't know. He's putting a chain on the door right now." A little later, she said, "He's closing the curtains—he doesn't want the public to know."

Later, Trekofski asked, "Why won't he talk to me now?"

Kim: "Why won't you talk to him, Jeff?" (To Trekofski) "He's told me to get off the phone and come in there."

Trekofski: "Pardon me?"

Kim: "He's told me to get off the phone and come in there. Wherever that is, I don't know, whether it's in my kids' room or my room, and he won't talk to me. No, he doesn't seem to want to, but he does have a sawed-off shotgun."

Trekofski: "Sawed-off?"

Kim: "I'm very scared for my kids."

After further exchanges, Anderson finally came to the telephone. Trekofski identified himself and said, "We'd like to settle things, you know, we would like to help out if we can."

Anderson: "I don't think you can. It's reached a desperate situation. Now, there is a possibility that I will give it some thought the longer you stay away. We both... Everyone sees these stand-offs on the news. We know how it happens. Let it happen like that for three or four hours. Maybe she will feel the pain and misery that I felt."

Trekofski: "Well, you are not going about it the right way, Jeff."

Anderson: "I'm sure they're pulling up right now outside. If they charge, if they do anything, I will have to hurt her. I will have to shoot her, then the children."

Trekofski: "Ah, don't do that."

Anderson: "There's a chance you can talk me out of it if you stay away. I'll keep in contact with you over the phone. Just stay away for now."

Anderson then hung up the phone. It was 11:16 a.m. By that time, RCMP officers had surrounded the townhouse. They made no attempt to enter because of Anderson's threat to shoot Kim and the children if police made any attempt to intervene.

At that point, Anderson entered the children's bedroom, followed by Kim. Lindsay was dressed in pajamas, holding a stuffed toy bear in her arms, and Juri was dressed in a night top and underwear. Kim instructed the children to move away from the window and sit on the lower bunk bed. Lindsay sat on the corner of the bed near the wall and Juri sat to the left of her. There was a deck of playing cards on the bed between them. Kim sat on a yellow milk crate at the end of the bunk bed, near the window.

Anderson pointed the gun at Kim and told her that they were going to talk. The room was small and hot, and he refused to let Kim and the children leave. For over an hour, he angrily denounced Kim's rejection of him. Why was she so indifferent to him? Didn't she see that he was in pain, how serious his condition was? Didn't she get his many messages, his letters? He asked about the things that he had always wanted to know, questions she had not answered in letters or over the telephone or at the door when he had called on her.

Kim sat sideways to Anderson, with worry and fear in her eyes. She sat leaning forward with her hands clasped, sometimes supporting her chin on her palm. As Anderson talked, she occasionally turned her head and made quick eye contact with him.

He asked her if she was aware that he had tried to do things "Jehovah's way." He said that he had tried to live up to her standards, to Witness standards. Why was she prolonging their separation? Didn't she see how miserable everybody was? It seemed like their marriage would be in limbo forever. Did she never plan to get back together with him?

Kim said something about having failed at two marriages, and said she would just as soon give up on marriage altogether. She then tried to distract him by asking him questions, mostly about his motorcycle holiday in the United States. The children began to complain that they were "hungry and tired." At one point, they asked Anderson if he was going to shoot them, to which Anderson said, "No, I love you too much."

Anderson told Kim how much he loved her, how much he loved the kids, how he wanted her and the kids and himself back together again. He asked her why she had danced with two Witness brothers at a congregation get-together, after he had specifically asked her not to. She replied, "Yeah, that was really dumb," and then repeated herself in order to indicate that she understood the gravity of his question. Meanwhile, the children had begun to relax, talking with one another and playing cards. Kim occasionally turned her head toward them, whispering, "I love you," or "Don't worry, it's okay."

Anderson wondered aloud if he'd always been a little crazy. He thought that perhaps their unresolved situation had brought the craziness to the surface. He apologized for what he was about to do, telling her he hoped he had enough courage to turn the gun on himself afterwards. He told her he feared that if he did not, the punishment would be worse—life in prison where a man could be raped and stabbed.

Anderson: "I'm so sorry. I have to do this."

Kim: "You don't have to do this."

Anderson: "No, I have to do this. I'm sorry, I'm a sick man."

Kim: "No you're not. You can get help."

He asked if she had ever loved him, and she told him that she had not loved him since she left him in Houston four years before. He asked why she did not love him now, why she had stopped loving him. Her last words were, "I don't know."

Anderson asked Kim for one last hug. When she refused, he started shooting.

The first shot hit the side of her face, spattering blood and tissue on the ladder leading to the top bunk bed. There was an eerie second of silence and delay before she fell backwards to the floor, flat on her back, feet to the door. Her hands fell evenly and close together just below her chest.

After Anderson shot Kim, the gun should have ejected the empty shell automatically, but did not because of the sawed-off barrel. So Anderson paused, turned the gun on its side and ejected the empty shell manually—a task that required time, mental acuity, control, and focus.

Anderson then turned, took a step to his right and brought the gun barrel up to Lindsay's face. She instinctively raised her hands, trying to protect her face or push the gun away. Eleven seconds after killing Kim, Anderson pulled back and shot Lindsay in the face.

Juri cowered on the bed, holding his dead sister, while Anderson again turned the gun on its side to eject the empty shell manually. Eleven seconds after killing Lindsay, he raised the gun to Juri and shot him in the face as well.

The gun was empty. Anderson ejected the third empty shell and loaded four new shells into the gun. Sixteen seconds after killing Juri, he stood directly over Kim's severely damaged head and shot almost straight down, narrowly missing his own foot (blood and brain tissue splattered on his shoes), and as he walked out of the room he noted blood was pouring out of Kim's head in a pool on the floor.

The gun was still loaded with three shells, which would have allowed Anderson to turn the gun on himself or shoot it out with the police surrounding the apartment, but he chose neither of those options. Instead, he calmly walked to the kitchen, put the loaded gun on the table and surrendered himself outside the front door on his knees.

He kept his arms raised to ensure that the police would not shoot him, and was arrested face-down on the front sidewalk. "I've done a terrible thing," he said. "I'm sorry I didn't have the courage to kill myself. I don't deserve to live anymore."

11

"ARE YOU THE FATHER of Juri and Lindsay Kostelniuk?"

My mind raced frantically through all the possible reasons for the RCMP officer's visit. Part of me sat across from him at the kitchen table, my body trembling in anticipation of what he was about to say. Another part of me stood in the corner of the room, calmly observing. I watched him struggle to maintain a professional demeanor, nervously fingering the piece of paper in his hands. There was no way to be prepared for what he finally said.

"I'm sorry to inform you that they and their mother, Kim Anderson, were murdered in Burnaby, British Columbia, at about 12:30 p.m. today. Jeff Anderson, Kim's husband, is in police custody."

The room careened, and a wave of nausea swept through my body. I felt fragmented, a part of me watching from every corner of the room.

"How... how did they die?" I managed to ask. "What kind of... weapon?"

The officer looked down at his piece of paper and cleared his throat. "It was a shotgun murder, sir."

Another wave of nausea. I held my stomach and doubled over in agony. "A shotgun?"

Marge's voice rose with violent emotion: "Why the children?" she cried. "What did they do...? Why...?" When I looked up, she was staring blankly at the officer, her face a distorted mask of horror.

The officer grimaced and shrugged his shoulders helplessly. "I'm sorry," he said. "That's all the information I have."

What could he say? What could anyone say?

CORPORAL TOM WAGNER, a forty-year old officer with the Burnaby RCMP Detachment, was assigned to be the primary investigator in the Anderson case. His superiors had initially assigned the case to someone else and Wagner was to be his supervisor. However, that officer was too emotionally overwhelmed by what he saw at the crime scene and was unable to continue on the case. Tom Wagner agreed to take over. "Somebody had to do it," he said.

While police surrounded the apartment in which Kim and the children were being held hostage, Corporal Wagner drove to Jackie Cole's home to bring her and her daughter Cindy to the RCMP detachment, both for their own safety and to obtain crucial information about Jeff Anderson. Wagner hoped that the hostage situation could be resolved without bloodshed, but he took care to change the police-car radio channel so that the Coles would be spared any reports of violence.

As soon as Anderson walked out the front door of the apartment, he was arrested. As the police handcuffed him, Anderson declared that he didn't deserve to live anymore and that he should be deported to Texas where they still had the death penalty.

The first police officer inside the apartment was horrified to discover Kim's body lying in a pool of blood on the floor of the back bedroom, her face and head gruesomely disfigured by two shotgun blasts at close range. However, it was only after running through the apartment, calling to the children that he discovered where they were. The bodies of Lindsay and Juri were on the bloodstained bunk-bed, their visages also disfigured from direct shots to the face. A toy teddy bear lie in Lindsay's lap, and Juri's arms remained clasped around his sister. A deck of cards were scattered between them. One of Lindsay's fingers had also been shot, probably as she held her hands to her face in a defensive gesture.

Wagner arrived at the crime scene after Anderson was taken away in a police car, and immediately entered the apartment with three other officers. The first things they saw were the shotgun on the kitchen table and some pieces of bread and jam—remnants of the children's breakfast.

The bodies were later removed from the apartment on stretchers, covered by thick blankets. A small crowd of neighbors and police officers stood transfixed. The media was there too with their television cameras.

Children were seen watching from their bicycles in the lane.

Meanwhile, Anderson had been taken to the Burnaby RCMP Detachment, where he was immediately administered tests to determine his level of sobriety. The tests showed that he was not inebriated and had not taken drugs of any kind. He remained calm and unemotional throughout the incarceration process, and slept peacefully for several hours after being placed in his jail cell.

THINGS HAPPENED VERY QUICKLY after the RCMP officer left our house. Marge phoned my mother and told her to prepare herself because we were coming over to give her some bad news. When we arrived at her apartment ten minutes later, she answered the door with frightened, frantic eyes. Afterwards, she sobbed uncontrollably in my arms, crying over and over again that there must have been a mistake. "Not my Lindsay and Juri," she kept saying. "Not my little grand-children."

The telephone rang and Marge answered it. An old friend from school—Dale Streich, now an RCMP constable living near Clandeboye—had been informed of the murders and arranged to visit us that evening. Marge then phoned my sister with the news.

As the initial shock began to wear off, a chasm of despair loomed before me. Determined to avoid what I knew would be a bottomless pit, I focused on my anger and anxiety—emotions that would lead to action and keep paralyzing depression and despair at bay. Marge had set us in motion by telephoning my mother and sister, and now I set to work to find answers, information that would help me put the pieces together and find some explanation for what had happened.

We took my mother home with us, where I made a series of phone calls. I started with RCMP Staff Sergeant Neil MacKay, head of the Burnaby General Investigation Section, who was able to provide me with a rough outline of what had happened that morning in Burnaby. He said that Jeff Anderson had held Kim and the children hostage for over an hour while the RCMP surrounded the apartment and waited for the Emergency Response Team to arrive. An RCMP negotiator made telephone contact but was not able to prevent Anderson from shooting and killing his hostages. When I told MacKay that our friend Dale Streich would be visiting us that evening, he indicated that as an RCMP officer, Dale would be able to take a written statement from us. Finishing the conversation, I got the distinct impression that MacKay felt deep regret that he and his fellow officers were unable to prevent the tragedy of that day.

Next, I called Kim's mother and stepfather. Norman Cole answered the phone, with a voice that was unusually low for such a cheerful man. When I relayed what I had learned from MacKay, he let out a long sigh. "Yes, it's quite a shocker all right." I wondered aloud why Anderson would do this after being out of Kim's life for such a long time and was stunned by what Norman told me: that Anderson had gotten back together with Kim over a year before, that Kim had left him for a second time shortly thereafter, that he had been living across the street from her, that Witness elders had already taken one gun away from him, and that my children had been in danger for some time without my know-ledge.

The rest I already knew from Sergeant MacKay, so I proceeded to question Norman about the actions of the RCMP, hoping to learn that there had been some mishandling of the situation, something that would explain how Anderson could have succeeded in doing what he did. Had the RCMP failed to act to save the hostages? Had they provoked Anderson into doing what he did? Norman assured me that the police had done everything possible and were not to blame in any way.

I then asked if Anderson had remained one of Jehovah's Witnesses after he and Kim separated. Norman told me that the Witness elders had initially assisted Anderson in getting Kim to reconcile with him but had counseled him to let her go after she had left him a second time.

"But was he still a Jehovah's Witness when he committed the murders?" I pressed.

Norman became hesitant and equivocal, saying that Anderson had not really attended Witness meetings with much regularity of late. My next question was more direct: "But was he still considered one of Jehovah's Witnesses?" Norman had to admit that he was. When I asked if anyone in the congregation had sus-pected Anderson might do something like this, he replied, "Well, we thought there might be some sort of blow up—but nothing like this."

I then asked to talk to Jackie, to whom I expressed my outrage and utter disbelief. I expected the same reaction from her, as Kim's mother, but to my sur-prise her voice remained very calm and composed. "It's all over for them now," she said. "We have to think about what's ahead for us, Jim."

I gasped at her response. At that point, Kim and the children had been dead only a few hours. How could she be so philosophical about their deaths?

I realized that Jackie was dealing with the tragedy in the only way she knew how: in the context of her beliefs as one of Jehovah's Witnesses. I remembered how passionately she had talked about the possibility of Witnesses being viol-ently martyred for their faith once the political and social disorder of Arma-geddon came about, how Witnesses should expect to have their faith tested by great hardship. I realized she had chosen to think of Kim and the children as having undergone a great test of faith—even though their murders had had nothing to do with religion. I also realized that she was telling me to worry about my own sinful soul and not the souls of my dead children, who were now more fortunate than I. They were now assured of a resurrection because they had maintained their loyalty to Jehovah, whereas I still faced eternal damnation if I did not act to change my point of view.

Her words fed the simmering anger in my heart. The deaths of Kim and our children were the senseless acts of a madman and had nothing to do with God. Juri and Lindsay had been robbed of their childhood, their adult life; they would never grow up, marry, and have children of their own—and for what? For some primitive tribal God who demanded the bloody sacrifice of innocents? Embittered thoughts flooded my mind. What kind of God would allow such a thing to happen? How could I have been so foolish as to believe in such a deity—in any deity? Where was Jehovah now?

The immensity of my rage frightened me, and I tried to hold it back. I told myself that I should understand how desperately Jackie needed the crutch of a religion at such a difficult time, how she needed my empathy and consolation, how devastated she must be beneath her calm exterior. I also had to admit that, my own feelings aside, I envied the power of her faith.

Continuing my search for answers, I asked Jackie what she could tell me about Jeff Anderson. Not surprisingly, at that point her philosophical demeanor vanished and her voice became hoarse with hatred. "The man's a pig," she said. "And Jim, he lies constantly." For the rest of our conversation, Jackie and I were on common ground.

As the evening approached, my mother Nellie insisted on going home to be alone, overcome by her own grief and exhaustion. Marge and I had found out all we could for now, and there was nothing further to do. No longer distracted by the activity of collecting information, Marge and I had to face what we had been avoiding all day. A deep and inexpressible sorrow descended on us like a pall.

When I was very small, Juri had asked me to explain the difference between "gone" and "dead." Over the years, the experience of being separated from my children had been almost unbearable. But although they were gone, they had still existed—both on this planet and in that part of my heart that grew along with them.

Now they were dead. Nothing would ever bring them back. Nothing would ever fill the empty hole at the center of my being. Nothing. Ever.

CORPORAL WAGNER RETURNED to the Burnaby RCMP Detachment just after 5:00 p.m., to conduct his interview with Jeff Anderson. When he arrived, another officer brought him up to speed on the case. He said Anderson had tested sober, had slept for several hours after his arrival, and had remained calm and unemotional.

The first thing Wagner noticed about Anderson was his hands, which were abnormally small and stubby for such a large man. The next thing he noticed *was his shoes, which still bore traces of blood and tissue from the crime scene. He ordered Anderson a change of apparel before proceeding with the interview.*

Wagner introduced himself to Anderson, and advised him of his right to legal counsel. Anderson chose to waive that right and agreed to be interviewed. Wagner later reported that he felt extreme disgust and revulsion towards Anderson, but nonetheless remained calm and professional throughout the interview. He understood that it was his job to exact a truthful and revealing confession from the suspect, and that he would have to gain Anderson's trust in order to obtain the information he needed. Outwardly, he talked to Anderson with compassion and sympathy, encouraging him to blame his victims for what had happened. Inwardly, he felt only contempt and an intense determination to get him.

The talk flowed freely as Wagner fed Anderson the sympathy he craved. Though Anderson initially spoke of his love for Kim and the children, he shed no tears and expressed no emotion or remorse for what he had done. Instead, he talked non-stop about all the wrongs that had been done to him by Kim, blaming her for everything that had happened that morning. He talked only of himself: of his pain, his depression, his loneliness, his rejection. As the interview continued, he blamed everyone and everything, from Jehovah's Witnesses to low blood sugar.

Near the end of the interview, Wagner asked Anderson how he felt. "Incredibly depressed and hopeless," he replied. "I feel like I want to be dead. I wouldn't want to live without her one way or the other anyway."

Wagner then asked if there was anything else he wanted to say.

"Not that I can think of," said Anderson. "Am I crazy?"

"It's not for me to judge," replied Wagner. "I'm not your judge."

DALE STREICH AND HIS WIFE Gwen arrived at our house later in the evening and did their best to distract us from our grief. We talked a great deal about the details of the case, and our conversation eventually turned to the question of Anderson's sanity.

Dale thought Anderson might be criminally insane, and I found myself agreeing with him. It was far easier for me to grasp the idea of someone killing in a moment of uncontrolled insanity than to comprehend the deliberate murder of two innocent children. I said that we would have to reserve judgment about Anderson's sanity and motives until we knew the results of his psychiatric examination.

Marge felt otherwise. "The bastard should be hanged!" she said. The rest of us sat up and looked at her.

Dale explained that a hanging would be unlikely, since the death penalty had been abolished in Canada since 1976 and there were no signs of its reinstatement.

"Someone should hang him anyway," Marge replied.

Dale tried to reassure her. "If it's punishment you want, he'll get it. Believe me, by the time he gets jerked around by lawyers, psychiatrists, the courts, Correction Services—he'll be punished plenty." His words were small comfort, though.

Gwen pointed out that the four of us had discussed the subject of capital punishment many times in the past. In those debates, Marge and Dale had always argued in favor of the death penalty, while Gwen supported abolition and I remained undecided. She now soberly remarked on "how glib people can be" when not affected by the tragedy of murder.

After Dale and Gwen went home, Marge and I lay awake for a very long time, unable to stop talking and thinking about the events of the day. The mercy of sleep finally arrived in the early hours of the morning when, empty and drained, we succumbed to the needs of our bodies.

CORPORAL TOM WAGNER *did not leave the Burnaby RCMP Detachment until well after midnight. During the previous week, he had logged many hours of overtime, and by the time he got home he was close to exhaustion.*

That morning's crime scene was one of the worst he had ever witnessed, and once home, he tossed back several shots of whiskey in an attempt to calm his frayed nerves. But nothing would prevent him from reliving the violent images he had seen that day, images that would continue to haunt his dreams for years to come.

Tom Wagner vowed that he would do everything possible to put Jeff Anderson away for a very long time.

12

As I EMERGED FROM SLEEP the next morning, the knowledge of my children's death floated to my consciousness like a nightmare. In my half-awake state, I tried to push the previous day's events back into my subconscious, and shape them into a harmless dream I could awaken from. But as I opened my eyes, I realized it was no dream; this was real and I had to face the day with fresh despair. At that moment, I didn't know how to endure the next ten minutes, let alone the rest of my life. I also didn't realize how much worse the pain would become.

I spent the morning wandering aimlessly around the house, finally fixating on the need to get to Burnaby as quickly as possible to gather more information, to get a clear picture of *what happened,* to make sense of the incomprehensible. I also wanted to attend a memorial for Kim and the children that was being held in Burnaby on September 2. With a sense of relief, I immediately busied myself making travel arrangements for Marge, my mother, and myself.

Later that morning, I received a call from the *Vancouver Sun.* The reporter wanted to know what Kim had been like as a person, but I found myself at a loss for words. After a few moments, I told him that she had been a devout Jehovah's Witness... and avid reader... born and raised in Burnaby.... He asked what kind of books she had liked to read, but try as I might, I couldn't think of a single author or title. After an awkward silence, the reporter suggested that I could call him back after I'd had a chance to collect my thoughts. I told him I would.

My sister Jeanette phoned that afternoon. I remember thinking how sad it was that it took a tragedy like this for her to break the Witness taboo against association. She hadn't known Kim or the children all that well, but was deeply affected by the news of their deaths. She was unable to stop weeping as she talked to me on the phone, and at one point tearfully expressed the firm conviction that she *would see* my children again on the day of the resurrection. I appreciated the comfort this notion gave her, but inwardly scorned it.

I wanted to tell my sister that the hope of an afterlife could not begin to address the atrocity of Anderson's actions, that the only issue now was justice on earth, not resurrection to a paradise earth. I wanted to tell her I was sick to death of hearing about Jehovah and his divine agenda for my children. But I did not wish to provoke an argument with her, and neither agreed nor disagreed with her statements.

My sister cautioned me against blaming God for what had happened. "A man did this," she reminded me. "Not God."

I was not so ready to let Him off the hook.

AFTER BEING INTERVIEWED *at the RCMP Detachment in Burnaby, Jeff Anderson was moved to the nearby Oakalla prison facility, a holding tank for prisoners awaiting trial. He was given a psychiatric assessment, the results of which proved inconclusive, and shortly thereafter was indicted on three counts of first degree murder.*

The day after Anderson's arrest and the removal of the bodies from the crime scene, the police allowed Jackie Cole to enter her deceased daughter's apartment. At first glance, everything looked much the same as it had before. However, she was not prepared for what she found in the back bedroom: the room was supposed to have been thoroughly cleaned, but she was horrified to see traces of blood and tissue still visible on the walls and floor. There was also evidence that someone—probably one of the investigating officers—had vomited in the room.

Jackie arranged to have her daughter's and grandchildren's belongings moved to her house, where they were stored in the basement. She carefully distributed Kim's houseplants around the house and watered them. In the days immediately following the murder, she would often go there to sit among the boxes. It was here that she expressed her grief and her rage, often growling like a wounded animal at the loss of her loved ones.

WE FLEW TO VANCOUVER on August 31, all of us now heavily sedated with tranquillizers. My mother's eldest brother Clare met us at the airport and took us to his home in nearby White Rock, where my dear Uncle Jim and Aunt Doris joined us later that evening. They were all a great comfort to us during the very trying days that followed.

At first, the talk at the dinner table was light and evasive. But it soon turned to what everyone had been reading in the newspapers and watching on television for the past two days. My Aunt Doris said this of Jeff Anderson: "He had the gall to say he didn't deserve to live now that he had killed three people. He could kill a woman and two children, but he didn't have the guts to turn the gun on himself. What a wimp!" To Doris, Anderson had no credibility at all, and his words rang hollow.

After dinner, feeling dizzy and nauseous, I went outside for some fresh air. I watched as the late summer sun set behind Clare's plumb trees, ripe with fruit. My Uncle Jim joined me later, lighting up a cigarette. "What a dirty son of a bitch," he said. "It's a rotten shame, this thing that's happened to you. But your best bet is to go home and forget the whole thing. Otherwise, if you think about it long enough, you'll go crazy for sure."

While in B.C., I telephoned Kim's father, Ken Evans, to see if he could provide me with any new information. Soon after we started talking, he made reference to Juri and Lindsay "praying to Jehovah" just before they died, and I felt my blood begin to boil. I'd heard enough religious sentiment, and without thinking, I snapped, "Well, your daughter sure married a winner this time, didn't she?" I hadn't realized until that moment how much anger I felt towards Kim, how much I held her responsible for the deaths of my children.

Nor did I realize how much I held myself responsible. An endless loop had been playing in my head since I had first heard of the murders, a tortuous litany of "if only I had done this... if only Kim had done that... if only..."

Ken naturally took exception to my remark and reminded me that it was not up to us to decide where the blame lay. He reminded me, as someone still sympathetic to the Jehovah's Witness position of neutrality in the affairs of government and institutions, that it was the "worldly authorities" who would decide right from wrong, and not us. He even questioned whether we had the right to blame Anderson at that point, saying, "Who knows? Maybe he's got a brain tumor and that's what caused him to do what he did." On the second point, I could not disagree, as I had already questioned Anderson's sanity myself. But as for neutrality in justice, I was anything but neutral. I knew exactly where I stood.

I phoned Norman Cole to get details about the Witness memorial to be held in Burnaby in two days' time. During that conversation, he asked if there were any possessions of the children that I might want, and I told him that I would appreciate having some of the photographs I had taken of them over the years. He promised to gather them together before we left B.C.

Marge and I were able to fall asleep that night with the aid of tranquillizers, but I found myself wide awake just before dawn, feeling as though I were gradually coming out of an anesthetic, suddenly aware of an acute, throbbing pain in my chest. As my grief finally broke, I began to weep, my body racked with sobs. Marge encouraged me to let it out, to voice my anger—something I had always found difficult to do.

I howled in hopeless agony, "I'm so bloody mad and I want to scream. But who or at what do I get mad *at*?"

The events of the next day only intensified the pain. We had looked forward to attending a memorial for Kim and the children that was being held in a large, new Kingdom Hall in Burnaby. However, when we arrived at the service with our relatives and some old friends from Vancouver—none of whom were Jehovah's Witnesses—we were completely unprepared for the callous and inhumane reception we received from those present.

Soon after taking our seats in the back of the auditorium, it became clear that the Witness rule against association would not be waived in a situation such as this. Former friends and relatives—even my father's brother, who had phoned me just the night before to offer his condolences—refused to acknowledge us publicly. Witness after Witness refused to meet my gaze or return my greeting.

The speaker began by reading a list of surviving relatives—a list from which my own name was conspicuously absent—and referred to my children throughout the service as Juri and Lindsay *Anderson*. A twenty-five minute long eulogy followed, in which Kim and the children were described as "faithful servants of Jehovah God" and assured of a resurrection. At no point was the manner of their deaths—and at whose hands they died—ever mentioned.

Later, I had the opportunity to talk with one of Lindsay's elementary school teachers who had attended the memorial and who had adored the children and watched them develop over time. She expressed the view that it was a "strange" and "bewildering" memorial, that it hadn't satisfied nor comforted her in any way. She said it was disturbing to leave out the overriding details of such an event, when the entire community—and not just the religious one—was so deeply affected.

When the service was over, we couldn't leave the Kingdom Hall fast enough. Marge pushed past an usher at the door, shouting, "I'm sick and tired of you bastards shitting on my husband!" I felt dizzy and nauseous and quickly walked to our station wagon, so I could lean on it for support. As we got into the car, we were approached by Ken Evans, who tried to persuade us to stay and talk to the congregation. I angrily told him that it was the worst memorial I had ever attended, and that we just wanted to leave, but he protested that we had misunderstood the nature and purpose of the service. "Witness funerals are not really meant to be memorials for the deceased," he explained, "but rather opportunities to praise and magnify Jehovah's name."

Marge abruptly cut him off, "Who gives a damn about your Jehovah, anyway?"

As we drove out of the parking lot, we saw the media with their television cameras on a hill just above us. At that moment, though, none of us thought of talking with them.

We fumed all the way back to Clare's house, taking out our anger on my poor mother, the only Jehovah's Witness present. That day was the beginning of the end for her, and she left the Witness faith soon after. It was also the beginning of the end for me. I had been passive for too much of my life, always taking the path of least resistance, but now I was determined to speak my mind. When we returned to Clare's house, I immediately contacted a reporter at the *Vancouver Sun,* but not the one who had first contacted me in Winnipeg.

The next day, I telephoned Jackie and Norman Cole to make arrangements to pick up the photographs I had been promised. When Norman answered the phone, he told me that he was sorry that we had been upset at the memorial service. It was too late for apologies. The front page of that day's *Vancouver Sun* would read: "Dad Laments Loss of Slain Children," and included a story in which I criticized the way in which Jehovah's Witnesses had stonewalled me from seeing—and protecting—my children, as well as their shameful behavior at the memorial service.

When I arrived at the Coles' later that morning, Jackie's friendly manner told me that she had not yet seen the newspaper headlines of that morning. She handed me a stack of photographs of Juri and Lindsay, her expression saying, "I wish I could give you more." As I looked through the photographs, I noticed a bruise under Lindsay's eye in one of the pictures and asked Jackie about it. She explained that the photograph had been taken "after the car accident." Apparently, Lindsay had been struck by a car while crossing the street in March 1984, suffering minor injuries, but this was the first I had heard about it.

"She lost a shoe during the impact," said Jackie, "and the funny thing was, as she was sitting there on the pavement, she was more concerned about getting her shoe back than anything."

Instinctively, I felt a panicky concern for Lindsay's well-being, which quickly turned to a feeling of helpless inadequacy. The accident had occurred over a year before and was now completely irrelevant. With deep sadness, I realized I would never have to worry about Lindsay and Juri's safety again.

Later that day, we received a visit from Corporal Tom Wagner, the RCMP officer investigating the murders. We were immensely impressed by him, sensing a large and generous heart beneath his brusque, no-nonsense exterior. To this day, I don't believe he really needed to interview us but only wanted to provide the information and perspective we so badly craved. And for that, I thank him.

At our request, Wagner walked us through the details of the case, telling us no less and no more than we wanted to know. He also expressed how much the murders had personally affected him and the other police officers involved, echoing the comments of Staff Sgt. Neil MacKay in the *Vancouver Sun*. "We feel terrible about this sort of thing," he had said. "The utter despair and frustration of not having been able to do something... No policeman would allow this to happen if he could prevent it. And that's the simple truth." Wagner also gave us his personal assurance that he would keep us fully informed of all developments in the investigation and the court proceedings to follow.

When Wagner asked about my relationship with Kim, I talked frankly about how difficult and headstrong she had been throughout our marriage and in the years following our divorce. Still nursing strong anger and resentment against her, I painted her in a needlessly negative light, and felt badly when Wagner then implied that Kim may have in some way contributed to her own death. "Maybe she was just too cocksure of herself," he said. "She should have realized that you have to be careful when facing an angry man with a gun."

JACKIE COLE WANTED TO KNOW why Jeff Anderson had killed her daughter and grandchildren, so she asked two Witness elders to visit him in the Oakalla prison facility where he was incarcerated after his arrest, to find out what they could about his motives and state of mind.

The elders were allowed to see Anderson in the visitation area, where he sat behind a double Plexiglas partition and answered their questions over a phone. He was in a kind of stupor that day, mumbling into the phone with his head down. When they asked what had caused him to begin shooting, he gave them the same explanation he had given to the police: he pulled the trigger because Kim refused to give him a hug. Jackie later commented that it was just like Kim to be so principled, and speculated that her daughter's stubbornness had probably not helped the situation.

The elders also asked Anderson if he had been led by evil spirits, to which he said no. A month later, they informed him that he had been disfellowshipped as one of Jehovah's Witnesses, although it hadn't yet been clearly established whether Anderson was criminally insane.

MARGE AND I MADE arrangements to have the cremated remains of Juri and Lindsay sent to us in Winnipeg, where we were determined to give them a proper burial and funeral.

While we waited for the remains to arrive, we bought a plot in South Foley Cemetery, located fifty miles north of Winnipeg and a half-mile from my grandparents' homestead. Relatives on both sides of my family had been buried there, including my father. I decided to dig the grave myself, with the assistance of my teenaged nephew Mark. Though it was a physically grueling job, it was something I needed to do. It was the last thing I could *do* for my children, even if it was only symbolic.

When we finished, Marge covered the grave with a waterproof tablecloth, anchored with four lime stones on each corner. "This is an upside-down situation, Jim," said my nephew. "Your children should have buried *you*."

The remains arrived by courier a day later, in the form of two small cardboard boxes glued together. The funeral service would not occur for a few days yet, and in the meantime Marge felt uncomfortable having the remains in the house. That evening, we took the boxes and two mahogany silverware cases to the basement of my mother's apartment building, where they would remain until the day of the funeral.

It was there that I prepared the remains for burial. When I gingerly opened the cardboard boxes, I found two smaller boxes inside. I thought of the shoeboxes I had used to bury birds on my family's farm, and marveled that my children could be contained in boxes even smaller than that.

Marge averted her eyes as I cut open the smaller boxes, and pulled out two plastic bags containing not ashes, as I had expected, but what looked like crushed calcium and porous bone. I was overwhelmed by a profound sense of helplessness and futility as I held my children in my hands, stunned that they—that anyone—could be reduced to little more than piles of dust.

The windowless, concrete-walled room was lit by a single bulb from the ceiling and grew extremely hot and humid. As I crouched down over the mahogany boxes, I felt a sudden sense of vertigo, like I was about to fall backwards into a void, and I had to steady myself. In that moment, I was a tiny, pathetic little man fighting against an irresistible force, a tiny inconsequential speck in a vast universe. My heart ached and reached out for the protective presence of God, but I found only silence and emptiness.

My hands fumbled as I tried to tie the plastic bags with string and Marge finally had to step in to finish the task. We then put the little bags in the mahogany cases and glued the lids tight. It was the last time I would touch my children.

The funeral service was held on September 14, 1985 at the church where Marge and I were wed four years earlier, and conducted by the man that married us, the Reverend Robert Burton. A group of close friends and relatives attended.

My sister Jeanette refused to come, not wishing to publicly defy the Witness ban on association.

After the service, my friend Dale Streich and nephew Mark filled in the small grave with loose ground, and arranged pieces of sod over it. Reverend Burton later commented that he had seen a family cover a grave on only one other occasion, in the case of an Aboriginal burial ceremony.

Afterwards, our friends and family joined us at our home, where we had prepared a lunch. We had also prepared a photo album of Juri and Lindsay, with pictures that dated back to their infancy, which we wanted our guests to look through and remember them by. But no one looked at the album, and no one discussed the children who had died. By the conversation in the room, you would never have known that a funeral had just taken place.

I later realized that this was to be expected; that the tragic death of such young children was a subject too painful for most people to discuss or think about, an area to be avoided at all costs. I felt that I was the only one who could even remember my children, and it seemed that their very existence on this earth was already quickly fading away.

My father, Michael Kostelniuk, the violinist in the middle of the frame. He enjoyed working in the fields by day and playing with his band at night. Clandeboye Community Hall (1949).

Nellie and Michael Kostelniuk (November 1938).

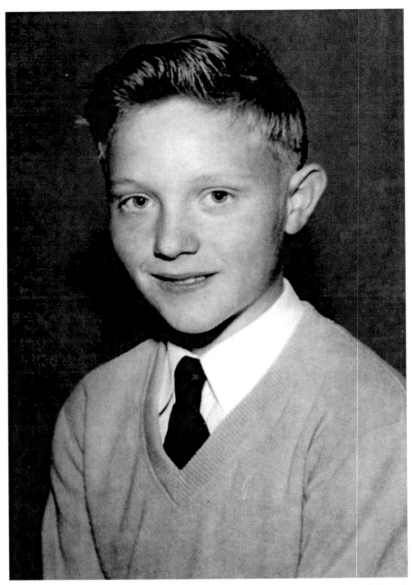

Myself at thirteen—I was a placid, imaginative boy and sang in the United Church (1959).

My sister, Jeanette Kostelniuk, at seventeen. She craved excitement and drove around
in fast cars with her friends (1957).

The day of my wedding to Kim. We looked happy, but we were really quite tense (January 27, 1973).

Kim Kostelniuk. She was a private person and rather camera-shy. I caught her here in an unguarded moment (1975).

Kim and myself at a Cariboo wedding, 1973. Kim never missed a chance to dance.

Kim, Lindsay, and Juri. Moments of joy after a heavy snowfall in the Cariboo highlands (1977).

Kim, with Juri and Lindsay. A single mother now, her children were everything to her (1982).

Juri and Lindsay. They were close from a very young age (1979).

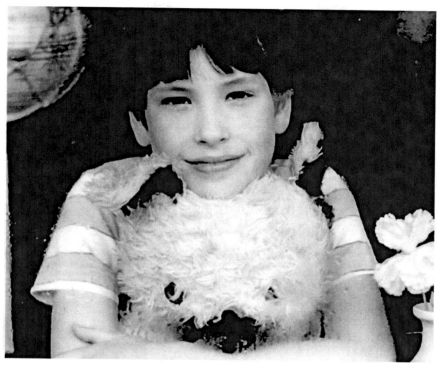

Juri—more dreamy than active (1984).

James and his Malamute pup Nikki, in Lone Butte in the Cariboo Mountains. Nikki had the most benevolent animal intelligence (1974).

Lindsay and Juri, gathering seashells near Bellingham, Washington. He was interested in marine biology (1979).

Juri, near Bellingham, Washington (1979).

Lindsay, unlike her mother, was never camera-shy. I taught her from infancy to enjoy having her picture taken (1985).

Lindsay, enjoying a holiday in Harrison Hot Springs, B.C. She looked and acted more like her mother everyday (1983).

Marge Kostelniuk—going out to a dinner party (1983).

Marge and Lindsay. Marge would
have made a good mother. Calgary,
Alberta (1982).

Lindsay and Juri; they were a pair (1984).

South Foley Cemetery in the rural Interlake of Manitoba. We visited the children's graves often then. Marge washed the stone and cut the grass over the grave. "It's all I can do for them now," she said.

Marge Kostelniuk on our front lawn with Gigi and Brandy (1991).

Marge and me with Gigi and Charlotte (2002).

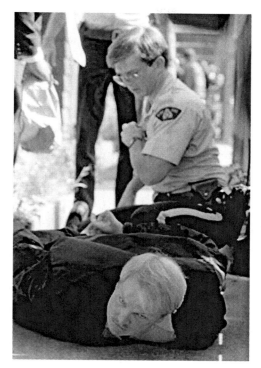

Jeff Anderson, at the moment of his arrest (Don Draper/*Vancouver Sun*).

Jeff Anderson being taken into the police cruiser on the day of his arrest (Don Draper/*Vancouver Sun*).

Jeff Anderson, later in prison (*The Province*).

Jeff Anderson, William Head Institution (2009).

13

A WEEK AFTER JURI and Lindsay's funeral, I began to experience increasingly disturbing dreams. Some of these nightmares involved violent combat and war-fare, where I was both hunter and hunted and the only choice was to "kill or be killed." Others featured menacing beings who threatened to kill me and my loved ones with a variety of weapons. During the night, the division between sleep and consciousness became increasingly blurred, and I sometimes exper-ienced hallucinations in my bedroom while seemingly awake.

I usually woke from these nightmares in a state of sheer terror, unable to go back to sleep. Not surprisingly, I began to have trouble falling asleep at bed-time—even with the aid of tranquillizers. The landscape of my unconscious had now become a dark and dangerous place I wished to avoid at all costs.

As time went on, even the daylight hours became imbued with violence and fear. My mind was frequently invaded by sudden images and fantasies. Out of the blue, I would find myself in that back bedroom with Kim and the children, seeing what they saw, experiencing the terror they felt, helplessly watching as their faces were blown apart again and again. When the doorbell rang, I would sometimes visualize a giant image of Jeff Anderson standing behind the door, a sawed-off shotgun under his arm.

Marge also began to experience nightmares and insomnia, and we both walked around during the day in a state of increasing mental and physical exhaustion. I now realize that these experiences were the result of having sup-pressed our intense feelings of rage and helplessness, emotional realities that fought to find some means of expression, if only in our dreams. However, at the time, we both tried to find some real way to resolve our anxieties.

I began nursing an absurd paranoid belief that Jeff Anderson would one day murder me in my bed when I least expected it, and expressed the desire to buy a gun to protect myself. Marge questioned my sanity as I tried to explain to her that I could not just wait around to be ambushed. But she herself obsessed about our house being broken into—something that had never happened to us—which led to the purchase of outdoor flood lights, extra deadbolt locks for the doors, windows and gates, and a high chain-link fence for the yard. These precautions somehow made us feel safe—or at least less vulnerable.

By October 1985, I was in desperate need of professional help. My mental and emotional condition had deteriorated to the point where I had trouble concentrating on my job as a bus driver; I would frequently burst into tears when I saw a little boy or girl who reminded me of Lindsay or Juri, and once or twice I lost my temper with passengers for no reason. I knew I could not go on as I was and persuaded Marge to see a psychologist with me.

During our first session, we must have overwhelmed the therapist with our intense outpouring of grief and despair. I remember how the poor man cautiously paused and took a deep breath before offering us a tentative comment: "You're very angry," he said. This was a reasonable observation under the circumstances, but Marge took extreme exception to it, interpreting his words as criticism. "Why wouldn't we be angry?" she fumed afterwards.

Nonetheless, she encouraged me continue in therapy if it helped. Looking back, I'm not sure that therapy accomplished much more than would have occurred naturally over time, but it certainly provided an important outlet for my feelings, as well as a distracting goal to work towards.

Over the next four years, I would indulge in almost every therapy imaginable—from past-life regression to meditative techniques to artificial brain-wave enhancers—in an effort to find the answer, the piece of the missing puzzle that would explain how and why my children had died, and perhaps miraculously restore them—and me—to life. It was an ongoing, relentless quest that stretched before me like a path I had no choice but to follow, no matter how pointless, ridiculous, and misguided it might have seemed to me and others.

IN OCTOBER 1985, Jackie Cole received a package in the mail that had been forwarded to her from Kim Anderson's address on Beta Avenue. When she opened the package, she was shocked to discover three letters from Jeff Anderson among the various bills. The letters were addressed individually to Kim, Lindsay, and Juri, and were written as though Anderson believed they were still alive.

When Corporal Tom Wagner was informed of this, he immediately suspected the letters had been written by Anderson in an attempt to establish an insanity defense. Though he did not believe that such a defense could ever succeed, in light of a recent psychiatric assessment that proved inconclusive, he

was incensed that Kim's mother had been subjected to such a manipulative act.
He immediately contacted Oakalla prison authorities to put a stop to Anderson's
nonsense.

IN THE MIDDLE OF OCTOBER, Marge and I placed a modest stone on Juri and
Lindsay's grave, a piece of grey granite engraved with two white doves and
olive branches. At the time, I wondered if their deaths would ever be laid to rest.
Despite psychotherapy and violent nightmares, images and fantasies continued
unabated, only occasionally relieved by dreams of Kim and the children.

In one of those dreams, Kim and I were in divorce court. I angrily accused
her of being cruel and unreasonable, and the judge expressed sympathy for my
claims. After leaving the courthouse, I followed her for a long time, until she
finally looked back crossly and spoke. "Don't follow me where I am going," she
warned.

In another dream, my children were in a room full of people, including my
father Michael. Lindsay was full of life and childish energy, and danced around
the room, to my father's delight. Juri, on the other hand, sat in a corner by himself. When I held him close and asked what the matter was, he said he couldn't
understand why he had been sent away while Lindsay had been allowed to stay
with us. In life, he had often expressed the belief that I loved Lindsay more than
him, and in the dream, I felt overwhelming pity for him as I tenderly rocked him
in my arms.

My emotional state began to affect my job more and more, and I became
very concerned about my ability to drive a bus safely. Marge was unemployed at
the time, but our relationship was becoming increasingly strained. We frequently
argued, our nerves raw and on edge, and I started to wonder if our marriage
could survive this much pressure. I became convinced that Marge would eventually leave me, a loss I did not think I would survive.

On my psychologist's advice, I decided to take a temporary leave of
absence from my job, a decision that turned out to be a blessing and a curse.

IN MID-OCTOBER, Anderson's defense counsel, G. Jack Harris, made the Reg-
ional Crown prosecutor's office an offer. He informed the Crown that, in order
to spare the taxpayer a long and expensive trial, Anderson was willing to accept
the lesser charge of second-degree murder. If accepted, the deal would mean the
difference between a twenty-five year life sentence without the possibility of
parole and a fifteen-year sentence with parole eligibility after only seven years.
The prosecutor's office told Harris that they would give his offer serious consid-
eration.

Shortly after, Corporal Tom Wagner barged into the prosecutor's office unannounced, interrupting a meeting in progress. Wagner picked up a copy of the Criminal Code and slammed it down on the lawyer's desk. "You don't even know your Criminal Code," he shouted. He angrily reminded the prosecutor that there was overwhelming evidence that Anderson's crimes had been planned and deliberate, and that in the case of murder involving a hostage-taking, Canadian law requires a first-degree charge.

The ruffled prosecutor indicated he would take Wagner's point into consideration. "You'd better take it into consideration," said Wagner. "Otherwise, I'll take it up with the Attorney General."

The Crown prosecutor's office subsequently declined Harris's offer, and the original charge of first-degree murder was allowed to stand.

THE BREAK FROM MY JOB was a relief, for I no longer had to worry about losing control of my bus and causing an accident. However, my psyche took advantage of the increased spare time to indulge in even more intensively obsessive dreams and fantasies. No matter what I was doing—resting on the couch, reading, watching television—suddenly and without warning I would find myself in the back bedroom with Kim and the children, reliving the horror of it over and over again. And I would feel the most overwhelming sense of pity and sadness for my poor children.

After a while, every time that would happen, I would experience excruciating pains in my chest, some of which were so severe that I thought I was literally having a heart attack or stroke. I had never experienced heart problems before, but nonetheless Marge persuaded me to make an appointment with a heart specialist, who conducted a series of stress tests and an EKG. In the end, the doctor diagnosed my problem as stress, and advised me to relax.

Marge was my anchor in the storm of my despair, and I clung to her physically and emotionally. Although deep in grief herself, she was always sensitive to my moments of deep mental darkness and never failed to help me through them. There were times when she held me in her arms as if I were a frightened child, until the agony passed and I felt safe once more.

Such physical and emotional pain as the result of the loss of a child, I was told by my therapist, would often result in the patient asking for any remedy, any drug, no matter how addictive, to take the pain away. Fortunately for me, I did not rely much on drugs or alcohol for relief, but turned to other ways of coping instead.

Corporal Tom Wagner continued to make heroic efforts to ensure that justice would be done for Kim and the children, and he and a newly appointed

Crown counsel, David Stone, kept us informed of developments in the case against Anderson. Both of these extremely professional men greatly eased our burden, as we never once doubted that they would do everything possible to ensure that Anderson received the punishment he deserved.

Once we learned that the Crown prosecutor would be proceeding with a charge of first-degree murder, there was nothing left for us to do but wait for the trial. In the meantime, I began to indulge in increasingly violent revenge fantasies and dreams. In one dream, I found myself alone with Anderson in a deep forest. He was unarmed, but I had a loaded pistol and had been instructed to kill him. I gave him a ten-second running start, and then hunted him down like an animal. At the end of my dream, I killed him execution-style, firing the pistol several times. In the days that followed that dream, I went over the details over and over again in my mind.

In another dream, I executed Anderson with a hunting rifle, just after the sun had set, as he stood with his back to the wall of my father's barn. Then I dragged the bloody body to the basement of my parents' farmhouse, the head banging on the steps on the way down. It was a bizarre dream, but nonetheless I enjoyed indulging in it later during the day.

Even though these dreams and fantasies gave me a strange kind of temporary relief, I worried about the pleasure and satisfaction I derived from them, and wondered if I was losing my mind. As one of Jehovah's Witnesses, I had always been taught to leave justice in God's hands: "Vengeance is mine: I will repay, says Jehovah." Yet here I was compulsively fantasizing about revenge on an almost daily basis. I had always believed in the principle of non-violence and turning the other cheek; now I questioned the solidity of my moral center. I knew that it was often only in the crunch that the foundation of one's beliefs were tested, and I knew I was failing the test miserably.

However, one day my mother Nellie surprised me by revealing that she too had revenge fantasies. "I would like to shoot Anderson three times while looking into his eyes," she told me without an ounce of shame or embarrassment. I then realized that we weren't immoral or crazy, just normal, decent people in a crazy situation. I came to see my revenge fantasies as a relatively harmless way of releasing the pressure of my rage—as long as I did not begin to consider acting out on those fantasies in reality.

IN THE SPRING OF 1986, Juri and Lindsay's paternal grandmother, Nellie Kostel-niuk, wrote a letter to the Watch Tower Society. In her letter, she sought spiritual support and advice to help her understand the tragedy of her grand-

children's death. She also wished to know whether Jeff Anderson was still considered one of Jehovah's Witnesses.

Two weeks later, she received a brief, unsigned reply from the Society's branch office in Toronto. The three short paragraphs of the letter counseled that it was best to put the whole matter in the past and "get on with Kingdom business." It advised her that "it is not beneficial to allow your mind to dwell on these matters, as you can appreciate. It is good to keep busy in Jehovah's service and trust in him and his promised hope of a resurrection."

Nellie left the Jehovah's Witnesses shortly thereafter.

THAT SPRING, I READ *Apocalypse Delayed: The Story of Jehovah's Witnesses*, an excellent book written by M. James Penton and published by the University of Toronto Press. Penton was uniquely qualified to write this scholarly overview of the Jehovah's Witness organization, both as a professor of history and religious studies at the University of Lethbridge, and as a disfellowshipped Witness himself who was born and raised in a Jehovah's Witness family and community. As the dust jacket of the book explained, the author's experience "combined the special insight with the critical analysis of an observer now at a distance from his subject." His book would come to have a profound effect and influence on me, helping me to better comprehend, both historically and sociologically, the organization in which I had spent more than sixteen years of my life.

Penton had previously written a book entitled *Jehovah's Witnesses in Canada*, published by Macmillan in 1975. At that time, Penton was a devoted Witness and the book was an apology for the Witness faith, emphasizing the important contributions the organization had made to the cause of civil liberty, via numerous court battles that successfully established their right to freedom of expression and the practice of faith.

However, he was also someone who openly criticized the organization, encouraging it to move in the direction of renewal and change. As a Witness intellectual, he was a member of a very small and distrusted group in the organization, and he was eventually disfellowshipped in 1981 for his radical views. This event created a major crisis in the organization that attracted a lot of media attention at the time. In 1981, the entire Penton family (including his wife, three children, and an uncle) and many of their close friends left the Witness faith in protest. A total of eighty-three Witnesses subsequently resigned from local congregations, and a number from Ontario and the state of Arizona followed suit.

I telephoned Penton soon after reading his book, and Marge and I subsequently visited him in Lethbridge, Alberta in May 1986. When we met Jim at his home, he embraced me heartily like a long-lost brother. He was a handsome, robust man who surprised me with his exuberant personality and southwestern accent—both acquired when living in Arizona as a young man. He seemed more like a Montana rancher than an introspective scholar, and we became fast friends.

We stayed with the Pentons for several days, during which we extensively discussed our mutual experiences with the Jehovah's Witnesses, as well as the tragic events of the previous summer. One morning, Marge showed Jim a photograph of Lindsay that we took during our visit with her in Calgary in 1982. I talked about some of the many pleasant and joyful memories I had of my children. Unlike the mourners at Juri and Lindsay's funeral, Jim did not avert his eyes from the picture, but instead looked at it long and hard and listened to our descriptions of the children with rapt attention. To our great surprise, this big, generous man whom we'd only known a few days burst into tears. "That poor, poor child," he said. "I'm so very sorry."

Jim did not realize what he had done for us in that moment. Up to that point, everyone around us, with the exception of my mother, had studiously avoided the subject of my dead children, as though they had never existed. Some people did so in a misguided attempt to spare us pain; others simply found the subject of death—especially the death of young children—to be too uncomfortable. Jim's response to our grief exemplified the advice given in Romans 12:15: "Rejoice with people who rejoice; weep with people who weep."

When we returned from our trip, I had an extraordinary dream about Juri and Lindsay, one that affected me on a deep level. The children and I were at a large indoor swimming pool, with submerged lights that illuminated the water. The water was a bright sea blue near the surface and darker in the depths. At one point, Juri dove to the bottom of the pool, where he disappeared for a long period of time before resurfacing in the luminous reflections of the water. He climbed out of the pool and walked towards me, reverently offering me a handful of glittering jewels and pearls retrieved from the floor of the pool. I was amazed by his find and touched by the generosity of his offer, and accepted the jewels gratefully.

Looking back, I realized that this dream represented a turning point for me. For the first time, I began to believe my children were safe in another dimension and I no longer needed to worry about them. I also felt that my son was trying to tell me that I should concentrate on my own healing—something I was still very far from achieving.

Despite some progress, I was still plagued by frequent nightmares. In one dream, I was surrounded by a thick, menacing cloud of black flies, which blinded me and prevented me from moving forward. In another, I discovered that my hands had been amputated and left to rot like old gloves. Torn by indecision, I knew that I must bury them, but at the same time, I didn't know how I would manage without them. Then, miraculously, a pair of new and rejuvenated hands replaced the decomposing ones.

When I awoke, I was horrified by the disturbing images of rotting hands, but realized that the dream held out hope for the future. Although I was still living with my emotional stumps, the dream told me something useful might one day grow there.

The painful, gaping hole in my chest was still raw and bleeding, but slowly, gently, almost imperceptibly, I began to feel the healing breath of God blowing through me.

One day that summer, Marge sat on our balcony with a cool drink in her hand, quietly weeping. It hit me at that moment to what extent she had put her own grief on hold during the past year in order to be the strong one for my mother and me. "I'm sorry," I said. "I didn't realize you were still mourning." Inwardly, I resolved to be as strong a support for her as she had been for me, and quietly thanked God for sending me this extraordinary woman.

Marge and I visited the children's grave on August 29, 1986, the first anniversary of their death. We had visited the grave many times that spring and summer, and each time Marge carefully clipped the grass that covered it. As I watched her cut every blade with perfect evenness, frowning with concentration, I asked why she always performed this task so thoroughly.

She sat back on her haunches and looked up at me. "Because it's all I can do for them now," she said.

14

AFTER RETURNING TO WORK in January 1986, I had looked forward to Anderson's trial with both anticipation and dread. While I had a deep desire to see justice done, I had an equally strong need to shield myself from further pain. I was already reliving my children's gruesome deaths on a daily basis. Did I need to hear them described in painstaking detail at a lengthy trial?

The only official role for me at the trial would be as a family member with a stake in the outcome, as the court did not require me as a material witness. On an emotional level, though, I believed that it was only my actual physical presence in the courtroom that would ensure justice for my children. I felt that my failure to attend the trial would be yet another way that I was not there for Juri and Lindsay. It was unthinkable that I should not be there.

However, when I sought Tom Wagner's advice in August 1986, he strongly recommended I not attend. A veteran of many murder trials, he doubted that I would derive any benefit from what I would hear, and was adamant that it would only cause me needless additional pain. Crown counsel Rick Miller expressed the same reservations, but also ventured the opinion that the trial might prove to be cathartic. "When the trial is over, you may finally be able to put it behind you," he suggested. However, when I asked what he thought we might learn from the process, he observed that trials often raise more questions than answers, leaving attendees more unsettled than satisfied.

Nonetheless, Marge and I continued to have an obsessive need to know the reason for Anderson's brutal act and on a deep level believed that the trial would tell us that. Against Tom Wagner's advice, I decided to take a two-week leave of absence from my job, and booked two plane tickets.

DURING THE FIFTEEN MONTHS leading up to his trial, Jeff Anderson's life was limited to sleeping, eating, and prison cleaning duty, with the occasional *distraction of a visit from his defense lawyer or a phone call to his mother in Texas.*

On the whole, Anderson adapted well to the strict regiment of prison life. Blond, blue-eyed, and white, with nice southern manners, he understood authority and his place in the pecking order. He got along well with the guards and avoided his fellow inmates, whom he considered dangerous criminal types, different from himself.

In the summer of 1986, Anderson began to receive regular visits from Wayne Northey and Arden Robertson, Christian sponsors who worked full-time for an agency that supported violent offenders. Anderson never again repeated his desire to be deported to Texas and receive the death penalty for his crimes. In fact, he subsequently entered a plea of not guilty to the charge of first-degree murder, and would be advocating at trial for the lesser charge of second-degree murder. Nonetheless, he confessed to his Christian sponsors that he deserved to die for his crimes, and he threatened to commit suicide by starvation.

Even sympathetic Christian men like Northey and Robertson doubted the sincerity of these statements, in view of Anderson's junk food addiction and expanding waistline, but they had made a commitment to help Anderson and promised to support him at his trial. They had no idea what the emotional cost of that commitment would turn out to be.

WHEN I TOLD MY SUPERVISOR that I would be taking a two-week leave of absence to attend the trial, he expressed strong reservations. He knew Marge and me personally, and had seen firsthand what we'd gone through in the past year. He told me frankly that he seriously feared the emotional and physical setbacks the trial would cause, and talked about how he had been affected by a rape trial he had attended a few years before. The victim was a friend of his, and for a long time afterwards, he had felt shaken and unnerved by the explicit detail and exposure to which the trial had subjected her and her loved ones. He urged me to consider how much worse a murder trial would be.

In the end, he asked me to discuss it once more with Marge. He hoped we would change our minds, but told us that if we were determined to go, he would honor our decision and make the necessary arrangements.

It was an agonizing decision. After much deliberation, we decided that our physical and mental health were more important than attending Anderson's trial; we didn't want to give up any more of our lives to this man. Yet a part of us would always feel guilty for not attending, and in retrospect I very much regret the decision we made.

At the time, I had no way of knowing how the details of the trial would pale beside the knowledge that was to come, how I would become increasingly driven by a deep, ongoing need to uncover every last detail of my children's deaths—including the minutiae of the killer's own mind.

THE TRIAL OF JEFFERY ANDERSON began on November 26, 1986, in an old court-house in New Westminster, British Columbia. It was presided over by Mr. Justice Josiah Wood, and attended at various times by Jackie and Norman Cole, Corporal Tom Wagner and his wife Theresa, and other RCMP officers involved with the Anderson investigation. The father of the murdered children was not in attendance.

The trial began with Anderson's not guilty plea to the charge of first-degree murder. He was fortunate to have been assigned Mr. G. Jack Harris as a defense counsel, an intelligent and articulate criminal lawyer with an excellent reputation. In his opening statement to the jury, Harris stated that there was "no defense" for what Anderson did, but questioned whether it constituted first-deg-ree murder. He went on to reassure the jury members that it was only a question of law; if they found for the lesser charge, it would not mean that the people Anderson murdered were in some way "second class," only that the crime did not fit the legal definition of a capital crime.

The only issues to be debated at the trial were (1) whether the murders were planned and deliberate, according to Section 247 of the Canadian Criminal Code; and (2) whether the murders had occurred when the victims were unlaw-fully confined, according to Section 214(5)(e) of the Code. If the Crown proved either of these points beyond a reasonable doubt, the defendant would be found guilty of first-degree murder. However, if Mr. Harris succeeded in convincing the jury that the murders had been a spontaneous act of passion, Anderson would automatically be found guilty of second-degree murder.

A very able and professional barrister, Crown counsel Rick D. Miller brought a certain emotional edge to his prosecution of Anderson. Tough, incisive, and self-assured, he painstakingly built a case against the accused, presenting irrefutable evidence that Anderson had begun writing his suicide letter to the Coles several months before the murders, had also purchased his first gun months before the murders, and had bought a second gun the day after his first gun had been confiscated. He also argued that Anderson clearly confined his victims against their will, with the intention to terrorize them and commit murder.

Miller called an RCMP corporal to the stand to tell the court what he and his fellow officers had discovered in the back bedroom after Anderson was *arrested. Reviewing the crime scene photos of the children, he described Lindsay's body slumped to one side of the bunk bed, her teddy bear still clutched in her arms. However, as he went on to describe the position of Juri's body beside her—how the boy's arms were still clasped around his sister—he suddenly became overwhelmed by his memory of the scene. Several women in the public gallery wept as the officer broke down and sobbed on the stand. Mr. Justice Wood called a brief adjournment of the proceedings.*

Arden Robertson and his wife Jean were in attendance that day as Anderson's Christian sponsor support team. They were decent people who firmly believed in a compassionate and restorative justice approach to violent offenders, and had committed their lives to that difficult work. However, they later confided to the children's father that they were horrified by what they heard on the stand that day. It must have tested even their faith and resolve.

ALTHOUGH MARGE AND I did not attend the trial, we were able to monitor its progress very closely, thanks to the kind generosity of Scott McRae, Editor of the *Vancouver Sun*, who made sure we received copies of the *Sun* reporter's daily, unedited notes by mail at no financial cost to us.

Marge and I anxiously awaited each mailing, and sat up late into the night discussing the most recent news of the trial. We were impressed with the work of Crown counsel Rick D. Miller and deeply moved by the RCMP corporal's spontaneous breakdown on the stand, which brought home how deeply the tragedy had touched the lives of *other* people in the community.

We were also rather surprised—and chagrined—that Anderson had been assigned such a reputable lawyer. Tom Wagner explained that we should be pleased; the Crown had gladly assigned Anderson the best lawyer available in order to reduce the possibility of later appeals based on incompetent representation. As the trial proceeded, we became increasingly confident in its outcome, and looked forward to putting it behind us.

DURING THE TRIAL, details about Jeff Anderson's crimes began to circulate among the prison inmates and guards. Each day after court, Anderson would walk the four flights of stairs up to his cell, and as he passed, some of the inmates would yell obscenities at him, calling him a coward and baby killer.

Though Anderson considered himself to be above the criminals around him, his fellow inmates placed him on the lowest rung of offenders: those who have committed crimes against children.

NOT SURPRISINGLY, throughout the trial I dreamt repeatedly of Kim, Juri, and Lindsay—and Anderson himself. In addition to frequent replays of that scene in the back bedroom, I experienced a number of dreams in which I was given the opportunity to save them.

In one dark dream, I visited Kim and the children in a rundown apartment. As I climbed the dilapidated steps to their door, I noticed two ragged old men sprawled outside on soggy, autumn leaves, staring vacantly. Once inside the apartment, I noticed that the children were extremely thin and shabby-looking, and appeared unusually subdued and frightened. Kim was pregnant with a third child and looked in very poor health.

Suddenly, Anderson burst into the room, violently knocking the door off its hinges. Not noticing me, he began to verbally abuse Kim and the children, who cringed as he ranted and raved. I stepped in as he moved towards them, certain that he would kill them if I did not intervene.

Desperate to calm him down, I noted that we were both dressed in blue bus driver's uniforms, and tried to use this as common ground. I told him that as a fellow professional driver, I understood the stresses of his job, but suggested it was wrong to take that stress out on his family.

However, as I talked, Anderson became increasingly enraged, his anger boiling over. I knew the only way to save my children was to kidnap them, and anxiously sought a means of escape...

TWO DAYS INTO THE TRIAL, Jack Harris called his client to the stand. Anderson testified for the better part of two days, as Harris walked him through the events of his early life, marriage, first separation, reconciliation, and final separation, as well as his involvement with the Jehovah's Witnesses, hoping to paint a picture of a confused and somewhat pathetic young man for whom the jury might feel sympathy.

He argued that Anderson's letter to the Coles was not the confession of a planned murder but a sincere suicide note, reflecting a genuine intention to take his own life; Anderson had no particular plan in mind when he walked over to Kim's apartment and had only taken the shotgun with him to demonstrate his seriousness; and that he had only locked the door and taken Kim and the children with him into the bedroom to keep the police out, not to intentionally confine them there against their will.

He went on to assert that Anderson had not shot his victims in a planned attack but in a sudden, explosive fit of rage after Kim refused to hug him. He suggested that the murders had been nothing more than a domestic dispute that might have ended peacefully had it not involved a deadly weapon that required the intervention of police.

THE DAILY REPORTS OF the trial did little to answer our questions about Anderson's motives and state of mind at the time of the murders. It was clear that his testimony on the stand was less confession than strategy, a well-rehearsed effort to escape the punishment he deserved—no more, no less. As Rick Miller predicted, the trial only succeeded in muddying my emotional waters; it did not help me to see any more clearly into the dark pool of Anderson's violent act, and only expanded the list of questions to which I was determined to find answers.

On cross-examination, Rick Miller drew a picture of Anderson as a spoiled, demanding child who grew up to be a controlling, manipulative adult. He dismissed Anderson's repeated threats of suicide as little more than calculated maneuvers, and demonstrated how he had taken advantage of Kim's religious beliefs and affiliation to force her return to him. Miller said Anderson began to plan the murder of Kim and the children after their second separation, when he was no longer supported by the Witness elders and had run out of ways to control and manipulate their relationship. He maintained Anderson had purchased and sawed off the barrels of two shotguns, not for protection or to take his own life, but to commit murder.

The murder of Kim and the children was characterized by Miller as a premeditated act designed to give Anderson ultimate control over Kim and the children—making him the authority to decide whether they would live or die.

On December 4, 1986, Jack Harris began his summation to the jury. He described Anderson in very unflattering terms, as "a failure who wallowed in self-pity for five years," as a troubled young man with pent-up emotions for which he had no outlet. Comparing him to a "plugged kettle," he tried to convince the jury that Anderson's "blow up" was inevitable and beyond his control. "If you are anywhere near that kettle when it blows, it's going to kill you," he said. "And that little, simple kettle can turn killer." According to Harris, Anderson was not a cold-blooded murderer, but a simple and pathetic man who simply "cracked" when he did not receive a hug.

The jury was not convinced. Two hours later, they found Jeff Anderson guilty of three counts of first-degree murder. Mr. Justice Wood asked an emotionless Anderson if he had anything to say before sentence was imposed.

"No, sir," he replied.

Justice Wood then sentenced Anderson to three concurrent life sentences for each count of first-degree murder, with no eligibility of parole for twenty-five years.

MARGE WAS RELIEVED by the news of Anderson's conviction, but for me it was an anticlimax. It did not bring relief, nor exorcise the demons of my mind. In fact I was very far from putting Anderson behind me, far from acceptance and peace, far from reconciliation with God or man. I was in prison, with no hope of parole.

15

WHY DID ANDERSON kill my children? Why did I fail to save them? Why did God allow them to die?

In the two years that had passed since the murders, every day my life had been framed by these three questions. They formed my first and last conscious thoughts, and continually looped back and forth through my subconscious like a monotonous chant. It didn't matter how many times I was told that the questions could never be answered. Still they continued, relentless and without relief.

In desperation, I returned to psychotherapy in January 1987. I repeatedly solicited my therapist's professional opinion of Anderson's state of mind and motives. Was he crazy? Did he know what he was doing? What would make someone commit such an unthinkable act? Week after week, my therapist patiently advised me that he could not diagnose Anderson without access to his file, that he probably suffered from a personality disorder and was not criminally insane, and it was impossible to understand an irrational act. Then the therapist would gently but firmly lead me back to the same place: "Anderson is not your problem, Jim. He can't provide you with the answers you're looking for any more than I can."

From there, we would go on to discuss my own feelings of guilt—for having failed to keep my family together, for not having fought harder for custody of my children, for failing to kidnap Juri and Lindsay when I had the chance. Time and time again, he would reassure me that I was not responsible for my children's deaths, that I could not have possibly foreseen what was to come, and that the only person to blame was Anderson.

The real question—the one and only question—hung suspended between us, unspoken and inexpressible. Why did God allow my children to die? If we live in a universe of meaningless chaos, one in which random acts of violence have no more significance than a dying star, then on what do we base our lives and our faith? Do we all exist under an illusory veil of meaning until tragedy rips it away? How does one continue without that veil? What was I living for, for God's sake?

But my therapist was neither priest nor philosopher, and did not attempt to probe the quick sands of existentialism with me. Instead, we discussed my healing, the various ways in which I could better love and nurture myself, calm my feverish mind, and let go of anger and fear. Our sessions usually provided a certain degree of temporary relief, but did absolutely nothing to stem the obsessive questions that had taken me hostage.

I had moved beyond my anger towards Kim and no longer blamed her for what had happened to our children. I now saw her for what she was—a victim. A victim of Anderson, first and foremost, but also the inevitable product of her own psychological scars, a damaging religious upbringing, an unsupportive religious community, and a probable chemical imbalance of the brain.

I had also moved beyond the desire for vengeance and no longer indulged in revenge fantasies that had obsessed me for so long. But Anderson still had a firm grip on my life and thoughts.

On March 15, 1987, journalist Jon Ferry published a series of articles in *The Vancouver Province* based on three separate interviews conducted with Jeff Anderson, prosecutor Rick Miller, and defense lawyer Jack Harris. The articles provided three contrasting portraits of Anderson, none of which provided me with any new knowledge or insight about the man who murdered my children. Rick Miller dismissed Anderson as a "self-indulgent psychopath" and a "conscienceless creep," while Jack Harris painted a picture of a troubled, pathetic man in need of professional help. Anderson himself parroted the rhetoric of his defense counselor, describing himself as "a plugged kettle ready to explode," a man who had gone through a difficult break-up and simply "needed to talk."

In March 1987, I found the name of Anderson's mother, Mildred Brader, while going through an old address book. Kim had lived with her shortly after her marriage to Anderson, and had provided that telephone number and address as a temporary place to send my child support payments.

I had never met Mildred Brader, but on an impulse, I dialed her number in Texas. I told myself that it would be a call of compassion, to see how she was coping with her son's imprisonment. Looking back, the call was obviously more about my need to communicate with Anderson himself than with his mother.

Mildred did not immediately recognize my name when I introduced myself on the phone, but then paused and caught her breath in surprise. When I told her the reason for my call, she explained, in a soft, Texas drawl, that she was fortunate to have two other sons to support her through this difficult time. When she asked after my own well-being, I talked about the effect Anderson's act had had on my life and mentioned that I was in therapy.

Mildred expressed her sympathy, and told me that she believed her son Jeff was "in agony" over what he had done. She told me that he often woke up in a cold sweat at night, terrified, and was himself seeing a prison psychologist. She also told me about her visit to B.C. in the summer of 1985, how she had pleaded with her son to "come home to Texas and forget all about Kim," and how he had remained "consumed" with the idea of getting back together with Kim and the children. "If only I had known what he was going to do," she said, "I would have brought that child home for sure."

Like me, she had at first blamed Kim for what had happened, but later realized how unfair it was to do so. When she attended Anderson's preliminary hearing in December 1985, she received a very thoughtful greeting card from Kim's mother, Jackie. "That card is something to treasure," she said.

When I asked Mildred if she was one of Jehovah's Witnesses, she said that she had joined the faith briefly many years before, which was how Anderson first got involved with the organization. She explained that she was now a Lutheran. When she asked if I was a Christian, I hesitated, but then replied that Marge and I were currently attending the United Church of Canada.

She reminded me that she, too, had lost a child; although she received weekly phone calls from Anderson, her son was "dead" to her. I wondered aloud what could have been going through Anderson's mind prior to the murders, thinking that Mildred might have some insight into his personality and character, but she was not able to tell me. "I guess that's why he's seeing the prison psychologist," she said. "To figure out why he did what he did."

Her next statement revealed just how simple her understanding of her son was: "It's so strange," she said. "Jeff loved those children as though they were his very own."

She seemed to understand my need to get answers from Anderson better than I did myself. She suggested that it might help if he were to write me a letter and try to answer some of my questions. I was taken aback by her suggestion, but convinced myself that it would be unkind—to Mildred—to reject it. I also told myself that it was unlikely Anderson would ever write such a letter. In the end, I told Mildred that I would read any letter that her son might send me.

Marge was nonplussed by my conversation with Anderson's mother until I told her the part about the letter. Then she stared at me as though I had suddenly grown two heads. "And what are you going to do with his letter when you get it?" she asked. I reassured her that there was nothing to worry about. I doubted

Anderson would actually write, and if he did, I could always send the letter back unopened.

As a kind of therapy, I had begun to keep a journal, recording my dreams, thoughts, and memories of Kim and the children. This activity led me to realize how little I knew about their lives after my separation from them. I began to translate the great void left by their murder into a lack of information without which I would never solve the mystery of their deaths. And I increasingly began to focus on Jeff Anderson as the only source of that information.

Around the same time, Marge and I started to attend meetings of The Compassionate Friends, a local support group for bereaved parents. The group had about a hundred members, most of whom had lost children either through illness, accident, or suicide. Although members of the group tried to be supportive and understanding, we were the only attendees, at the time, who had lost loved ones through the act of murder, and it was difficult for them to relate to our experience. Nonetheless, we continued to attend the meetings regularly for a time, for lack of an alternative.

In early April 1987, I went to the mailbox to collect our mail, and among the various bills found a thick, white, business-size envelope neatly addressed to me. The upper left-hand corner read: "Jeff Anderson, Kent Institution, Agassiz, British Columbia."

My heart pounded in my chest and a rush of revulsion and fear flooded my body. As I traced my finger over the blue ink of the envelope's script, I thought over and over again, *The hand that wrote this, murdered my children… the hand that wrote this, killed Juri and Lindsay…*

I tried to appear calm as I walked into the kitchen with the letter, not wanting to upset Marge more than necessary.

"It's here," I said.

"What's here?" she asked.

I cleared my throat, and extended the envelope towards her. "The letter."

After a brief pause of incomprehension, Marge's eyes widened with horror. "What are you going to do?" she asked.

I shrugged my shoulders. "It can only be an apology," I said. "I can't think what else he would want to say to us." I stared at the object in my hand. "I guess I'm going to read it," I said, and left the kitchen.

My hands were shaking as I sat on the edge of our bed, fingering the envelope, overwhelmed by a dizzying mixture of emotions: horror, curiosity, anticipation.

The letter was dated April 2, 1987, and written on six pages of white, foolscap paper. It began with "Words cannot begin to express the anguish for the horrible thing I've done," and ended with "I beg your forgiveness, if that's ever possible." Everything in between read like something written for a prison psychologist, liberally peppered with therapy buzz words like "immaturity... self-deception... need for control... blaming behavior... self-justification..." At the end of six pages of intellectual rationalizations, I had no sense whatsoever of the man's character, personality, or emotions.

I initially discarded the letter, but my continuing need for information—and meaning—kept drawing me back to it. Although Anderson's letter was not very self-revealing, he did demonstrate a willingness to discuss the details of the murder, and I started to wonder if he might open up to me in future communications. His letter also helped me to dispel the larger-than-life monster of my fantasies and nightmares, and with it, the irrational fears associated with him. And although I was impatient with the letter's tone, I took what appeared to be a remorseful apology at face value. It made me think there might be a human being with whom I could make contact, who might have the humanity to tell me what I wanted to know.

Anderson's request for forgiveness raised another hope. The meaning-lessness of my children's murders had cast me adrift, spiritually, and I longed to believe in goodness again, to have a concept of God in my life. At a time when I most needed the comfort of spiritual belief, I could find no foundation on which to base such a belief. Desperate to associate some meaning, some good with the horror of my children's deaths, I began to hope that forgiveness might be my road back to a normal existence—the life I knew before the unthinkable happened, before the veil was ripped away. Having rejected (or at least survived) the alternatives—vengeance, madness, suicide—I began to convince myself that forgiveness of my children's murderer might be the magic cure that would lead to the healing my therapist kept talking about.

I was a desperate man ready to try anything. I made the decision to reply to Anderson's letter about a month later.

I had already read a little about the concept of restorative justice—a formal, therapeutic relationship whereby victim and offender work together to effect a healing based on remorse and forgiveness—and I latched onto that phrase as a way to explain my correspondence with Anderson. But my decision to engage with him was less than altruistic. At best, I hoped that wearing the mask of Christian forgiveness would eventually restore my faith. At worst, it was a face-saving way to rationalize my obsessive need to fill in the pieces of the puzzle, to obtain the information I so desperately needed, to communicate with the man who had last seen my children alive.

The first exchange of letters, in the spring of 1987, began a correspondence that would drag out over five years. It also began a bizarre journey into the life and mind of Jeff Anderson, one that would eventually reveal all of the information I hungered for—and cruelly tear away the last veil of illusion that remained in my life.

16

BETWEEN MAY 1987 and November 1988, I received letters from Anderson at least every two weeks. Although they were usually excessively long and tedious documents, they met a number of my emotional needs. I usually responded with relatively short replies every third letter or so, which encouraged him to keep writing.

During the first year of our correspondence, Anderson's letters actually helped to calm my fears and anxieties. They were articulately composed, and their smooth, non-threatening expressions of remorse and sympathy were like a soothing balm. In a bizarre way, they made me feel safe, in that they reassured me that Anderson could not hurt me and my family any further. They also held out the promise of transforming the enormity of what had happened to me into something more psychologically manageable. If Anderson could be reduced to human dimensions, it might be possible to rid myself of the monstrosity that had held me hostage for the past two years.

I was encouraged in this direction by more than one person. In therapy, my somewhat liberal-minded psychologist promoted the view that Anderson was a human being like any other, who had simply "fucked up royally on one occasion." I had also become friendly with some people associated with the Mennonite Central Committee, an organization dedicated to the view that criminals are victims of their society and environment. One of the members of that organization, Wayne Northey, was particularly influential. He was one of the Christian advocates who supported Anderson (and other offenders) in prison, and he strongly encouraged the restorative justice aspect of our correspondence.

Another influence was Wilma Derksen, the author of *Have You Seen Candace?* Wilma's fourteen-year-old daughter was abducted and murdered in 1984, and her response to that tragedy had been dramatically different from my own. A deeply Christian woman, she immediately expressed public forgiveness for the unknown person who had killed her daughter, and subsequently became a leading spokesperson and advocate for the healing power of forgiveness. I first met Wilma when she joined a bereavement group for homicide victims that Marge and I began in August 1987.

A month earlier, one of the leaders of the Compassionate Friends bereavement group received a call from the Victim Services section of the Winnipeg Police Department. They were calling on behalf of a woman who had recently lost her sister and niece in a domestic homicide, and were trying to place her with an appropriate self-help group. Marge and I agreed to meet with her, and shortly thereafter began hosting a small group of homicide survivors in our home. As the group grew, it began to meet in a local Mennonite church under the name of Family Survivors of Homicide.

Wilma Derksen later described those meetings in a newsletter. "Once every two weeks we would brave the cold weather and get together jut to tell our stories. We planted a tissue box on the coffee table and sometimes we used them, sometimes we didn't. Our simple guidelines were that we would honor each other's stories, validate each one, never impose our own beliefs, values, or ideas on others, and keep the stories confidential. It was truly a healing experience. We bonded in a way that I had never experienced before."

It was strange, becoming intimate with people through the common experience of tragedy, but the main benefit of our meetings was the opportunity to experience our losses in an open and public manner. In the September 1997 issue of *The Atlantic Monthly*, Eric Schlosser wrote about a convention of an organization called Parents of Murdered Children, and his words eloquently captures this shared experience: "One after another the faces of murder victims are projected onto a large screen—hundreds of faces, most of them young. This could be a slide show at a college reunion, cheery and nostalgic, except all these young people are dead. The effect is overwhelming. The convivial spirit of a typical American convention gives way to the sorrows of a congregation of the damned. As the face of each murder victim appears, a family member lights a candle. Before long the ballroom is full of grown men and women who are crying, lit by flickering candlelight, in a modern ritual that oddly evokes the ancient meaning of the word 'victim': one who is sacrificed."

It took a great deal of dedication, hard work, and commitment to establish our group, and Marge and I and other volunteers ran ourselves ragged to the point of burnout. However, in the summer of 1988, we were fortunate enough to receive a $20,000 grant from the Victims Assistance Committee of Manitoba, which greatly relieved the pressure. Through this financial support, the group was able to acquire a full-time staff person and an office equipped with a small library.

Wilma Derksen became an active and driving force behind the organization, and I was impressed with the extent to which forgiveness had helped her deal with the death of her daughter. It became a seductive concept for me; like revenge, it represented a quick fix, with the potential for immediate emotional gratification. Hungry for the healing power it promised, I committed myself to continuing my correspondence with Anderson.

Early in our correspondence, Anderson often mentioned the Bible, God, heaven, hell and the afterlife. To him, they were all wrapped up together under the banner of "faith." My belief in an afterlife was awakened, and that belief was supported not only by the Bible, but by powerful dreams of Kim and the children, in which they seemed to be communicating with me from another dimension—that they were safe—and that I too would be safe someday. I told Anderson about these dreams and asked whether he too experienced dreams of Kim and the children. He wrote that he had not, but wished that he had. I wondered if he would *really* ever want to meet his victims again in the life to come—after what he had done to them. It occurred to me that a murderer's past will haunt him to his grave, and especially at the time of his death.

Obviously, he had a strong need to believe in something. He could no longer subscribe to the beliefs of Jehovah's Witnesses, and so it was evident he adopted some form of Protestant evangelism. But with every new bit of faith he acquired, contradictions multiplied in his mind. He no longer wanted a faith based on "a foundation of ignorance" or "blind faith," so he started to read Bible literature brought to him by his Christian sponsors, Wayne Northey and Arden Robertson. "You should see the 8 Bibles and ump-teen Bible books & literature I have," he wrote. "…you'd think I was a Bible-thumping Hell preaching Baptist." But he had doubts. In his first letter to me, he wrote: "I hope it brings comfort to you to know they [Kim and the children] are in a far better place with God. I want to believe that, and mostly I do, but sometimes I'm not sure." He later wrote that he was sometimes skeptical about Christianity and the existence of God.

In my efforts to encourage him to believe in *something*, I wrote: "I know what you mean about [doubts in] God. We yearn for redemption, for a better place than this one, because this one can be hell—we both know that—but I have learned this, Jeff, and I'm not trying to hand you my religion because we've both had enough forced religion—if there is a hell on earth, there is also a heaven… There is love and redemption for you and for me."

Later, Anderson described himself as an agnostic.

Nevertheless, I encouraged him to share the details of his life with me, in the hope that his letters would reveal some common ground on which I might relate to him as a human being. I was completely unprepared for the common experiences that the letters brought to light. It was extremely unsettling to discover parallel patterns in our lives, as I read about the circumstances of Anderson's childhood and adolescence, his involvement with the Jehovah's Witnesses, and his relationship with Kim.

My overriding motivation and need, however, remained the harvesting of information. For me, the devil was in the details, and there were a lot of them. I believed that it was in the details of Anderson's life that I would at last find the answers to the questions that haunted me. What makes one man capable of committing murder, and another man not? What made this man capable of killing my children?

JEFFERY LYNN ANDERSON WAS born January 2, 1959 to Mildred Morene Brader, a thirty-seven year old woman from the poor side of town. His father was Hershel Gary Anderson, a sewing-machine repairman, ex-boxer, and alcoholic.

Anderson described his mother as a "loving, generous and hardworking" woman who would do anything for her children, and his absentee father as "a mystery." Mildred and Hershel separated a few months before Jeffery's birth, and eventually divorced. Father and son met each other only once, when Jeffery was three months old, in a Texas prison where Hershel was doing time for writing bad checks.

Mildred already had two older sons, Luke and Don, from a former marriage, and raised all three children on her own. She and the children lived in an old two-bedroom bungalow on the southeast side of Houston, a low-income area of the city. A proud woman who preferred work to welfare, she worked long hours at physically demanding jobs—like a bakery—while the older boys attended school and Jeffery stayed with a babysitter. Believing his mother's long absences meant she didn't love him, Jeffery would often stand by the window and cry as she left for work, wondering if it might be the last time he would ever see her.

When Mildred was home with Jeffery, she frequently indulged him with his favorite foods, and he learned to comfort himself emotionally by overeating. As a result, he quickly became an overweight boy who was teased and made to feel ugly by other children, which made him feel increasingly angry and resentful.

By the age of six, he started to develop aggressive behavior towards other children. He would dare his babysitter's children to step in front of passing cars, jealous that they had a father and he didn't. He frequently vandalized other children's toys, simply because he was feeling "lonely," and once hit a girl with a slingshot "because she looked like she was happy and having fun." Jeffery also began to set fires as a way of gaining attention, once in the tall grass near his kindergarten class and another time in the local grocery store. The fire department was called in the first incident, and although the fire did little damage, it gave Jeffery a feeling of power that he liked.

Jeffery's two half-brothers, Luke and Don, were nearly a generation older and had already left home when Jeffery was still young. Don was a bit of a "hell raiser," a rebel who worked as a boiler-maker after a stint in the Navy, and had a love of fast cars. Luke was the more stable and mature of the two, a happily married man who eventually became a skilled machinist with his own machine shop. Jeffery would later claim that he looked up to Luke as a father figure, but he did not seem to emulate him in his behavior.

Jeffery suffered a serious car accident at the age of seven, which resulted in a broken thigh bone and a three-month stay in the hospital. The experience was traumatic for him; his entire left leg and part of his right leg had to be encased in a cast and kept in traction, followed by a period in a wheelchair, then on crutches. For the first two weeks, his mother visited every day, and thereafter about every other day. Despite her efforts, he felt lonely and abandoned.

After Jeffery's physical recovery, Mildred became briefly involved with the Jehovah's Witnesses, and would take Jeffery with her as she preached door-to-door. Although she left the organization after two months, she continued to maintain certain Witness beliefs and practices throughout her life. Although Jeffery would sometimes receive Christmas and birthday presents, Mildred, for the most part, tried to uphold the principle of not celebrating these so-called pagan holidays, a practice that made him feel different from other children and families. She also firmly believed in the coming Apocalypse, a belief that she passed on to her son.

Jeffery grew up believing the world was going to come to an end before he reached adulthood, and that he would probably not be one of the saved. He believed this to such an extent that he made his mother promise to give her consent for him to marry at age seventeen, so that he could experience wedlock before the world ended. She granted his request.

Jeffery would frequently run away from home and school for days at a time, usually hiding behind the garage or under the house. He would steal food from a neighbor's house and sleep on the cold ground, watching family and friends search for him from his hiding place. He later explained that he ran away in order to get his mother's attention and to manipulate her emotions; as long as he stayed away, she would remain worried and frantic, and he enjoyed the feeling of control this gave him.

Soon, the attention he gained from these episodes was not enough. Jeffery began to feel increasingly distant from his mother and emotionally dead inside. He became disrespectful towards her and refused to help out at home in any way. At thirteen, he met an older boy of seventeen with whom he would go for joyrides and shoplift pornographic magazines from corner grocery stores. It was at this time that he began to masturbate and develop intense sexual fantasies.

At around age fourteen, Jeffery developed an intense interest in radio and began to dream of a career as a disc jockey. Though his family strongly discouraged him, he would spend endless hours imitating the DJs he listened to, reading books on the subject and talking to local DJs on the phone. One day, a DJ invited him to sit in on his nightshift at a local station, which for a time became a regular Saturday night event he found "thrilling."

He also developed an interest in football, trying out for and making his junior high school team. Playing football challenged him both physically and mentally, and allowed him to experience a sense of camaraderie with his peers. His success at football greatly increased his self-confidence and self-esteem.

However, at the age of fifteen he began to feel increasingly fearful about his future, and began to obsess about the radical violence he saw at school and throughout the country. In a search for answers, he began to read various Jehovah's Witness books that his mother still had around the house, and became convinced that the current unrest signaled the beginning of "the last days." He also became preoccupied with surviving the coming "Armageddon."

In an effort to become one of the saved, he began to attend meetings at a local Jehovah's Witness congregation, where he was showered with attention and praise for his decision to serve Jehovah. It was more attention than he had ever received in his life, and he found it intoxicating. Within a few months, he was baptized in the swimming pool of a local Holiday Inn as a fully dedicated Jehovah's Witness.

During this period, he began to distance himself from his peers at school. He came to realize that football was "too aggressive and violent for a Christian," and that rock music was not of Jehovah. He quit the football team and gave up his dream of becoming a DJ, and for the next few years struggled to earn the approval of God and his fellow Jehovah's Witnesses. He attended three Witness meetings a week, preached door-to-door on weekends and on the days in between pursued personal Bible studies and socialized with other Jehovah's Witnesses. The transformation was dramatic. Almost overnight, he had gone *from being a deeply troubled young man to "an energized spokesman for God," who no longer worried about his future.*

He also developed the classic "us" and "them" attitude of a Jehovah's Witness, believing himself to be vastly superior to the worldly, non-Christian heathens around him. He refused to salute the flag in school or complete assignments involving the theory of evolution, and prayed to be the victim of violence at school so that he could be a martyr for his faith.

He soon found that he was not able to live up to the standards he had set for himself—especially when it came to his sexual desires. No matter how much he tried, he was unable to give up his obsessive sexual fantasies and masturbation, and out of guilt and shame eventually stopped attending Witness meetings. But Jehovah's Witnesses had become the focus of his entire life and when he left the faith, he soon became deeply depressed. At one point, he attempted suicide by swallowing a bottle of over-the-counter sleeping pills.

Although he was no longer a practicing Jehovah's Witness, Jeff still believed in Witness doctrine. He knew he was a doomed sinner who would die by the age of eighteen, and believed he had no future. As a result, he decided to quit school at sixteen and spend a year working at various low-paying jobs while still living with his mother. He took the jobs mostly to appease his mother and to buy expensive toys, such as a Honda motorcycle, a stereo, and a CB radio.

He met his first girlfriend at age seventeen through CB radio, and it was with her that he had his first sexual encounter. The relationship did not last long, since she did not live up to his ideal of the perfect Witness sister-wife. He briefly revived his dream of being a DJ when he landed a job with a country music station in nearby Baytown, Texas, but he was not as experienced as he had led the station owners to believe and was fired after only one show. These experiences led to another period of depression, during which he again attempted suicide with over-the-counter sleeping pills.

His brother Luke then gave him a part-time job at his machine shop, and with it the opportunity to learn a valuable trade, but Jeff wasn't interested and did not last long at the job. He began a relationship with another girl whom he had also met through CB radio. Thanks to Jeff's feelings of sexual inadequacy and fear of rejection, this relationship lasted only two months.

Feeling directionless and longing for intimacy, Jeff returned in desperation to the Jehovah's Witness community after a two-year absence. His prime motivation was to find a sister-wife with whom he could have the ideal Witness family. When attending meetings, all he could do was fantasize about the young women in the congregation. He even started to drive to other Kingdom Halls in the city, where he would park outside the building and watch, through his car windshield, as "sisters" entered and left the meetings.

At age eighteen, he was still living with his mother and spent most of his time eating junk food, watching television, and going to porn films. His attempts to date non-Witness women were inevitably disastrous; after a particularly humiliating experience with a young woman who laughed at his sexual inadequacy, he became even more convinced he needed a Witness wife who would be kind to him. The search for the perfect sister-wife would become the main obsession of his life—and would come to symbolize the answer to all his problems.

At nineteen, things began to improve somewhat. Jeff obtained an FCC radio license and landed a weekend job as a disk jockey for a radio station in Conroe, Texas, a small town seventy miles outside Houston. The pay was low, but the job gave him the opportunity to gain experience and confidence. His brother Don co-signed a loan that enabled him to buy a car with which to commute to his job. He also met an attractive "sister" at a Kingdom Hall meeting in Conroe, whom he tried to impress with a gold necklace stolen from a local department store. It didn't work—the girl refused him, telling him he was "too fat." The experience led to another period of depression, during which he quit his radio job in Conroe and returned to his old ways.

With no job, Jeff was unable to keep up the payments on his car, and it was eventually repossessed. After months of unemployment, he became more and more depressed and overweight, and often considered suicide. He also used to shoplift small items from stores. One day, he stole an expensive camera, which he hid in his closet and never used. Unfortunately, someone witnessed the theft, and a few days later, his sister-in-law told him that the local sheriff had been asking to see him. Terrified of being arrested, Jeff decided to leave town.

A year earlier, he had met a Witness family from Maui who had encouraged him to come and visit them there. And so, with little more than $300, a suitcase and the clothes on his back, he decided to move to Maui to "make a fresh start." He didn't tell his mother where he was going until the last minute, from an airport telephone.

Jeff Anderson arrived in Maui in the spring of 1980. Although he no longer considered himself much of a Jehovah's Witness anymore, he immediately phoned the family he had met the year before, who directed him to a local bed-and-breakfast that catered to vacationing Jehovah's Witnesses. He decided he would play the part of a dedicated Witness in order to stay in the good graces of the local community and derive whatever benefits he could from that association.

He was twenty-one years old, a self-described "criminal and liar" who had never lived apart from his mother or held a job for more than a few months. But he hoped that Maui would be the place to find the sister-wife who would turn his life around.

The next morning, he met Kim Kostelniuk, who had also come to Maui to find the Witness man of her dreams.

17

MARGE WAS WARY ABOUT my correspondence with Anderson. However, she shared my need for answers and became drawn into our correspondence in spite of herself. Though she never asked to read any of Anderson's letters, she did not object when I offered to read portions of them aloud to her. And although she herself never wrote a letter to Anderson, she did on more than one occasion dictate some words for me to include in my letters to him. As a result, Anderson began to address his letters as much to Marge as to me, and seemed to instinctively recognize that he would need to gain her trust in order to fully gain mine.

Marge remained deeply skeptical about the whole letter-writing process, yet she fully supported my need to engage in it. I desperately needed to be able to forgive Anderson, needed him to become a safe, productive and law-abiding citizen. I convinced myself that I was acting out of true altruism and sincere goodwill, even though the words of my letters revealed the true motivation behind my need for forgiveness and redemption. "By forgiving you, I can begin to forgive myself, and maybe God will be able to forgive me too."

With the disturbing parallels between our lives—the confusion and alienation of our childhoods and adolescence, our early obsessive involvement with Jehovah's Witnesses and subsequent marriage to the same woman—I had started to view Anderson as a dark shadow of myself. I thought that if I could come to understand what had led Anderson to do what he did, I might also understand the choices and mistakes of my own life. If I could forgive him, maybe I could relieve my own guilt for having failed to protect my children. And if Jeff Anderson could be forgiven by me, maybe he could be forgiven and redeemed by God—and maybe, just maybe, redemption existed for me.

At the same time, my desire to see Anderson as human and forgivable conflicted with my need to uncover the truth of what happened in that back bedroom on August 29, 1985. I had a compulsion to know every detail of the last sixty minutes of my children's lives, from the only living person who could tell me—their murderer.

In a bizarre way, I wanted Anderson to punish me with the details of my children's deaths. As I read his description of the way he had neared Lindsay's face with the barrel of the shotgun before pulling back and shooting, the way Juri had wrapped his arms around his disfigured sister with "fear and panic" in his eyes, it did not occur to me that Anderson might take pleasure in relating these details to me—only that I deserved to suffer as much as my children had on that terrible morning.

Yet no matter how much Anderson told me, I could not shake the feeling that there was still a vital missing piece of the puzzle, something I had yet to discover. In the summer of 1987, I received a letter from Anderson telling me that a local professor of criminology was writing a book on murder in Canada and the professor's assistant had recently interviewed him in prison. The letter deeply disturbed me on two levels. Anderson made a bizarre reference to the interview having been his "best," making me wonder what other interviews he had given since being imprisoned. He also proudly declared that he had been "totally open and honest about everything." I couldn't help but wonder if Anderson had revealed something to the interviewer he hadn't revealed to me.

That something never came to light, and towards the end of 1988 I felt that the purpose of my correspondence with Anderson was coming to an end. I told myself—and others—that this was because we had now completed the full circle of forgiveness and redemption, and there was no reason to continue our interaction. In fact, I found Anderson's letters increasingly disturbing and had started to feel deeply conflicted about his reported rehabilitation—a goal that I ostensibly supported and had invested in emotionally, yet could not fully accept and believe.

After his murder conviction, Anderson had been moved to Kent Institution, a maximum security prison that represented a major improvement over Oakalla. At Kent, he had the opportunity to attend classes, had access to a decent library, and had the privilege of using a fully-equipped gym—with a yard the size of a football field—for a full ninety minutes each day. He no longer had to share a bunk with another inmate, and his ten-by-seven-foot cell was furnished with all the conveniences of an average college dormitory room: bed, metal table with drawers, bookshelf, clothes cabinet, bulletin board, desk lamp, radio, black-and-white television set, sink, medicine cabinet, toilet, and a two-by-four-foot window that could be opened for ventilation.

At the beginning of our correspondence, I was impressed with the degree to which Anderson seemed to take responsibility for what he had done. On a number of occasions, he expressed the view that he should receive the death penalty for what he had done, that there was a deep "injustice" in his continuing to live after he had taken the lives of Kim and the children. He also expressed the view that his twenty-five-year sentence was "a mere token gesture of debt... an insult to the value of the precious lives taken, and the victims left behind." He left no doubt he believed prison was where he belonged.

When I asked him about his trial, he wrote that "it was a useless battle from the start," and if he had it to do all over again, he'd rather avoid a trial.

During this time, he expressed how low he felt—very low. Since August 29, 1985, it was as though he was living in a time warp, "not living but merely existing in some altered state... like a disembodied spirit." He wrote about the "constant melancholy" he felt—for example, when staring out the window or when he would hear some meaningful song on the radio that would bring memories of Kim and the children rushing back. "So often," he wrote, "I don't feel worthy to be part of the human race, more like some bug or animal that should be squashed or killed."

When he wrote in this vein, I actually pitied him. I couldn't begin to understand how it would feel to walk in his shoes, and continue to live knowing what he'd done.

Yet as time went on, he expressed the same views and feelings less and less. Instead, he began to complain about his inability to "relate" to his fellow inmates, how he lacked their "criminal mentality." He also expressed the desire to be moved to a medium security prison where he could enjoy more privileges and "personal space."

In the fall of 1987, Anderson transferred to the Regional Psychiatric Centre (R.P.C.) in Abbotsford, B.C., which he excitedly described to me as a "really wonderful" place. He said the staff, nurses, and psychiatrists all mingled freely—and "respectfully"—with the inmates, how he was allowed to have potted plants in his nice "well ventilated" cell, and how he had access to a large yard and most of the facility, and now ate off "real plates" with "real silverware." He reported that he was allowed to work at the center's large greenhouse and had the opportunity to use the extensive educational facilities, including a library and gym as well-equipped as one in any high school. He described this new prison as a place for "those who admit they have a problem and want to help themselves," and hoped I would be pleased with his good fortune.

In June 1988, he reported that his sense of self-worth had improved significantly and he had learned to be less "self-critical" about his past mistakes. He proudly announced a whole catalogue of the "self-improvement" courses he was taking, including a psychology correspondence course from a local university and prison courses such as Life Skills, Speech Craft, and Substance Abuse (for his problem of overeating). He boasted that he was now working part-time as a tutor to other inmates, and reading books onto cassette tapes for the blind.

Shortly before Christmas 1988, he said the R.P.C. would be holding an open house social for inmates' families, children, and friends. To my horror, he told me he would be "official babysitter" for the visiting children during part of the open house. "I see it as another chance to prove that I can be trusted and am not dangerous," he wrote. "I consistently shatter the public's stereotype image of what a murderer... is supposed to be like." I was utterly baffled by the fact that R.P.C. staff would put a child murderer—no matter how rehabilitated—in charge of children. However, much to my relief, I later learned that Anderson had been too "depressed" at Christmas to fulfill his babysitting duties.

In a later letter, he excitedly told me that he had applied for a transfer to an even better facility. If Kent seemed more like a college dorm than a prison, and the R.P.C. the equivalent of a rehab clinic, then William Head Institution on Vancouver Island sounded like the Club Med of prisons. Anderson told me it was situated on "over 85 acres of land... part of which is exposed to open coastline, making it possible for inmates to fish and swim... And I understand one can roam through the woods for hours without ever coming in sight of a guard tower. Can you believe it?" He boasted that inmates were not usually transferred to William Head until they had served at least eight years of their sentences, but that he had earned the opportunity to go there after serving only three years.

The letters were becoming hard to take. I decided I had learned as much as I would from Anderson, and told Marge that I wished to end the correspondence.

However, since the spring of 1988, Anderson had been trying to persuade Marge and me to visit him in prison, and had sent us the appropriate forms. I was opposed to such a visit, feeling it would be redundant after my long, exhaustive, and ultimately unproductive correspondence with Anderson. What could either of us say that hadn't already been said on paper? Marge felt otherwise. She expressed the view that anyone could write convincing letters, and wanted to meet Anderson in person, to see for herself the extent of his rehabilitation. She wanted the opportunity to observe his eyes and his body language, where she knew a person's true nature and character could not be so easily concealed.

I reluctantly agreed, hoping that the visit would be a positive conclusion to everything I had accomplished over the past two years and would provide everyone involved with a sense of closure. But when I told Anderson that we had made formal application for a visit in June of 1989, he made a disturbing request that caused me to question his motives. He asked if he could "invite the media to record our historic meeting" in order to "further public awareness of victims' rights and plights." I told him that the presence of the media would be highly inappropriate, and Marge and I would go through with the visit only if we were assured complete privacy.

In April 1989, we received a visit from a local federal parole officer, who had been asked by the R.P.C. to do a community assessment report on us prior to our being granted a visit. Gabrielle Thiessen was a pleasant, socially graceful person who immediately put us at ease. She got down to business by bluntly asking why we wanted to visit Anderson. After she was satisfied about our motives, she expressed her concerns. She was not as convinced of Anderson's sincerity as I was, and questioned whether he was attempting to use me in a bid to gain privileges or even achieve early parole; she also suggested that my forgiveness of him was not helping the progress of his prison therapy. However, she did not dissuade us, and in the end indicated that she would not oppose our request. We were subsequently told we would be allowed to meet with Anderson on June 12, and that our meeting would be facilitated by Anderson's psychiatric worker, Karen Harvey.

When we arrived at R.P.C. that morning, we were surprised by the attractive landscaping surrounding the complex, which looked less like a prison than a holiday resort. After we parked the car, we signed in at the security gate and passed through a metal detector before being escorted to an electronic gate, where we were greeted by Karen Harvey. A sensitive young woman with a soothing voice and wholesome face, Harvey led us to an outer visitor's room of the complex, where a security officer would remain seated behind a glass partition throughout our visit.

Harvey talked with us for over an hour, expressing some of the same concerns as Gabrielle Thiessen. She talked about the programs Anderson was enrolled in while at R.P.C. and the difficulty he had in adjusting to prison life. She explained that he was at R.P.C. only temporarily for special observation and treatment, and would soon be returning to Kent, where he would once again be housed with the general population. Harvey indicated that most of Anderson's problems in prison had to do with the fact that he set himself apart from other prisoners and saw himself as different from the common criminal element, an attitude that did not sit well with other inmates. She told us he so hated the idea of returning to Kent, that he had made a desperate application to be transferred to the lower-security William Head Institution on Vancouver Island, an application that would never be approved at this early stage of his sentence. When the transfer was subsequently rejected, he had attempted suicide with an overdose of antidepressant pills.

Of course, I had not been aware of any of this. In his letters to me, Anderson had written extensively about the success of his therapy programs at R.P.C. and the degree to which he had come to recognize the seriousness of his crimes and the "garbage thinking" that had led to them. Harvey painted quite a different picture. She explained that Anderson seemed to feel that he should set his own agenda at R.P.C., that he knew better than the prison therapists what was best for him. While he seemed to understand certain concepts on an intellectual level, it was clear that he did not seem to grasp the full import of his crimes, nor their devastating effect on others. This was in direct contrast to his early letters, of course, in which he constantly expressed extreme remorse for what he had done both to me and my children—once even asking me to shoot *him* in the face with a shotgun, which he felt was the only just punishment due him.

Finally, Harvey warned us what to expect when we met Anderson, explaining that he was surprisingly presentable and well-spoken, with a likeable personality. She reminded us that we should not let his manner and appearance allow us to forget the grim reason he was in prison. Finally, she paused and took a deep breath, and told us it was time to bring Jeff into the discussion.

She returned a few minutes later with a large, overweight man who resembled the picture I had seen in Kim's apartment six years before. He wore a standard green uniform and soft shoes that looked like sneakers. As I looked at his clean footwear, I remembered how Anderson's shoes were the first thing Tom Wagner had noticed before interviewing him—how they were still spattered with blood and brain tissue from the crime scene and had to be changed before the interview could proceed.

When I looked at Anderson's face, I did not see the intimidating monster of my nightmares and fantasies, but a visibly nervous, rather infantile-looking man with a pale complexion and thinning hair. I remember thinking I could probably kill him with my bare hands if the opportunity presented itself.

I shook Anderson's hand and Marge followed suit. Like Wagner, I noticed how incongruously small his hands were in relation to his body. Anderson sat opposite us, with Harvey sitting off to the side. An awkward moment of silence followed, during which Anderson fidgeted nervously while Marge sat, rigid and silent, and Harvey observed.

Anderson spoke first, in a soft, Texas drawl that was strangely calming. He tentatively asked me about our victim's support group, Family Survivors of Homicide, and for a while, the two of us engaged in small talk about that enterprise. He listened and smiled at the appropriate moments, and then suddenly said, "You know, I'm really very nervous."

As he shook his head and looked down at the floor, I told him that we were also nervous. He told us that he was ready to hear our "personal criticisms" of him—he was "well-prepared" for what we might have to say.

I turned to Marge. "Well, now is your chance," I said.

She did not hesitate, but dove right in. Looking directly at Anderson, she said, "Is that what you want, Jeff—for me to hurt you?"

Anderson responded by sitting upright in his chair.

Marge continued, "You don't know how many times I've cursed you, Jeff. I get the impression you're an intelligent man. What I want to know is… why didn't you just walk away from Kim? Why did you kill the children? Your argument was with her, not them…." She leaned forward intently. "Do you realize I would have been a good mother to those children, that I would have cared for them dearly?"

Anderson nodded his head as she spoke, yet offered no answers. Marge continued to speak in this vein until she suddenly stopped, seemingly unable to go on. She quickly composed herself and continued. "Last October 24 would have been Juri's fourteenth birthday," she said. "That day was very hard on Jim. The holidays are also very tough. Do you know what an emotional wreck Jim has been since this happened? I've had to keep both him and his mother going. Our marriage will never be the same. It's survived, but there's been a big strain."

Marge paused and took a deep breath. Anderson remained silent. She went on to talk about the children's funerals. "With the Witness funeral in Burnaby, the strain only got worse. Do you have any idea how that felt? I didn't mind being ignored by the Witnesses—after all, I was only the stepmother. But to be the children's father, who had traveled all that way—just to be shunned. When we buried the remains, Jim's own sister refused to come to the funeral because it was held in a church."

Anderson seemed to relax somewhat when the subject shifted to the Jehovah's Witnesses, no doubt thinking this could mean an area of common complaint between him and Marge, but I quickly shifted the subject back to Anderson himself.

I bluntly asked what could possibly have been going through his mind the day of the murders. I told him that I was able to understand some aspects of him, but not others. In our correspondence, I had empathized with the failures of his early life and could relate to his feelings of depression, loneliness, and rejection, but I could not grasp how a man could ruthlessly kill a woman and two defenseless children. I asked him to explain how he could ever follow through on such an impulse. "Was it like the impulse to commit suicide," I asked, "in the sense that you could see only one inevitable choice?"

Anderson answered my question calmly. "No," he said. "Suicide is the result of not being able to live with the pain."

He then went on to repeat what he had told me in his letters: he had made the choice to kill Kim and the children in retaliation for what he perceived as their rejection of him. Almost as an afterthought, he quickly added that his act was, of course, "wildly out of proportion" to any wrongs suffered by him. I wondered whether he truly believed that or whether it was how his therapists had taught him to think and talk about his crimes.

At that moment, I pitied him, and told him so.

Anderson then asked if he could show us some pictures of Kim and the children. When we agreed, he brought out a photo album containing pictures of his wedding to Kim in August 1981. He handled the album with great care; he delicately placed it on the coffee table in front of us and slowly turned the pages with his soft, stubby fingers, as though it were a revered holy book. He pointed out what a "beauty" Kim was, and described her in glowing terms as a "rare gem" and the "ideal Witness wife."

As I looked through the album, I was surprised to see photos of the children I hadn't seen before, photos in which they looked so... alive. At that point, Karen Harvey drew in for a closer look. Color rushed to her face as she looked at the pictures. "Why, they were beautiful children," she said.

We had been there for about forty-five minutes, and it was clear that we were not going to learn anything new from our visit. As the meeting wound down, Marge told Anderson that she was disturbed by the way he seemed to idealize Kim, and advised that a more realistic picture of her might help him to understand his own behavior and actions better. "In the end," she said, "you put Kim down in the ground. So stop putting her on a pedestal, like she was some kind of saint. It's not going to redeem you now." She also warned him that we did not want to see any media coverage of our visit, and asked that everyone present send their written impressions of the visit for the record. Anderson readily agreed to do so, as did Harvey.

After an uncomfortable pause, Anderson looked directly at Marge. "I would like to say at this time that I feel you would have made a good mother to Juri and Lindsay," he said. I told him how helpful our correspondence had been in helping to resolve my anger and grief, and he agreed it had also been essential to his own healing.

Then, with a perfectly straight face, he added, "You know, as for victims, I've got the best!"

His comically bizarre statement made Marge laugh out loud and left me speechless.

"Well," said Anderson. "I'm glad you have a sense of humor about it."

After Anderson had left the room, Harvey expressed admiration for my forgiving attitude.

"It's been the answer for me," I said plainly, but was starting to feel less and less sure about that. We were debriefed by Harvey for about half an hour, and finally left the facility with a tremendous feeling of relief.

We then drove to a restaurant in nearby Aldergrove, where we ordered lunch and B.C. apple ciders. To our surprise, we found ourselves feeling quite triumphant and elated. I was happy to have brought a long and difficult process to an end, but Marge was feeling somewhat different.

She told me that she had been quite surprised by Anderson, speaking seriously and thoughtfully of his seeming intelligence, the respectful way he had spoken to us and how considerate he had been of her feelings. "I think he is basically a good person who went astray," she said. "He's certainly much too soft to survive in a place so full of tough criminals."

I was aghast. I remembered Karen Harvey's words of warning: how easily Anderson could fool people with his nice, Southern manners and smooth personality, how he could make people forget why he was in prison in the first place.

"What on earth do you mean?" I asked incredulously, amazed that Anderson could fool Marge, of all people.

"Well," she said uncertainly, "he's not... violent. Not vicious and cold-blooded like other criminals."

"But he *is* violent," I protested. "He killed three people—viciously, and in cold blood!"

I couldn't believe what I was hearing. Marge—who had always been my reality check—seemed to be implying that Anderson's act had been some kind of temporary transgression, that he was now returning to his decent self and was not a real criminal after all. It was not a view that Marge would hold for long, but I was deeply shaken by the effect Anderson had had on her—and wondered how many other people he might be able to fool.

Suddenly, the possibility of early parole for Jeff Anderson didn't seem like such a far-fetched possibility.

18

AFTER OUR VISIT WITH ANDERSON, Karen Harvey had asked if we knew about the book being written by Simon Fraser University professor Neil Boyd, entitled *The Last Dance: Murder in Canada.* She went on to tell us that Anderson had been interviewed for the book, as well as for a subsequent television documentary by the same name.

I vaguely recalled Anderson telling me that he had been interviewed by a young woman for the book. At the time, I didn't think anything would come of it and put it out of my mind. My curiosity aroused, I told Harvey that I would obtain a copy of the book as soon as it was available. I also thanked her for alerting us to the documentary, which we did not know about. We both thanked her for steering us through a difficult meeting that day.

When we returned to Winnipeg, we quickly settled into a quiet routine, relieved that our association with Anderson was now in the past. I told Anderson I saw no reason to continue our correspondence after the closure of our visit, and looked forward to a new phase of my life in which he was no longer such a frequent topic of conversation.

I should have realized Anderson had invested too much in our relationship to let it go that easily. I soon received a small package from him in the mail, one that not only contained one of his typically long, rambling letters, but also a audiocassette tape labeled "Interview: March 22, 1987." His letter told me it was a recording of a radio interview that I might find interesting.

I was immediately curious—yet wary. I wondered why he hadn't told me about the interview before and why he was sending me a copy now. I later realized that it was probably a calculated attempt to keep our correspondence going—knowing I would find the contents of the tape hard to ignore—and also in keeping with the increasingly confessional nature of his correspondence.

The tape confirmed what I had expected: Anderson's interviews with Neil Boyd and his assistant were not the first he had given since being incarcerated. The interview on the tape comprised part of a CKO phone-in, radio talk show program hosted by John Gilbert, which was broadcast nationwide on March 22, 1987. Incredibly, the host of the program was both against capital punishment and in support of shorter prison terms, as was the majority of the program's all-male callers. Throughout the broadcast, Anderson was portrayed as an unfortunate man who had simply cracked one day, an otherwise non-violent individual who no longer posed a threat to society, yet was costing the taxpayer close to $50,000 a year to keep in prison.

Anderson was interviewed by Gilbert over the phone. The beginning of the interview was reassuring, for despite the program's obvious agenda and a certain amount of self-pity on Anderson's part, he seemed to admit that he deserved the life sentence he had received. When the radio host asked how Anderson felt about such a long prison term, he said serving life was worse than death by execution, in that he had to live with what he'd done every day. He told Gilbert that serving "five thousand years" in prison could never compare to the degree of his own self-punishment. He also pointed out that twenty-five years was just an arbitrary figure, and that no sentence could ever be sufficient payment for the lives he'd taken—a view that I could not have agreed with more.

But the remainder of the interview stunned me. When Gilbert pressed Anderson to talk about how he would face the next twenty-three years of his sentence, Anderson's real agenda became obvious. After some hesitation, he stated he couldn't believe he would ever have to serve his full sentence, and informed the audience that he would be eligible for a judicial review of his parole ineligibility after serving fifteen years.

At this point, neither I nor Gilbert—nor the majority of Canadians—were aware there was any way someone convicted of first-degree murder without the possibility of parole would ever be considered for early release. As I subsequently found out, Anderson knew what he was talking about.

When the Trudeau government in Ottawa had abolished capital punishment eleven years before and replaced it with minimum twenty-five-year sentences for first-degree murderers, the legislation included what has become known as the faint hope clause—a stipulation that a lifer could ask for a judicial review of his parole ineligibility after serving fifteen years of his sentence. In 1987, no one had yet become eligible for a judicial review, but it was something that lifers looked forward to with anticipation, and Anderson was no exception.

Anderson went on to suggest to the radio audience that he should be given the opportunity to earn his way out of prison; there was no point in spending

$50,000 a year to keep someone like him in prison for twenty-five years. He maintained—and his host and the people calling in agreed—that an early release was the least expensive and most sensible option available under the faint hope clause.

I felt as though I had been kicked in the stomach. Anderson had participated in this interview just prior to the time he'd been writing letters to me expressing extreme remorse, letters in which he told me over and over again that he deserved the death penalty and should never get out of prison, that it was unjust he should live under any circumstances when Kim and the children's lives had been so brutally taken.

With a sickening feeling, I remembered the warnings of Gabrielle Thiessen and Karen Harvey. Had I in fact been duped by Anderson and co-opted into his agenda for early release? Had I unwittingly undermined my future ability to fight against such a release?

The interview only got worse. Encouraged by the host and caller's support, Anderson went on to stress that he had come from a good family with no history of alcoholism, drug abuse, or insanity; he was a normal man who had simply been pushed too far and had acted quite uncharacteristically when he committed murder. He advised women involved in separations and divorces not to be cruel in dealing with their spouses or boyfriends, and to be more kind and sympathetic to their feelings of rejection.

His message was clear. If Kim had been a kinder, more sympathetic person, Anderson would not have been pushed to do what he did. Anderson was not responsible for the murders—Kim was.

Karen Harvey's words rang in my ears: "He does not seem to grasp the full import of his crimes, nor their devastating effect on others…"

Not long after listening to the radio tape, I became aware that Anderson had also been featured in a CBC television show called *Pacific Report*, which was aired in February of 1987. I immediately obtained a copy of the program from the CBC and sat down to watch it with a feeling of dread. The title of the program itself—"Male Rage"—provided a clue as to what I could expect, and so I was not surprised to see and hear a Jeff Anderson angrily blaming Kim and the children for what had happened and portraying himself as the real victim.

When the interviewer asked Anderson what had caused him to finally pull the trigger, Anderson again blamed Kim, saying it was because she had refused him a hug. In a letter to me about the same time, Anderson had written, "True, I asked them all for one last hug… but that didn't really make me shoot." In that same letter, he told me that he had felt compelled to carry out his plan. "I was afraid I wouldn't do it, so I did it." Yet even that statement didn't explain *why* he did it; it only says how *determined* he was to do it.

Anderson even contradicted himself in the television interview. When asked why he shot the children as well as Kim, he said, "Because they were there, I guess," but added, almost as an afterthought, "Maybe they represented rejection, too." The section ended with Anderson lecturing the audience on the dangers of obsessive love, telling them anyone feeling that way should get professional help before it led to disaster.

I was now even more convinced than ever that the murders had been pre-meditated, and was once again haunted by the feeling that there was a missing piece to the incomprehensibility of Anderson's act. If the murders had not been an act of insanity or passion, why had Anderson believed it necessary to kill not only Kim, but Juri and Lindsay too? Why were the murders carried out with such deliberateness? A feeling of rejection—especially rejection by children— wasn't enough to explain it.

Still reeling from the impact of Anderson's interviews, I was then surprised to receive a telephone call from Neil Boyd. He began by apologizing for inter-rupting my Sunday, and explained that he was in the process of putting together the documentary version of his book *Last Dance: Murder in Canada*—in which Anderson was a subject—and wanted to know if I would contribute photographs of Kim and the children. I knew Boyd to be a respected criminology professor and author, and liked and trusted him immediately. Though I had not yet read *Last Dance: Murder in Canada*, and did not know what approach Boyd had taken and would take in his depiction of Anderson, I felt his documentary had the potential to be an important educational tool. Therefore, by the end of the conversation, I agreed to assist in any way I could.

Boyd told me that he had conducted an in-depth, hour-long interview with Anderson, but only about eight minutes of the interview would appear in the final documentary. He also told me that the documentary would be aired sometime in January 1990, and that the book was already available in book-stores.

I knew Boyd was making a concerted effort to be sensitive and discreet during our conversation, but nonetheless I could not help feeling that he was holding something back when he talked about Anderson. At one point, he men-tioned my restorative justice relationship with Anderson, commenting that he would find it difficult, if not impossible, to take such a forgiving approach.

I was deeply curious to see how Boyd would portray Anderson in his book and documentary, and purchased a copy of *Last Dance: Murder in Canada*. I was quite puzzled when I initially perused it. The book discussed a number of murder cases that had taken place in Canada, from manslaughter to first-degree murder, but I could find no mention of Anderson in its pages. I concluded that for some reason, Boyd had decided to include Anderson in the documentary but not in the book, and set the book aside to read properly later.

Shortly thereafter, I received yet another letter from Anderson, this one containing a bizarre offer. He explained he was earning modest wages from his part-time laundry job in prison, which came to about $140 per month, and wanted me to have his monthly checks as restitution for the pain he had caused me. I was appalled—by the ridiculousness of the offer, by the implication that my forgiveness could be bought, and by the obvious manipulation behind it. By this time, I was painfully aware that the restorative justice aspect of our relationship was all one-sided. No amount of money could restore my children to me, yet my acceptance of Anderson's hollow gestures of remorse could potentially restore him to freedom.

After much soul-searching, I decided I could no longer participate in a process that I no longer believed in, and on September 2, 1989, I wrote to Anderson to refuse his offer and again request an end to our correspondence. In the same letter, I mentioned Neil Boyd's documentary and casually mentioned that I was surprised Anderson was not included in the book by the same name.

It was a casual remark that I would regret for the rest of my life, for it would inadvertently force Anderson to surrender the missing piece of the puzzle I had been trying to wrest from him for the past two years. And like an immovable object that suddenly gives way, its impact was violent.

Anderson's reply was immediate. He said he understood my confusion and explained that Boyd had used pseudonyms in his book; that he and Kim were in fact featured in the first chapter as Gordon and Gail Parker. He went on to apologize for not having been completely honest with me and for my having to find out the truth this way.

My heart pounded in my chest. I threw the letter down and looked for my copy of Boyd's book. As I started to read the first chapter, I could see that Gordon Parker was indeed Jeff Anderson, and Boyd's account of events leading up to the murders accurately reflected what I had learned from the police and from Anderson himself.

However, as I read on, I discovered that Boyd's account briefly touched on an aspect of the case about which I knew nothing. As I read the following sentence, the numbing disassociation I had experienced when I learned of my children's murders was cruelly absent. This time, the pain was immediate and brutal:

"[Gordon] sexually molested his step-daughter, feeling that he was being deprived of sex with his wife…"

19

AFTER HER MARRIAGE to Jeff Anderson in August 1981, Kim Kostelniuk knew that she had made a terrible mistake, and lived in constant fear and anxiety through-out the next two months of their marriage. Anderson had lied to her about his financial affairs and she soon had barely enough money to feed her children. Her feelings of disgust and revulsion towards him only deepened her natural aversion to sex, and Anderson would sometimes become violent when she refus-ed his sexual demands.

One night, Anderson left their bed around 2:00 a.m., angry and frustrated that Kim had refused him yet again. Later, Kim's four-year-old daughter Lindsay came into the bedroom, asking her mother for "some panties" because "somebody was touching me." After Kim led her daughter back to bed, she angrily confronted her husband. Anderson admitted that he had crawled into Lindsay's bed for comfort, but insisted that he had only hugged her in a non-sexual way.

Kim left Anderson shortly thereafter, living in Calgary for a time before fin-ally returning to Burnaby, B.C. in the fall of 1982. In March 1984, Anderson followed Kim to Burnaby, where he gained the sympathy of the local Witness elders, who pressured her to take him back. Fearing congregational discipline, or even disfellowshipment, she reluctantly agreed to resume their relationship.

One morning after Anderson moved into Kim's home in Burnaby, Lindsay told her mother that she had had "a dream" about someone being in her bed and touching her "privates." Not long after that, both Juri and Lindsay reported that Anderson had exposed himself to them.

Kim felt trapped. She feared for the safety of her children, but also feared being rejected by the religious community that was the center of her life. At the urging of her mother, she arranged a meeting between herself, Anderson, and the congregation elders. She told Anderson of the meeting, which gave him time to prepare his story for the elders.

In past meetings with Anderson and the elders, Kim likely tried to persuade the elders that there was a scriptural basis for her being allowed to leave her marriage. She probably pointed out that although Paul stated in I Corinthians 7:10 that a wife should not leave her husband, he also went on to say that "if she should actually depart, let her remain unmarried..."

However, because elders were governed by Watch Tower policy in such matters, they could not condone a woman leaving her marriage unless her husband had been guilty of adultery. With no indication of that, she was obligated to stay with him.

But now, something far more important than her crumbling marriage was at stake: her children were at serious risk of sexual abuse and they needed protection and safety. In desperation, she angrily revealed Anderson's sexually inappropriate behavior, confident that the elders would not force her to stay in a situation that was unsafe for her children.

However, Anderson managed to convince the elders that he was innocent of Kim's accusations. Kim had expected the elders to support her, but instead they angrily denounced her. They implied she was lying, that she had always had a problem accepting male authority, and that she had failed to fulfill her marital duties to her husband. They finally reduced her to tears, and she had no choice but to return home with Anderson, broken and defeated.

Afterwards, Kim fell into a deep depression, and began to see suicide as her only way out. Friends and family eventually persuaded her to seek outside help—a resort frowned upon by Jehovah's Witnesses.

On July 20, 1984, Kim sought the advice of a social worker at the B.C. Ministry of Human Resources. The social worker listed "possible sexual abuse" as the cause for Kim's visit, and advised Kim that the protection of her children should be her primary concern. Though sympathetic to her situation, he told Kim that she would have the weekend to consider appropriate action before the Ministry would be forced to intervene. In the meantime, at his insistence, she reassured him "that she would not leave the children with Jeff and would be sure they were protected and safe at all times." She was instructed to call him the following Monday to let him know her choice of action.

On July 23, Kim called the social worker to tell him that she had taken his advice and left Anderson, and would keep him apprised of the situation. By November 7, Kim's file with Family Services had been closed, with a note that said "there are no protection concerns at this time."

"[GORDON] SEXUALLY MOLESTED his step-daughter…."

There is no way to express the helpless devastation that those words brought into my life. My quest for the truth had opened a Pandora's Box that could never be closed again. It led me to the unbearable knowledge that my children—and Lindsay in particular—had suffered more than I could ever have imagined, that I had failed completely and on every level to protect their fragile young lives. It is a failure and guilt that I will never escape from or be able to forgive myself for.

Early in the murder investigation, Tom Wagner had made a passing reference to Anderson having exposed himself to the children. I had almost forgotten about it. Why had I not asked him to elaborate? Was it because it seemed a relatively trivial and unsubstantial matter at the time, in comparison to the murders themselves? Was it because I knew I could not possibly deal with any more pain than I was already experiencing? Or was it deliberate blindness?

Wagner's comment had obviously contributed to the nagging questions at the back of my mind over the past two years. And now that I had found the missing piece, it had to be faced and examined, no matter how painful.

Anderson had freely confessed his pedophilia to Boyd's assistant, and now that the book was out, he could no longer conceal it from me—hence his quick response to my letter and desperate attempt at damage control. He knew our restorative justice relationship had been founded on the assumption of absolute honesty and trust, and he would now have to explain why he had not disclosed this crucial information. He also knew how much the information would bring his crimes into focus, for it provided clues about his possible motives for killing Kim and the children.

He came to regret it, though, claiming to have admitted it first to his prison psychologist at Kent Institution because he had held that total honesty was a kind of "miracle cure-all drug" that would make everything all right. But there was another side to it. Because pedophilia is the Scarlet Letter of our generation, "you'd almost rather die than have your dirty little secret made public." When the story followed him from Kent Institution to R.P.C. "like a dark shadow," he realized that total honesty wasn't the miracle cure-all drug it was cracked up to be, implying he would have been better off keeping the secret to himself.

And now that the secret was out, it had come to me.

Anderson began his next letter by telling me that he had deliberately withheld the information for my own good, in the interest of sparing me additional pain. He also implied that his prison psychologist had supported the concealment, and in the end he had concluded that what I didn't know wouldn't hurt me. "You'd never find out, I figured."

Then came the inevitable pleas for forgiveness. While he could not expect me to take the new information "lightly," he hoped that I would be as "understanding" with this as I had been with everything else. He also expressed the extraordinary view that "Marge, being a woman, may have a harder time with this," and told me how important it was to him that he not "lose her trust and support."

He then went on to admit to the molestation that had occurred in Houston, and at my insistence, related the events that led up to the incident. Having been denied sex by Kim, he needed "sexual gratification... something to make me feel good," so he went into Lindsay's room and molested her while she slept. When she awoke, he panicked and quickly left the room, terrified she would tell Kim. When confronted about it, he denied having touched Lindsay sexually, but was never quite sure whether Kim believed him. From that day on, he feared that she would expose him one day, and he resented the power that gave her.

He said that when Kim threatened to tell the elders about what he had done, he became angry that she was trying to ruin the new start they were making and was terrified he would be exposed as a fraud. He was desperate to save face and determined to do everything in his power to convince the elders that Kim was not telling them the truth. Kim had told him about the meeting in advance, so he had had "plenty of time to work on sounding innocent."

The elders interviewed Kim first, and while there is no doubt that she accused Anderson of sexually inappropriate behavior, the specifics of her accusation are unclear. In his letter to me, Anderson confessed to the Houston incident, but denied that there had been any sexually inappropriate behavior with the children after he reunited with Kim in Burnaby. However, one of the elders who had been present at the meeting later reported that he could only remember Kim mentioning that Anderson had exposed himself to the children, and her voicing a "suspicion" that other incidents may have taken place. He had no memory of being told of any specific molestation of Lindsay, and maintained that he and the other elders would never have counseled Kim to stay with Anderson if they believed there was a genuine risk of sexual abuse.

What transpired in the elders' subsequent interview with Anderson is equally unclear. The elder I spoke with reported that when they confronted Anderson about exposing himself to Lindsay and Juri, he insisted that he had only been teaching them "about the birds and the bees." When the children subsequently confirmed his story, the elders felt that Anderson had simply shown "poor judgment" in his teaching method. They gave him "stern counsel" about the inappropriateness of his behavior, but concluded there was "no basis for anything more to be done about the matter."

Whatever transpired in those interviews, Anderson felt that his efforts to convince the elders of his innocence had succeeded beyond his "wildest dreams." He confessed to feeling a sadistic pleasure when the elders attacked Kim instead of supporting her, after all the pain and humiliation she had put him through. *This is fucking great,* he thought. *I have her right where I want her now.* During the car ride home, he felt power and control, and delighted in her discomfort. "Can you imagine how alone and hurt and misunderstood she must have felt?" he asked me.

His sense of control did not last long. Afterwards, Kim withdrew into an angry and cold shell, making sarcastic remarks like, "You're the boss, Jeff," and "Sure, I'll spread my legs for you like a good little Christian wife." In the end, he felt angry, helpless, and humiliated, and grew increasingly fearful that she would leave him again—and this time, he would not be able to get her back. On the morning that she moved out, he warned her not to "pull a Houston again," but convinced himself that she wouldn't dare risk the wrath of the elders again. When he returned that night to an empty apartment, he experienced a complete and final loss of control, and his world came crashing down.

Once the vile truth was out, Anderson's subsequent letters to me grew more and more bizarre and confessional, as though he believed that finally revealing his true feelings and nature to me would somehow inspire my sympathy and understanding. While the letters horrified me, the information in them finally helped me to understand the sequence of events that led to my children's deaths.

Anderson told me that he could not believe it when the elders were unable to force Kim to return to him, and he became enraged when they eventually advised him to accept the separation. Snooping among the things Kim left in the apartment, he ran across a letter from a Witness sister, telling Kim that Witness elders were not always right and urging her to do the best thing for her and the children. The letter included a brochure about the dangers of pedophilia. Anderson's fear of being exposed grew to the point of paranoia. "It is such a terrible taboo that you'd almost rather die than have your dirty little secret made public."

He confessed that he first began to fantasize about killing Kim after she told the elders about his sexual molestation of Lindsay. Even though the elders had not believed her, from that point on he feared that she might reveal the secret to other people and convince them of his guilt. He wanted to keep her quiet and punish her for shaming him, and he began to fantasize about all the ways he could kill her: by hitting her from behind with a frying pan, by poisoning her, by hiding in her apartment and bludgeoning her while she slept, by strangling her or drowning her in the bathtub. He also fantasized about sexually violating her while she was unconscious or dead.

He also revealed that more people might have died on August 29, 1985, if the RCMP had not intervened when they did. He told me that he had often fantasized about "walking into the Kingdom Hall with a shotgun and shooting everybody," and that he had planned to rape and murder Jackie Cole and her daughter Cindy after killing Kim and the children. He had a full box of cartridges and a fast motorcycle waiting outside, and the Cole residence and Kingdom Hall were only a few city blocks away. I could not help but wonder what might have happened that day if Kim's mother had not called the police when she did.

His letters also suggested that there might have been a purpose to his killing Juri and Lindsay as well. He explained that it had always been his intention to kill everybody, but he did not want to give Kim that impression in case she panicked and overpowered him before he had a chance to kill the children. He explained that he shot Kim first for that reason only, "otherwise I would have wanted her to watch the kids being killed—the ultimate revenge on her." He also admitted that, contrary to his earlier claims that he had intended to commit suicide after the murders, he in fact had a strong desire to witness the public reaction to what he had done.

Even more bizarre, at the same time that Anderson felt compelled to confess these details to me, he also sought to reassure me that his years of prison therapy had cured him of his previous problems. He told me that the first thing he had to do when he arrived at Kent Institution was to write a 120-page autobiography detailing his life and crimes, through which his psychologist became aware of his sexually inappropriate behavior with Lindsay. Anderson said he regretted having given that information so freely, for it followed him to R.P.C., where he was required to participate in a sex offenders program. While he admitted that "it was good to be honest because it forced me to deal with a past problem," he went on to say he would "now rather forget about it since I no longer feel it's a problem for me..."

He also tried to impress upon me the danger he would be in should he be transferred back to Kent Institution with a pedophile label attached to him, and asked that I not publicly discuss the information he had given me. He told me that Neil Boyd had agreed not to include the information in his documentary for that very reason. Anderson's Christian sponsor, Wayne Northey, contacted me shortly thereafter. He convinced me there was a basis for Anderson's fear, explaining that prisoners have their own code of morality, with "diddlers" (child molesters) viewed as the lowest of all life forms. However, as it now seemed unlikely that Anderson would be sent back to Kent—he would probably eventually be transferred to William Head Institution, the medium-security facility—I was puzzled by the urgency of his request.

Anderson subsequently admitted that he was also concerned should his family—and his mother in particular—find out about his pedophilia. And of course, that concern extended to the public. At the beginning of our correspondence, I had warned him that I was working on a manuscript and that some of the information in his letters might someday be used in a published book. At the time, he told me he had no concerns whatsoever, asserting "The truth… doesn't do an injustice to anyone. The injustice is done when truth is smothered over with ignorance, or is forgotten about when it has the potential of helping others in all kinds of ways." At the time, he strongly encouraged me to write a revealing book that would "celebrate the lives of Kim and the children."

However, his support of the truth had undergone major modifications since then—as had his earlier professed support of his own incarceration. These days, his main concern seemed to be for his own safety and well-being.

While I had no desire to protect Anderson, I also did not want to have his death on my conscience. At the time, I had no desire to make my daughter's molestation a matter of public knowledge anyway, and therefore reassured Anderson (and Northey) that I would not discuss it publicly. I believed my reassurance would put an end to Anderson's public relations concerns, but that was not to be the case.

In January 1990, the documentary *Last Dance: Murder in Canada* was finally aired on The Knowledge Network. Written by Neil Boyd, Director of the Criminology Research Centre at Simon Fraser University, and directed by Michael Doherty, it received excellent reviews and subsequently won an award of excellence at that year's AMTEC Media Festival. A critic at the *Vancouver Sun* described it as "a calm, reasoned look at different types of murders… the opposite of all that excitable, hyped-up violence on American television."

The documentary did not receive a positive review from Jeff Anderson. Although he had fully cooperated in giving the interview used in the documentary, and Boyd had honored his agreement not to mention the sexual molestation of one of the victims, Anderson was "shocked" by the final product. He would subsequently undertake a one-man campaign to try and stop the film from being broadcast again. After two years of harassment from Anderson, Boyd finally agreed to delete the section on Anderson from the film!

20

ANDERSON SAW *Last Dance: Murder in Canada* when it was first aired in British Columbia, but it was not aired in Manitoba and it was several months before I had the opportunity to view it myself.

In the meantime, Anderson wrote to me about the documentary, complaining that seeing it had forced him to "relive" the events of 1980 to 1985. He took particular exception to the fact that the film included pictures of Kim and the children, asserting that it "somehow seemed wrong" to have their images "splashed across the TV screen for the whole world to see." He reported that he immediately wrote to Neil Boyd to express his concerns about the documentary, and had to undergo special group therapy sessions at R.P.C. in order to deal with the intense feelings of depression that it aroused.

In a letter of reply, I explained that I myself had contributed the photographs of Kim and the children because I wanted the audience to see them as more than just another murder statistic—I wanted them to be the beautiful, vibrant individuals they had been. I told him that while I was sure the program was disturbing for him personally, I really couldn't understand his objection to the pictures. It wasn't as though the documentary had shown photos of them after they had been shot and disfigured. Surely he realized Kim and the children would be subjects of the documentary (in addition to Anderson himself) when he so enthusiastically agreed to be interviewed.

Last Dance: Murder in Canada was aired a second time in April 1990, and Anderson forced himself to watch it again. This second viewing upset him even more than the first, and he immediately obtained an advance program list from The Knowledge Network to find out when it was due to be shown again. In a subsequent letter to me, he angrily wrote that when he had agreed to be interviewed for the documentary, he had thought it would have a limited audience and would be used only as part of the Open Learning Institute's system of telecourses, not broadcast on public television. He then went on to describe the reaction of some of what he called his peers, at which point I finally began to understand the source of his discomfort.

Anderson had earlier described to me the sex offender program he was enrolled in at R.P.C. He explained that he was required to participate in daily two-to-four-hour long group therapy sessions with other sex offenders, and these sessions could be quite "intense." At that time, he did not seem to mind the group therapy, saying, "I get along with the guys well, they're more my type... For the most part everyone is intelligent and has excellent verbal and writing skills."

The men in the program were required to read their autobiographies in front of the group and members of the staff, and to keep daily logs or diaries, which were also read aloud on a daily basis. Anderson reported that "nothing gets held back" and that "every imaginable deviant sexual fantasy is openly discussed and worked on..." He also said the staff encouraged the participants to confront one another's "thinking errors." According to Anderson, being in the sex offender's program was like being in a fish bowl where every thought and action was closely scrutinized and analyzed.

Anderson told me that he had viewed the documentary in the company of some of the men in his group, men who "know me and care for me." According to Anderson, these fellow inmates already knew about his crimes through group therapy, yet for some reason, the documentary caused them to "feel angry" at him. I couldn't help but wonder whether he hadn't been completely candid with his peers, whether they had in fact confronted him with his failure to be fully honest with them after viewing the documentary. He said that the documentary made him feel "naked, bare and vulnerable to the core, my personal life splashed on the screen with no control from me." I suspected Anderson had hoped to put his own spin on his story when he agreed to be interviewed by Boyd and was disappointed with the less-than-flattering result.

My suspicions were confirmed when I finally viewed a copy of the video myself. *Last Dance: Murder in Canada* is a well-made and fascinating documentary that examines the different degrees of murder through four separate cases and interviews. Anderson's crime is presented last, with the following preface by Boyd: "Murders in Canada are rarely calculated acts of punishment, cases in which men impose what they consider just penalty on those who have wronged them. We conclude with Jeff Anderson, a murderer who falls into that category... a man who killed his wife and stepchildren in a planned and deliberate manner." The camera then shows images of Anderson being handcuffed on the ground by police while he calmly tells his captors, "I don't deserve to live."

Warm and glowing photos of Kim and the children fade in and out of the segment, and a videotape of the Cole family attending the Jehovah's Witness memorial is also featured. The visual images are certainly unsettling for the viewer. However, as I watched the video, it soon became clear that it was Anderson's own interview that was most disturbing, not only for the audience, but for Anderson himself. The camera vividly captures and reveals what Anderson was able to skillfully conceal on paper—and what he thought he would be able to conceal on film. By the end of the documentary, there could be no doubt in anyone's mind that Jeff Anderson is a chillingly detached, psychopathic killer.

The interview is jarring and disturbing on many levels. Anderson skillfully mimics the physical components of certain qualities and emotions, such as intelligence, rationality, horror, and remorse. His expressions and gestures are enacted with the precision and timing of a trained actor—a grimace and clenched fist here, a weary sigh there. But the viewer is instantly struck by the lack of any genuine feeling behind the gestures. Throughout the interview, Anderson discusses his brutal murder of three people whom he supposedly loved in a detached and analytical manner.

The interview also glaringly reveals Anderson's agenda for early release, and what Karen Harvey referred to as his "failure to grasp the full import of his crimes." The only time that one senses any real feeling from him is when he begins to question the fairness of long sentences for first-degree murderers. At that point, a note of escalating anger appears in his voice as he expresses the view that sentences should be applied "on an individual basis," that "the system leaves no room to take into account if [a prisoner] feels remorse, if they've applied themselves while in prison... There's just this all-encompassing twenty-five years for anybody and everybody... and I think that's very unfair." His anger almost turns to derision as he points out what he assumes is obvious to everyone watching: "I will be doing the same amount of time as a Clifford Olson will do—possibly—and I see us as the difference between day and night. Yet the system doesn't allow for differences in personality like that..."

With cocky and deluded self-confidence, Anderson believed that he would be able to convince viewers of his rehabilitation through the sheer strength of his personality, and would be rewarded for his ability to act innocent, just as he had been by the Witness elders. He believed his interview with Boyd would be a good PR opportunity.

After viewing himself in the documentary, even Anderson was able to recognize that he had given a less-than-convincing performance. Having failed to manipulate the situation to his advantage, he now focused all of his manipulative powers on Neil Boyd, in an effort to get rid of the evidence that was so damaging to his agenda. Over the next five years, Anderson would become increasingly obsessed with the documentary, writing Boyd and others increasingly numerous and harassing letters demanding that the program no longer be shown, that its frequency be reduced or that his interview be cut.

Despite my request for an end to our correspondence, over the next three years Anderson continued to send me letters, the contents of which became more and more outrageous and difficult to stomach. In June 1990, he excitedly told me about his new computer, on which he was now able to write letters and play computer games, and later told me how much he was enjoying his new stereo and CD player. He also mentioned a brief relationship with a "lady friend," who for a time had written to him through the personals and visited him in prison. With giddy infatuation, he described how, during one visit, they had "talked non-stop for two hours and maintained almost constant eye-contact."

In January 1991, Anderson wrote to tell me of his "graduation" to Mission Institution, a medium-security prison that was one step closer to his dream of being transferred to William Head. Like a college student resolving to work hard during summer vacation, he said, "Mission has a new sex-offender program and I intend to dive right into that without taking a break…" Once there, however, he complained bitterly about his new "classmates," who he considered different from himself, both in their lack of intelligence and tendency to minimize their crimes.

He also described his daily routine at Mission. He would get up at 8:00 a.m., skip breakfast (not being "a morning person"), and attend group therapy from 8:30 a.m. until noon. Lunch was at 12:35, after which he was required to attend another hour of therapy. The rest of the afternoon was free, and he would usually socialize, go for a walk in the yard, play on his computer, or watch television. Dinner was at 4:50, after which he would usually watch television until after midnight. On weekends, he was allowed to sleep in and spend time pursuing his own activities.

During this peaceful routine, he often tried hard to impress upon me the danger of his environment, where "general population" and "protective custody" prisoners (mostly sex offenders and diddlers) were not completely separated and shared some of the same facilities. He said the population inmates were in the majority and tended to resent protective custody prisoners, and this situation had led to a number of scary incidents. He indicated that there was an unofficial segregation rule among the prisoners, whereby sex offenders were not allowed to eat at the same table as "solid cons," and told me that he had once made the mistake of breaking that rule with the wrong guy: "[The other prisoner] wanted me to leave his table because I was a sex offender," he wrote. "When I politely asserted myself and insisted that nobody owns the tables and chairs, he got angrier and louder and threatened me... I wasn't willing to call his bluff and risk the consequences, so I moved. I felt humiliated..."

In November 1991, Anderson boasted that he was now considered a "treated sex offender," since his most recent "lab test" showed his "criminal thought patterns and arousals" were low and his "appropriate thoughts and arousals" high. However, in February 1992, I received a letter in which he angrily reported that he had been "kicked out of group therapy."

According to Anderson, his group therapist had insisted he end a relationship he had developed with a young criminology student visiting the prison. When he resisted her interference in his private life, she accused him of "acting superior." He concluded that his healthy self-assertiveness was obviously threatening to the therapist and that the situation represented a power struggle between them. At that point, I remembered Karen Harvey's observation that Anderson wanted to set his own agenda at R.P.C. and that he believed he knew better than prison therapists what was best for him.

Though I grew weary of receiving these tedious and offensive letters and could have taken steps to ensure that he no longer wrote to me, there was a part of me that did not want to lose the continuing opportunity to monitor him. As long as I received letters from him, I knew that he was still safely in prison where he could do me and no one else any harm. I was still working on a manuscript about my children's murders and viewed Anderson's letters as potential valuable research and documentary material.

However, by 1992, I had reached a serious impasse with the book. Although I had reassured Anderson and his Christian sponsor Wayne Northey that I would not publicly discuss Anderson's molestation of my daughter, I no longer felt that I could write something of integrity and value without a full and honest treatment. Not able to write a book in which I would essentially be involved with covering up the pedophilia that Anderson had confessed to me, and also unable to callously disregard repeated concerns about his safety, I finally shelved the manuscript indefinitely.

When I told Wilma Derksen—a Christian advocate of forgiveness after her daughter was abducted and murdered—about my dilemma with the manuscript, even she thought that I was carrying "forgiveness" too far. "Some day, Jim," she said, "you're going to have to decide which side you're on." Those words shook me. But nothing about the situation was easy, so I continued to do nothing about it. It hadn't occurred to me that writing and publishing the truth about Anderson was not necessarily the same as seeking revenge.

I also spoke about the situation with a local publisher of a small literary press, Joan Parr, who had been reading rough drafts of my manuscript. She said that I needed to tell the whole story in order to "clear the air." Otherwise, I was liable to join the "Men's Club." She was right; it just hadn't sunk in yet. If I wasn't already in the Men's Club, I was definitely supporting a conspiracy of silence where Anderson's crimes against children were concerned.

By September 1992, Anderson's obsession with Neil Boyd's documentary had intensified. His letters began to include increasingly hysterical tirades against its further broadcast, describing it as "something that has grown into an unstoppable monster [which] eats at me like a cancer." However, he assured me that his concerns were not for himself, but for Kim's family. "All I can think of is how in the hell this may be affecting the Coles and Ken Evans." He worried that the documentary's frequent airings continually called up unpleasant memories for them and only served to victimize them over and over again.

When it became clear that his efforts to get the documentary squashed were not succeeding, he then turned to me for assistance. "My heart tells me that this documentary has had its run and should be fazed out now, but Neil Boyd does not see it that way. He keeps pointing to the fact that you have not opposed it, ignoring the impact on the Coles and Evans as if they do not exist..." He continued by saying that he felt "...confused, worried and frustrated over this, and I've decided to leave it up to you, Jim." He wondered if my feelings about the film were the same as before. If I told him that I still wanted the documentary to run because it helped me in some way, he would pursue it no further.

Shortly after receiving that letter, I received a phone call from Neil Boyd himself, asking whether I was concerned about the documentary. I reassured him that I completely supported *Last Dance: Murder in Canada* and did not object to it in any way. Afterwards, I wrote an angry reply to Anderson, pointing out there was no reason for him to defend his victims in this matter as I fully supported the documentary and Kim's family was not even aware of its existence (when I phoned Jackie Cole in January 1998 and asked her about the documentary, she said she'd never heard of it). I also pointed out that the film did not reveal his child molestation, and since concerns about his personal safety seemed to have been unfounded, I could see no reason why he should be so concerned.

Anderson's reply was immediate. With patronizing psychobabble, he expressed the view I was clearly "angry and protective" about the documentary, and it was "still important" to me. For those reasons, he promised that, for my sake, he would "cease any further efforts to have it phased out." However, he then went on to write another two pages of haranguing complaints about it, and in the future would write to me again and again on the subject.

In October 1992, I sent Anderson what I hoped would be my final letter on the subject. I impatiently explained that I supported Boyd's documentary; it filled a gap for me—a gap that had been left as a result of my having to shelve my book project for his safety. I told him I considered the matter closed and insisted he no longer write to me about it.

Nonetheless, I received a disturbing letter from him two months later. "It is the *frequency*, not the portrayal of this very public reminder, that strips away the right of Kim's family to remember and grieve privately," he wrote. "The film is now so public that I think it borders on cruelty." He went on to write that he would be very surprised if Kim's family and friends felt different about it. "I suspect that this would be confirmed if you were ever to make a phone call to them regarding this matter."

I was alarmed and angered by Anderson's attempt to manipulate Kim's family through me, and told him so. "Forget about the Coles and the Evans," I wrote to him. "I don't think you're the best person to be defending their inter-ests. In fact, they'd probably be appalled that you were looking out for them." I advised him to separate himself emotionally from Kim's family once and for all. "Your ties with [them] were cut when Kim left you the second time. The day of the murders, those ties were shattered forever. It's best to accept that fact. Don't fool yourself into thinking that because you're concerned about them, that it's okay. You're going the wrong way if you do."

He had written letters to Jackie Cole in the past—which she refused to read—and obviously hoped I would speak to her on his behalf. His urgent need to get rid of the documentary as a constant reminder of his crimes dovetailed nicely with his need to gain not just my sympathy, but Kim's family's as well. We could all potentially play a part in either helping or hindering his agenda to obtain early release. Boyd's documentary presents Jeff Anderson for what he is—a psychopathic killer who can provide no reasonable excuse for having so brutally, heartlessly, and deliberately taken the lives of a woman and her two innocent children. Although the documentary does not identify him as a sex off-ender, it is linked to Boyd's book, also entitled *Last Dance: Murder in Canada*. Anderson knew that it would not be hard for anyone to make the connection between Jeff Anderson the murderer and Gordon Parker the pedophile. His greatest hope was to have one or more of his victims' relatives vouch for his parole eligibility at his hearing. At the very least, he needed them not to oppose his application for parole.

He made this very clear to me in one of his earlier letters. In it, he commented that he could not blame me if I spent the rest of my life "declaring to the world and to the parole board what a piece of shit I am... You have that power and sometimes it scares me to death." He wrote that if either I or the Coles ever became vocal against him, he would never see the light of day again. "You literally have my life, or at least where I spend it, in your hands..."

In the same letter, Anderson told me he felt "sad and frightened that so many people really believe that longer sentences will make the streets safer," and predicted that a policy of longer incarceration for sex offenders would "backfire on society some day." His vehemence and certainty about this made me uneasy at the time, but I didn't fully realize why until I saw the Boyd interview. In it, his prophecy took the form of an ominous threat, when he warned the audience that he and his fellow murderers would "eventually get out"—and that "society will pay one way or another."

Much as I wanted to continue to monitor Anderson's movements, I was finally no longer able to take the strain of dealing with his relentless correspondence. In January 1993, I once again informed him that I no longer wished to receive letters from him, and shortly thereafter received a heartfelt goodbye. "I love you man," he wrote. "And I don't want to do anything to hurt you further."

Thinking about the catastrophic effect of Anderson's so-called love for Kim and the children, I recalled the ironic poster slogan about domestic abuse, with the caption that said: "Love sometimes hits like a ton of bricks." Anderson's love was something I could do without.

* * * *

IT HAD NOW BEEN more than seven years since an RCMP officer had brought me the news of my children's deaths, and more than five years since I began corresponding with Anderson. With the receipt of his January 1993 letter agreeing to a termination of further communication, Marge and I breathed a huge sigh of relief. By that time, we were no longer involved with Family Survivors of Homicide, the support group that we had founded in Winnipeg. It was now in the capable hands of Wilma Derksen, and Marge and I looked forward to turning our attention to the quality of our day-to-day lives.

Although the quiet routine we fell into was uneventful and relatively dull compared to the tumultuous events of the previous seven years, we could not have been happier. We were able to spend more time enjoying one another, our friends, our home, and our three rambunctious Bichon Frisé pups: Brandy, Gigi, and Charlotte. I had come to accept that the gaping wound of my children's deaths would never fully heal, and recognize and appreciate the unique ability it gave me to empathize with the pain of other human beings. I had also come to terms with my own reasons for having pursued a relationship with Anderson, recognizing that it was somehow necessary for me to uncover the truth behind my children's murders in order to get on with my life.

I had also begun to make my peace with God. After so many years of being exiled in the wilderness of my grief, I tentatively began to experience the world as a place that might contain more than just chaos and despair. I began to hope that it might also include order and meaning—even beauty.

Three years later, I experienced a vivid dream about Kim and the children. It took place on the fields of my father's farm. I was sitting on his tractor, an orange, model Z Minneapolis Moline with a huge yellow umbrella that provided shelter from the hot summer sun. Juri and Lindsay climbed aboard and begged me to take them for a ride. I let out the clutch and moved the tractor slowly forward. As the children squealed with delight, I looked up to see Kim walking towards us, her face glowing with health and radiance. When she came near, I cut the engine and we all got off the tractor and walked towards the house. Kim and I were no longer married, but had become the best of friends. All the hard feelings arising out of our divorce and custody concerns were gone, and there was a warm sense of forgiveness between us.

The dream was deeply moving on several levels. Awakening, I wept with a sense of loss mixed with relief and wonder. It also left a lingering sense of nostalgia and yearning. In its bright, friendly, and fertile landscape, Juri, Lindsay and Kim were once again my family and loved ones. It aroused a strong and burning desire to do something important for them. In the months that followed the dream, my mind turned again and again to the manuscript gathering dust on my shelf...

21

BY THE SPRING OF 1996, I had experienced three peaceful years in which the name of Jeff Anderson was rarely heard or spoken. Though I continued to struggle with ongoing feelings of loss and guilt that remained more than ten years after my children's deaths, their murders had ceased to be the center and focus of my life. Marge and I were now living relatively quiet, working-class lives, dreaming of the day we might retire to a small villa in Mexico, like our good friend Jim Penton and his wife Marilyn.

However, the calm surface of our lives was unexpectedly disturbed on June 12, 1996. That day's *Globe and Mail* newspaper reported on a new bill before the House of Commons in Ottawa, one that proposed important changes to Section 745 of the Criminal Code. Bill C-45 was introduced in response to concerns about parole eligibility—an issue that I would find impossible to ignore—and sparked a national debate about the appropriate punishment for killers. Out of the blue, the subject of Jeff Anderson—and murder—had once again invaded our lives.

Bill C-45 was designed to make it harder for convicted prisoners to obtain early release through the faint hope clause of the Criminal Code. At the time, Section 745 of the Code stipulated that first-degree murderers could automatically ask a jury for parole-ineligibility reduction after serving only fifteen years of a statutory twenty-five year sentence. If passed into law, Bill C-45 would make it impossible for multiple murderers to apply for early release, and would also introduce two new procedural hurdles for other first-degree murderers. It proposed that before a convicted murderer could have his request heard by a jury, he would have to first persuade the chief justice of a superior court that he had a reasonable basis on which to persuade a jury that he should be allowed to take his petition before the National Parole Board. It also proposed that in the event that the prisoner overcame that hurdle, he would then have to achieve a unanimous jury decision instead of the current two-thirds requirement.

Section 745 of the Criminal Code came up for revision in 1996 largely because of Clifford Olson, Canada's most notorious serial killer at the time. In a short period of time between November 1980 and July 1981, Olson abducted, raped, and murdered eight girls and three boys between the ages of nine and eighteen years of age, all in the Fraser River Valley area of British Columbia. Once in custody, Olson confessed to the murders, but in most cases, the police had no bodies to confirm what he had told them. As a result, the police and Crown struck a controversial deal with Olson that outraged the families of his victims and the general public. In return for leading the police to his victims' bodies, a fee of $10,000 per body would be paid to Olson's wife and son, a pay-out that eventually totaled $100,000.

In 1982, Clifford Olson was sentenced to the worst sentence allowed under Canadian law: life imprisonment with no eligibility for parole for twenty-five years. That sentence was undermined, however, by his right to apply for early release under the faint hope clause. Then Justice Minister Allan Rock hoped to push Bill C-45 through the House of Commons before August 1996, the earliest date that Olson could make such an application.

The main impetus for the bill came from Victims of Violence, a national victims' rights group run by Gary Rosenfeldt and Sharon Johnsrude, the step-father and mother of Olson's third victim, sixteen-year-old Daryn Johnsrude. The group argued that allowing Olson to apply for early release would simply provide him with an opportunity to indulge his notorious love of publicity, forcing the families of his murder victims to relive his crimes yet again. The public also worried that dangerous criminals like Olson might actually be released into the community through this loophole in the law.

The western-based federal Reform Party, which held significant representation in Parliament, joined Victims of Violence in advocating that the faint hope clause be scrapped altogether. The Bloc Québécois, on the other hand, opposed the proposal, advocating uncomplicated, universal judicial reviews for all convicted murderers for rehabilitation purposes. The majority Liberal government responded with the compromise of Bill C-45, but was unable to get it passed into law until January 9, 1997, several months after Clifford Olson had already made his application under the old rules of the Criminal Code.

As a result, Olson did not have to pass the procedural hurdles required today. In August 1997, he represented himself during a lengthy judicial review. Although his chances of persuading a jury to allow him to make an application to the National Parole Board were virtually nil, anger and outrage were expressed by victims' rights groups, the Reform Party, the Canadian Police Association, and the general public that Olson had been allowed to make an application at all. These events resulted in a strong backlash across Canada against all convicted murderers.

Bill C-45 proposed that multiple murderers would no longer be allowed to make an application for early release. I initially assumed this meant that after the bill was passed, there would no longer be any hope of early release for Jeff Anderson, no matter how faint. I subsequently discovered that was not the case. While the new procedural hurdles would be retroactive for all convicted murderers, the no-review restriction against multiple killers would not; in other words, the new procedures would apply to all first-degree murderers no matter when they were convicted, but only multiple murderers convicted since the passage of the bill could be prevented from making application for early release.

The reason is that the Charter of Rights and Freedoms prohibits the retroactive or *ex post facto* imposition of laws which may deprive persons of rights that they have held under previous legislation. What it all came down to for me was that Anderson, convicted prior to any amendments to Section 745 of the Criminal Code, could still make an application to have his parole ineligibility reviewed. If Bill C-45 were to become law, though, he would have to pass the difficult new procedural hurdles before the Parole Board would hear his application.

In the midst of the national debate that erupted over this issue in the spring of 1996, it was not at all certain that Bill C-45 would make it into law. If the bill failed, Anderson would have the right to have his application heard directly by a jury, and would have to convince only two-thirds of that jury to allow him to make an application directly to the Parole Board. The earliest date he could begin the process would be August 2000—only four years away.

I was jolted by the realization that Anderson might actually succeed in gaining early release within a few short years. He had worked hard to fashion himself as a model prisoner, completing every rehabilitative course and psychological program available in the hope that it would help him earn his way out of prison. He had been building his case for years, and I knew he would make his application as soon as it was legally possible. I also knew how easily his smooth manners and appearance could persuade people into thinking he was a non-criminal who had simply made an unfortunate mistake—instead of a cold-blooded killer who probably still posed a serious threat to society.

On June 22, 1996, I wrote a letter to the Minister of Justice in Ottawa, opposing the early release of first-degree murderers under any circumstances. I received a reply on July 30, 1996, signed by Herb Gray. The letter included an informative fact sheet regarding Section 745 of the Criminal Code, and assured me that under the current and proposed provisions of the section, "some murderers will never be released." It also emphasized that legislation had been introduced to improve sentencing and conditional release, and that further reforms were being discussed to deal more effectively with high-risk violent offenders. The end of the letter reassured me that "the opinions of Canadians like you, who have become familiar with the criminal justice system through no fault of their own, will be carefully considered when decisions are taken regarding additional reforms." Gray's letter seemed genuine and more than just political rhetoric. As a result, I started to believe that I might be able to make a difference by speaking out on this issue.

In the summer of 1996, I became aware of a four-page paper that had been written and distributed in August of 1996 by the Church Council on Justice and Corrections. It was entitled "Judicial Reviews For Those Who Murder: The Faint Hope Clause," and it came out strongly against Bill C-45. The paper included a June 18, 1996 brief to the House of Commons Justice Committee that claimed "judicial reviews are working," and warned that the government's proposed amendments to the Criminal Code would result in "profound human and financial costs that will make our ineffective criminal justice system even more retributive and our communities even less safe." It also included an out-of-context quote from Sister Helen Prejean's book, *Dead Man Walking*, in which she states: "I cannot believe in a God who metes out hurt for hurt, pain for pain, torture for torture. Nor do I believe that God invests human representatives with such power to torture and kill…"

I subsequently sent a copy of the paper to Wayne Northey, one of Anderson's Christian sponsors and the editor of *Accord*, a Mennonite Central Committee pro-offender newsletter that covered justice issues. I knew that Northey took a keen interest in the debate over Bill C-45 and wished to cover both sides of the issue. Therefore, I suggested that he publish my June 12, 1996 letter to the Justice Minister as a response to the Council's paper. He readily agreed to publish my letter, but with one condition: that I not use Anderson's name "out of courtesy and concern for his privacy and safety." Marge had also advised me to think seriously about whether I really wanted to "open this Anderson business up again after putting it all behind you."

After so many years of relative peace of mind, I was once again facing that familiar rock and hard place, torn between placating those around me and doing what I knew to be right. Wilma Derksen's words rang in my ears: "Some day you're going to have to decide which side you're on." This time, the choice was crystal clear: I resolved that my responsibility to Kim, Juri, and Lindsay, as well as to society in general, must take precedent over all other concerns.

I subsequently called David Roberts, a journalist with the Manitoba bureau of *The Globe and Mail*, who later published an article entitled "Parole Bill 'Better Than Nothing'" in the September 17, 1996 issue. The article was a sensitive but hard-hitting piece about the issues surrounding Bill C-45. Roberts specifically referred to Jeff Anderson, and quoted me as saying: "Is it fair for an offender to serve a mere fifteen years for killing three people? As an alternative to the death penalty, a non-negotiable, long-term sentence is reasonable retribution."

I subsequently received a number of offers to be interviewed about Bill C-45 on both radio and television, but turned them down. I felt Robert's article had more than adequately expressed my point of view, and I instead began working on my manuscript again, which I felt would be the best means of addressing the issue in the long run.

A month later, I received a letter from Jeff Anderson. I was not entirely surprised, as I had half-expected him to respond to the *Globe and Mail* article, but I was completely unprepared for the contents of the letter that he had so painstakingly composed on his computer over several days, before and after reading the article.

His letter began with a condescending lecture on crime and punishment, one that spoke against "vindictiveness" and in favor of "compassion." He pointed out that my attitude seemed to have changed "from positive to negative," and that I no longer seemed to believe in a "healing justice system." The letter then adopted an accusatory tone. Why was I saying mean things about him in the newspapers? Why hadn't I considered the progress he had made in prison, the many courses he had completed, all of the therapy he had received, and the "good works" he had done over the past eleven years? Why wasn't I focusing on those positive things instead of his crimes? Was it because he had written to the Minister of Justice on his views of Bill C-45? Was it because of Neil Boyd's influence and the controversy over the documentary, *Last Dance: Murder in Canada?*

He also reminded me that he was basically a good and decent person, quite unlike his fellow inmates. "Most men in prison are very manipulative, deceptive, and demanding," he informed me. "The hope of freedom drives them, not the hope of reconciliation or making amends. They are consumed by their little self-centered world... and don't give a damn about their own victims." He pointed out that very few of them "voluntarily subject themselves to grueling therapy programs," or "demonstrate remorse," or "speak out for victims"—as he himself had done.

He claimed, on one hand, that serving fifteen years for killing three beautiful people—five years for each person—seemed grossly inadequate. But on another level, "the benefits of incarceration had been acquired." Lessons had been learned. Tears had been shed. Maturity and insight gained. "The skills needed not to reoffend had been learned and maintained over many years." Serving more time served no purpose, because "vindictive justice is all that remains..."

As for his victims, he missed them terribly. "I would gladly be a scapegoat, wave my judicial review, or kill myself if I thought for one second it would honor or resurrect Kim and the kids." Then he added that they were gone and some day we would be gone too. "You can spend the rest of your life trying to avenge their deaths," as he implied I was doing, or we could celebrate their lives in a more positive way.

He didn't seem very sincere about waving his judicial review, any more than he had been about killing himself. What he did seem truthful about was getting out of prison as soon as possible. For him, the victims, sadly, were dead now for eleven years and it was high time we, survivors and offenders alike, got on with life. In other words, if *he* could recover from *his* loss of Kim and the children, why couldn't the rest of the world recover also? Why, after eleven years, was this still a problem?

It was not the counsel I would have accepted from a therapist, much less from Jeff Anderson. It was the wrong counsel. And it was plain to see what bill of goods he was trying to sell.

I knew that Anderson had finally achieved his goal of being transferred to William Head Institution, a medium-security prison on Vancouver Island, in September 1995. In his letter, he emphasized how much he "deserved" to be there, how he had "earned" it. He then treated me to a long and detailed account of William Head, as though the relative un-prison-like nature of his current surroundings would somehow convince me of his own un-criminal-like nature.

William Head deserves its reputation as a soft Canadian prison; it does not even remotely resemble the concrete fortresses that we usually associate with penitentiaries. Situated on a beautiful 85-acre peninsula that juts into the Strait of Juan de Fuca near Victoria, it features a conspicuous absence of confining barriers. Gone are the traditional cellblocks with tiers housing sixty or more inmates, with clanging steel doors, barred windows, and numerous guard posts. Instead, the design is more reminiscent of upscale campus housing, featuring three units containing two communities. Each community has four two-storey duplexes (eight five-man residences) and a community building that houses the unit's staff offices, common areas, a boardroom, recreational areas, and laundry facilities. The institution is secured by a fourteen-foot fence only where the peninsula is not bounded by water. Guards have firearms, but do not carry them inside the facility.

Prisoners are allowed many recreational privileges, including golf, tennis, softball, volleyball, floor hockey, weight training, aerobics, soccer, pool, and even salmon fishing, in season, from a nearby wharf. Educational and vocational programs include university correspondence courses, life-skills courses, cognitive-skills training, pre-employment courses, as well as employment training in such areas as carpentry, electrical technology, horticulture, and car repair. There is also a William Head on Stage theater program in which inmates together with actors from the local community produce plays twice a year.

Anderson's letter included photos of William Head's beautiful natural surroundings, as well as the smiling faces of Anderson himself and his fellow inmates involved in various activities such as sharing a Christmas dinner together with all the trimmings in their "private" duplex dining room. There was another photo of Anderson relaxing on a park bench, enjoying a coffee, with the magnificent ocean and the mountains behind him—images that bore a closer resemblance to summer camp than a penitentiary.

However, Anderson later qualified that William Head, for all its amenities, was still a prison. He claimed he would rather work his butt off for minimum wage, sleep in a car in the middle of winter, and eat cold beans from a can in exchange for the simple freedoms most people take for granted.

It was all too much. After three years of freedom from Anderson, I was sickened by his letter and the knowledge that his safety was no more at risk than my own. I resolved to purge my life of Anderson once and for all, and to continue with the manuscript I had shelved so long ago.

After photocopying Anderson's letter and photos for my records, I turned the originals over to Gabrielle Thiessen, the parole officer we had met earlier in Winnipeg, who returned them to William Head authorities with the specific instructions that Anderson never be allowed to communicate with me again. Shortly thereafter, the victim liaison coordinator at William Head, Jan Frazelle, assured me I would no longer receive correspondence from Anderson, but would continue to receive notifications that victims are entitled to under the Corrections and Conditional Release Act.

I was finally reassured that I no longer needed to be concerned about monitoring Anderson's activities and whereabouts. Prison authorities would immediately notify me in the event that Anderson was transferred to another institution, or escaped, or was granted some form of release, in which case I would be informed of his location and the conditions of his release. I would also be informed of any applications for parole, and the dates and locations of any related hearings.

Anderson was eligible to apply for parole-ineligibility reduction in August 2000. While I would have preferred there be zero possibility of early release, I was relieved that the new amendments to the Criminal Code significantly reduced that possibility. Under the new law, Anderson first had to make an application to a chief justice. If the chief justice approved his application to a jury, he would then have to convince *all twelve members* of the jury to allow him to appear before the National Parole Board, based on the following criteria (a) his character, (b) his conduct while serving his sentence, and (c) the nature of the offence for which he was convicted. Should he convince the jury of his worthiness, he would then be allowed to make an application to the National Parole Board. However, the jury would also determine when he would be allowed to make that application, and could, for example, stipulate that the application be delayed indefinitely. In either case, a successful application would not determine whether or not he would be released on parole, only establish an earlier date by which the National Parole Board would be required to review his case.

The courts and the Parole Board are separate entities. Under specified conditions, the law gives the latter discretion to grant or deny parole. Unlike the courts, the Board's primary responsibility is the protection of society. A decision of the Board is an independent assessment of the risk that an offender may pose to the community at large and is not bounded by the strict rules of evidence and reasonable doubt that operate in the courts.

The passing of Bill C-45 in January 1997 certainly succeeded in making the faint hope clause of the Criminal Code even fainter for Jeff Anderson. Yet I believed at the time (and still do) that any possibility of early release for Jeff Anderson—no matter how faint—represents a serious risk to society.

And I will never stop reminding judges, juries, and the National Parole Board of that fact.

22

MANY CRITICS BELIEVE the Canadian criminal justice system is in a credibility crisis. That viewpoint is argued by law professor David M. Paciocco in his 1999 book, *Getting Away With Murder: The Canadian Criminal Justice System.* Paciocco asserts that a criminal justice system that has lost public confidence is a lost system, and points to the strong public perception that some offenders are treated harshly while others are not treated harshly enough.

Though I have read a great deal in the past few years about crime, punishment, and justice, I do not claim to be an expert on these subjects; nor do I believe there are easy answers to the complex issues they present. If anything, the more I learn about the justice system, the more I realize how very complex its workings are. However, I do believe that my experiences over the past fifteen years have given me a unique view of certain aspects of the justice system, which is one of the reasons I felt compelled to write this book.

There are two very polarized groups in Canadian society when it comes to the subject of crime and punishment: those who feel that criminals should be given the harshest sentences possible, then locked up and forgotten about; and those who believe every effort should be made to rehabilitate offenders. Of course, it can be demonstrated that neither approach is completely effective, for society has to deal with a wide variety of criminals and criminal activities as it does people in general.

As a secondary victim of violent crime, I have examined punishment options from every possible viewpoint and have come to some clear conclusions:

Do I support the reinstatement of capital punishment? No. Like many others, I believe our society has evolved beyond such primitive and barbaric expressions of justice, and agree the death penalty is as immoral as the crime it seeks to punish.

Do I support the harsh treatment of criminals? No. I cannot believe in cruelty for the sake of cruelty, and have to support more progressive prisons if only because they are less dangerous for prison guards and staff to administer.

Do I still support restorative justice? Yes, I do, but only insofar as it works. It has been demonstrated that a certain percentage of criminals can be rehabilitated and become productive members of society, but the effective identification of which criminals fall into this category is still pretty much a guessing game. Do I think it is worth the effort and expense to try and reach that percentage? Absolutely.

The type of criminal I am concerned about falls into a much smaller percentage of those who commit murder: those who have been convicted of first-degree murder. In fact, my interest is limited to an even smaller percentage of that narrow category: those killers who have committed the most heinous kind of first-degree murder, who by the very nature of their acts and inability to grasp the full import of their crimes cannot possibly ever be considered capable of rehabilitation. In this group fall multiple murderers (such as Jeff Anderson), who kill more than one person; serial murderers (such as Ted Bundy and Jeffrey Dahmer), who kill many individuals over a period of time; mass murderers (such as Marc Lepine), who slaughter a large group of people in a single, violent episode; and child killers.

This small group of criminals is guilty of crimes so deliberate, vicious, and cold-blooded that there must never be any possibility of their release from prison. Yet such crimes are not properly defined within the Criminal Code. The worst sentence that can be imposed by any judge in Canada is life in prison without the possibility of parole for twenty-five years. Of course, just because a prisoner has the opportunity to apply for parole does not mean that his freedom will automatically be granted, and there are some criminals—such as Clifford Olson and Paul Bernardo—who we can be reasonably confident will never get out of prison. However, as far as the public is concerned, *any* possibility that such offenders could be released—no matter how small and distant that possibility might be—is too great a risk to be tolerated.

There is a saying that it is not enough for justice to be done; that in order to be effective, justice must be *seen* to be done. I believe that society is crying out to see justice done in the case of those criminals whose acts deserve our greatest denunciation and punishment. In order to restore some sense of balance to the criminal justice system, there must be real and unequivocal consequences for such acts. As Paciocco has said, "With rare exception, we should hit those who kill intentionally and hit them hard... Why? Not because it will make society safer, but because it is the right thing to do."

Prior to Canada's abolishment of the death penalty in 1976, such criminals would have been sentenced to death. First-degree murder represents five percent of all homicides, and those who commit multiple murders fall into the unofficial category of the worst of the worst. Forty or fifty years ago, they would have been the few killers among a hundred selected to hang for their crimes.

I am not in any way proposing a return to capital punishment; I continue to view it as a method of punishment that is neither effective nor civilized. I do believe that we have not succeeded in replacing it with an alternative that adequately meets the needs of society—not only its need to be protected from the worst of the worst, but to also witness the *appropriate* punishment of such criminals.

As Paciocco has suggested, the current justice system takes a contradictory, schizophrenic approach to first-degree murder, one that is reflected in the Criminal Code's faint hope clause. On the one hand, it expresses society's abhorrence of intentional murder with provisions of long, minimum sentences for murder. On the other, it worries that those so convicted may not be dangerous enough to justify locking away for so long a time. When the Code seeks to punish intolerable acts of brutality that society cannot accept, it also simultaneously undermines that objective with the universal promise of parole in the name of rehabilitation and good behavior.

In its brief opposing Bill C-45, the Church Council on Justice and Corrections supported its argument with the following quote from Sister Helen Prejean's celebrated book *Dead Man Walking:* "I cannot believe in a God who metes out hurt for hurt, pain for pain, torture for torture. Nor do I believe that God invests human representatives with such power to torture and kill..." However, as I pointed out in my letter to the Justice Minister in Ottawa, the Council's use of that quote was taken out of context, and did a great disservice to Prejean's well-thought-out and sophisticated thinking on the subject of punishment.

Sister Prejean is a well-known opponent of capital punishment, but clearly would have supported the provisions of Bill C-45. Though she objected to the death penalty as a punishment "as excessive as the original crime it punishes," she also expressed the view that "it is excessive that those convicted of so heinous and irrevocable crime such as murder should be made to serve only a few short years in prison... Measured retribution is attained, I believe, by sentencing which requires *non-negotiable* long-term imprisonment for first-degree murder..."

I agree with Prejean on both points, and strongly recommend that Canadian judges be given the option to sentence all first-degree murderers to non-negotiable natural life sentences with no parole or release, and that the worst of the worst—multiple, serial, mass murderers, and child killers—be given such sentences automatically, without exception. I am also strongly against the practice of allowing those guilty of more than one murder or rape to serve each sentence concurrently—that is, allowing a criminal who receives three twenty-five year sentences (for killing three individuals) to serve those sentences at the same time, so that his maximum time in prison is only twenty-five years, rather than seventy-five years. It is a practice that reduces the value of individual human lives, and seems to have more to do with prison costs than with justice.

I am not in favor of longer sentences for all crimes, and continue to support the possibility of rehabilitation for the majority of offenders. In fact, I would actively support replacing sentences for non-violent offenders with community service and financial restitution in order to relieve our already overburdened, overcrowded, and expensive prison system. I believe that in most cases, prison should be a last resort, reserved for the most violent and dangerous of criminals.

David M. Paciocco writes that "the more gentle among us have an abiding but naïve belief that we can rehabilitate our worst offenders, even against their will." I propose it is high time we stopped wasting our precious resources on psychopaths who can never be reformed and safely released into society, and instead reallocate those resources to members of society who can really benefit from our help.

EPILOGUE

As THIS BOOK WAS nearing completion, my agent, Victoria Ridout, wrote to Jeff Anderson to seek permission to publish some of his letters in full. In two meticulously written letters of reply, Anderson politely expressed regret that he was unable to grant such permission. He stated that doing so would be "irresponsible," since portions of his letters to me included "self-reported inaccuracies and exaggerations regarding (1) the pre-meditated nature of my crime; (2) self-reported sexually deviant behavior; and (3) my life with Kim and the children."

When asked why he would have made such self-damaging confessions if they were not true, Anderson reported that he had "perjured" himself in his letters "in a desperate attempt to appease the bizarre demands of certain influential prison therapists." He claimed that he and his fellow prisoners had been pressured to "pad one's story and fabricate facts" and faced serious consequences if they did not. Those consequences included "reduction in pay level; negative psychological reports; transfer to higher security; and *no support for parole* (italics mine)."

Anderson claimed that "published information of an erroneous or sexual nature will present an undue risk to my personal safety and jeopardize [my] long-term rehabilitation." In light of those concerns, he suggested that Ridout forward a copy of the manuscript to him before publication, so he could "correct the inaccurate content."

He also said that he would be forwarding extensive documentation to support his claims, such as "documents for Correctional Service of Canada staff; psychological reports; and newspaper clippings." That documentation was never received.

To make the matter absolutely clear, at that point in time, Anderson was in total denial that he had done anything sexually inappropriate to either one of his child victims. He had now reversed the earlier confessions of child molestation of Lindsay that he had given to his prison therapist at Kent Institution, to Neil Boyd's assistant, Liz Elliott, and to me. Now he was telling a different story.

Jeff Anderson had the right, under the current Section 745.6 of the Criminal Code, to make an application for parole ineligibility reduction in August 2000. To my knowledge, he never did. Perhaps under the amended rules and new procedural hurdles, he saw the futility of convincing a chief justice of his worthiness to approve his application.

* * * *

WHY DID I WRITE this book? That is a difficult question to answer, but I'll try.

Two days after Kim, Juri, and Lindsay were killed, Marge and I went for a walk along the beach near English Bay in Vancouver. The world no longer seemed a safe place. It felt to me as though my physical surroundings were tilting, swaying out of proportion, and I sank to the ground to regain my balance. From that pivotal point in time, I realized I wasn't the same person anymore, either psychologically or spiritually. The world was no longer stable and I felt a sense of vertigo.

For quite some time, I tried to restore my previous view of the world as a place where children could walk the streets or play at home in safety. I tried conventional religion, past-life regression, brain-wave enhancers, hypnosis, and regular therapy. Although these methods gave me some temporary relief, I found that writing was the best kind of therapy. It was a way of shining a light on the darkness, of bringing the truth to light.

In writing, I was able to put the whole experience into perspective, somewhat like laying out a deck of cards into its respective suits. Accepting the death of my children—especially because it was so violent—has been difficult, if not impossible, to do. Writing was a way of restoring the dead, of making them live again. They now had voices where otherwise there was only silence.

Writing has also given me a voice, a way of becoming. It's made me grow.

The need to memorialize my children in written form, as a labor of love, was not the only reason I wrote. The guilt about not being able to save them from their fate was also a big motivator.

I believe that writing, for many authors, is a compulsion. That was especially true for me, to the extent I felt the book had "chosen" me. Before long, it had a life of its own, and I went with it.

To write about my loss caused me to be vulnerable. Paradoxically, though, I've found strength too. While there is a wound inside me that will never heal, some living, healthy part of me wants to show that I'm not finished. I still need to share the load with others, and every reader takes a little of the weight from me.

Yet despite my best efforts to uphold the victims and speak for them, to find some measure of healing and justice, to cast a light in shadow and find meaning in chaos, to tell the story and share my sorrow, I expect no easy resolution.

Last summer, I read *The Old Man and the Sea,* and identified with the old Cuban fisherman in the story. In it, he hooked a huge marlin which pulled his little skiff way out to sea, beyond where other fishermen would dare go. He fought sharks and eventually lost the fish—except for the skeleton and tail—trying to bring his catch to shore. Although in that condition the fish no longer had any commercial value, the old man wasn't defeated. He had proved his courage in that terrible ordeal.

I'm coming in to shore.

James Kostelniuk
Winnipeg, Manitoba
June 2000

AFTERWORD

As I WRITE THIS chapter—and it looks as though it won't be the last—Kim and the children have been gone nearly 24 years. That's a long, long time. A lifetime. Many things have happened since that fateful day in August, 1985. So, here is a summary of events before and after the first publication of this book in September 2000.

Back in September 1999, I met Jack Montgomery, a silver-haired Crown Counsel with a stellar reputation who had spent most of his professional career prosecuting high-profile homicide cases in Winnipeg courtrooms. He had recently retired from criminal work and had taken up writing. A true crime book had just been released with a local publisher based on one of his cases, called *She Was Only Three*, and he was busy working on another. With his extensive background in criminal law, I knew he would be an excellent adjudicator for my book, and so I gave him a rough draft of my manuscript to read. The first thing Jack said to me after reading my manuscript was: "I can't believe the way the Jehovah's Witnesses treated you at the funeral of your children—and in a house of *God!*" He went on to say that my book should be published by a Toronto publisher to give it the national exposure it deserved. "You must publish this book," he said, "otherwise you'll be lying on your deathbed one day and saying to yourself, 'I sure wish I had published that book.'"

Montgomery was from the old school of justice stretching back to the days when we still had capital punishment in Canada. He and his wife Jennifer were childless, but through their charitable work with children's organizations, especially at Christmas time, it was obvious they loved children. Of Anderson, he said to me gravely, "He should have been hanged by the neck until dead. That way, justice would have taken care of him, and you could have moved on."

I took Montgomery's advice and found a Toronto publisher. He was always there for support, throughout the editing, publishing, and publicity that followed.

He would often phone, and with his razor-sharp wit begin the conversation by saying, "How is the salmon fisherman?" referring to how prisoners at William Head Institution were allowed to fish for salmon in season.

Of course, knowing that capital punishment would probably never return to our criminal justice system, he advised me to attend one if not all of Anderson's parole hearings—something that seemed so far off, I hadn't given it much thought. More than once, he said, "You *will be there* at his parole hearings, won't you, Jim?" Not fully appreciating the gravity of what he said, nor the long road ahead of me, I solemnly agreed that I would. But I wanted to know why— what reason had I to go? How could victims win, after all, when the system seemed so stacked against them? "Why?" he echoed in his typically booming voice. "Because you've got *righteousness* on your side." That was new to me; I had never thought of the situation in terms of good and evil before. Could there be something or someone bigger than me at work here?

This book was originally published in hardcover by HarperCollins Publishers Ltd., in Toronto. The book launch was held at McNally Robinson Booksellers at their Grant Park location in Winnipeg. There were over one hundred people in attendance. My wife Marge and her elder sister Shirley sat with my mother Nellie at a table near the podium. My own sister Jeanette had already passed away in March 1996 of ovarian cancer. She was 55. A faithful Jehovah's Witness to the end, Jeanette would have undoubtedly been conspicuously absent that evening. Some fellow workers from Winnipeg Transit were there, as well as workers from Marge's beauty supply community, and other friends and relatives. Many present were from the greater community, undoubtedly alerted by journalist David Robert's timely front page article in *The Globe and Mail*, about the book prior to its launch.

Then I went on a book tour of Vancouver and Toronto, speaking about it with several media personalities and writers.

Wolves Among Sheep, between the hardcover edition and a later mass market edition, sold close to 7000 copies.

Writing and researching the book was a long and painful process; publishing it was liberating. A young woman who had been in line to purchase my book said to me later, "I had a confused adolescence, just like yours." When you write about tragedy and loss, you hit a universal chord. I received calls and letters from readers across the country. The book formed a conduit to the community. For many people, including those I had never met, their kind words were like a healing balm. Publishing the book was the right thing to do, a way of unburdening myself.

For a long time after the book was published, it felt as though we had completed a long, hard journey. But, as I was to discover, the journey was far from over. This chapter, the story of parole, began four years before the publication of the book itself. In October 1996, I got a phone call from Sherry Brown, a victim's coordinator with Correctional Service of Canada in Abbotsford, B.C. She called about putting a red flag in Anderson's file blocking any further correspondence with me, something I had requested after receiving his last letter that September. Brown had a way of talking with victims about their rights, of informing them and helping them to feel cared for and involved; she had a gift. For the most part, she seemed genuinely interested in the book I was writing.

In January 1998, I stayed at the home of friends Wayne and Esther Northey in Langley, B.C. While doing research in the area, I visited the National Parole Board's headquarters in Abbotsford, where I met Sherry Brown and Fraser Simmons, the Regional Director at that time. Simmons went the proverbial extra mile and sent a greeting card and phoned me on August 29 to see how we were doing. Such thoughtfulness restored my faith in the system. Actually, I had never lost faith in the system; people working in it enhanced it. Many others, too numerous to mention, from the National Parole Board and from Correctional Service of Canada phoned and wrote over the next decade. They were doing their jobs, first and foremost, as victims' workers. But there were times I sensed they were going beyond the call of duty and that they really cared. And for that, I am truly grateful.

A long line of sporadic correspondence about parole and escorted temporary absences began in October 1996, when I got a letter from Jan Frazelle, Victim Liaison Coordinator at William Head Institution, where Jeff Anderson was incarcerated. I was reminded that "twenty-five years without the possibility of parole" didn't necessarily mean what it said. Anderson would be eligible to apply for unescorted temporary absences and day parole in August of 2007, and for full parole in August of 2010. Frazelle, who provided a telephone number, was always there to hear my questions and concerns and to talk with me. She said that as a registered victim, I would be notified by Correctional Service if Anderson was transferred or escaped prison or was granted any form of release such as a Work Release or any special passes under the warden's authority.

I received a letter from Fraser Simmons in Abbotsford, B.C. and a package of background material on the operation of the National Parole Board. He wrote that dates and timetables set for the offender's conditional release "are review dates only and do not necessarily lead to release. The most important consideration the Board applies to every case under review is the safety of the community. The Board *always denies release if there is reason to believe that the offender will commit a new offence* (italics mine). Since this offender is serving a life sentence, he will remain imprisoned for life unless the National Parole Board grants him some form of conditional release."

Concerned that Anderson might re-offend if released, I went to my lawyer and had her make notarized copies of Anderson's letters to me, in which he confessed to sexually molesting Lindsay when she was four years old. I was concerned that with his history of pedophilia, he might be of risk to women and children, especially if he manipulated them with his phony, nice guy image—and especially if he withheld the whole truth about himself, which from his past record he was inclined to do. I mailed those letters by Express Post to Fraser Simmons, who put them in Anderson's file.

Sherry Brown submitted the entire book, *Wolves Among Sheep: The True Story of Murder in a Jehovah's Witness Community*, as my victim impact statement.

In August 2001, I retired from my job at Winnipeg Transit and went on a pension. Marge continued to work part-time in the beauty supply business until May 2004. In February 2003, I landed a part-time job with the Canadian National Institute for the Blind, as a driver for their rehabilitation workers. In July 2004, Marge and I both moved to a retirement village outside city limits.

In August 2004, Marge's sister Shirley died at age 69. She had suffered from lymphoma for five years. As Marge's only sibling, we had taken her for chemotherapy, medical tests, and other treatments during her illness. In December of the same year, my mother Nellie died of complications due to congestive heart failure at age 85. She had suffered with heart disease for seven years. We were deeply saddened by the passing of these two women; they were the last of our immediate family. They had shared Christmas, Easter, and birthday parties at our home for years and now we missed them terribly.

In July 2004, I received a phone call and a letter from Debra Kihara, Regional Communications Officer with the National Parole Board in Abbotsford to inform me of two significant changes to the Board's policies in the past few years. She wrote, "For many years, victims and others who wished to do so, have been able to send information for the Board members to read before they make decisions on this offender... As long as the Board is able to provide the offender with a copy of the information, the Board may consider information *from any source* (italics mine)." Under a new Board policy defining the word "victim," Marge could also apply for victim status. "In other words," Kihara wrote, "persons who are not relatives of Kim Anderson or your children may now ask for victim status and in turn, ask for notification throughout a sentence and/or ask to present statements at our hearings." She went on to write that "Since 2001 July victims have been able to present statements at our hearings. Adult victims may observe the hearings and read their statements in person or observe the hearing and be present while their taped statements are played." Further, she suggested that if I were to read my entire book aloud at Anderson's hearings, it would be difficult if not impossible for the Board to accommodate. "You may wish to prepare a shorter statement if you want to do a presentation at the hearings."

Kihara, aware of my concerns should children be exposed to Anderson, either in an institutional setting or in any kind of unsupervised, conditional release, urged me to make a record of those concerns in a short victim impact statement to be shared with Anderson and his case management team. To Kihara, this scenario was positive in that it allowed Anderson's CMT time to work with him on these issues in the years prior to his first parole hearing.

In June 2005, I prepared a brief, three-page victim impact statement for the Board and submitted it to Debra Kihara, to be shared with Anderson and his case management team, and to be placed in his file. It read in part: "The problem with Jeffery Anderson... is his frank discussion of the sexual molestation of my daughter, Lindsay Kostelniuk, when she was four years old. To my knowledge, although Anderson was never convicted of a sexual offence, it is that admission of guilt, or perhaps the denial of it, which causes me concern... I have heard through a prison official at William Head Institution that Anderson has since denied the sexual molestation of Lindsay. Why does he make such a horrendous admission and engage in extensive therapy, if he is not a sexual offender? ... I am not saying that sexual abuse is the reason Anderson killed, but by his own admission, it had something to do with it." I concluded by saying that "my greatest concern is for the safety of the community in the event of Anderson's parole—and that means any community, province, or state where he may be released. I am concerned that, despite the many programs completed in prison, Anderson has not come to terms with his crimes, their impact, nor the reasons for committing them."

I put the whole matter aside until August 2007, when I received a phone call from CSC to the effect that Anderson would soon be receiving a series of ETAs (escorted temporary absences) from William Head to nearby Victoria, B.C. In the first year, Anderson received about 16 hours a month of these ETAs in total, including travel time, for trips to Victoria. ETAs are officially granted to offenders so they may receive medical treatment, have contact with family members, undergo personal development and/or counseling, and to participate in community service work projects. In Anderson's case, his package-specific

ETAs, approved by the warden, were most likely for counseling, community programs outside the Institution, and for religious services and/or contact with brethren at a church of his choice.

The ETAs, which by January 2009 numbered around 79, with 379 community access hours, continued to grow in number. Their purpose was mainly to ease the offender slowly into the community, with the benefit of an escort to watch him at all times. In October 2008, I received a phone call, followed by a letter, from Sarah Robertson, Regional Communications Officer with the National Parole Board in Abbotsford. She advised me "that the Board received an *application* to consider this offender [Anderson] for **day parole** (to live in a halfway house). The Board has accepted the application and has *tentatively scheduled a hearing to take place in **February 2009** at William Head Institution near Victoria, B.C.*" I was reminded of the information the Board considers about the offender during hearings. Before making each decision, the Board carefully considers all available information about the offender, including any information from victims, the offender's criminal history, police reports, psychological assessments, judge's remarks at the end of sentencing, professional appraisals of the offender's conduct while incarcerated, an assessment of the potential risk to the community if the offender was to be granted conditional release, and a report on the investigation of the offender's release plan and the community resources available to him.

Initially, Marge and I had no intention of attending Anderson's parole hearing at William Head. I had previously submitted my book and a short form victim impact statement to the Board which would undoubtedly be read by them prior to the hearing. As Sarah Robertson pointed out, I had the option of observing the proceeding from a local parole office in Winnipeg via video-conferencing equipment, and that's what we decided to do. On January 16, 2009, Robertson wrote, "However, please note that with any technical equipment, there is always the possibility of malfunction and we cannot guarantee that if this was to occur, that you would be able to observe the hearing." In another letter, Robertson suggested that if we planned on attending the hearing that I should ask at least one other adult to accompany me. She also suggested that the federal Department of Justice in Ottawa had a fund to cover victims' travel expenses to attend National Parole Board hearings; however, a victim must be registered with the National Parole Board or the Correctional Service of Canada in order to apply. "**You are already registered with the Board,**" she wrote in bold type.

When Robertson phoned later to enquire about our decision whether to attend the hearing or not, I turned to Marge with my hand over the receiver and asked her the same question. "Let's go already," she said. That was it; we made our decision to attend the parole hearing in person with Marge acting as an observer and my support person.

I didn't expect much from this parole hearing, and told Robertson so. I expressed the view that after all his ETAs, the Board would probably be lenient and grant Anderson day parole. She gently encouraged me by saying that although staff members are not allowed to discuss in advance whether caseworkers will recommend a release—according to the Privacy Act—Board Members would discuss such details openly at the hearing. In other words, Robertson and other members knew something I didn't—something that would be revealed later. And what I heard her say, without saying it, was that Marge and I should be there to hear it.

Marge and I flew to Victoria and stayed in a hotel near the waterfront. Early on the morning of February 4, 2009, we took a taxi to downtown Victoria, where we picked up my cousin, Agnes Stewart, who came along as an observer, and proceeded about a half-hour distance in the morning darkness down Metchosin Road to William Head Institution. After signing a visitor's log at the security gate, we deposited any purses, wallets, and/or briefcases in lockers (cell phones, pagers, cameras, and recording devices were prohibited in the institution). We were, however, allowed notepads and pens to make notes. Arriving an hour early, we were escorted to a conference room by a correctional officer, where he made coffee while we waited for Carol Baldwin, Manager of Assessment and Intervention at the Institution, to arrive.

Baldwin arrived just before 8:00 a.m. She had been expecting us, but was surprised to see us so early. A courteous and upbeat woman, she lifted our spirits and made us comfortable during this stressful time. She took us to the empty room where the hearing was to take place and explained the seating arrangements. This room was adjacent to her office, separated by a locked door. We went to her office, and sat down on sofas across from her desk. One of Baldwin's assistants brought coffee, a platter of fruit, and some Danish pastry—a bit of unexpected hospitality. Sarah Robertson, a professional looking young woman, arrived from Abbotsford with a technical assistant especially designated to record the hearing. They had come all the way from the mainland. Between Robertson and Baldwin, we were briefed on the role of observers—how we were to remain silent during the hearing so as not to jeopardize the outcome. We were told about the format of the hearing, the factors the Board would access, the terms the Board would use, and the type of release being considered. Because of the Privacy Act, Correctional Staff couldn't discuss any treatment the offender had received prior to the hearing, nor could they disclose whether caseworkers were about to recommend a release or not. All these facts were about to be discussed publicly during the hearing.

A correctional officer, or CO, joined us in Baldwin's office. Because Marge knew that Anderson had a computer, she asked if offenders at the institution were allowed access to the internet. "Absolutely not," he said. "Some of them do have computers, but we never allow that." Close to 9:00, as we were about to enter the hearing room, I took a deep breath.

"Are you nervous?" the CO asked.

"No I'm not," I said. "Anderson is the one who should be nervous. He's the one who has something to prove."

As we entered the hearing room, Baldwin and Robertson joined our group at the back. The CO sat off to the side. Two other observers from the community, a man and a woman, sat directly in front of us. Next, there was a table with Anderson, seated between two men. To his left sat his Institution Parole Officer. To his right was his pastor. All three sat with their backs to us. At the front of the room were three Board members, facing us. A woman sat between two men. From our position, we could clearly see the Board member's faces from across the room. As a full-time member, the woman on the Board had been a CSC parole officer from 1975 to 1993 in the Abbotsford and Victoria areas. From 1983 to 1985, she had worked as the Manager of the Pandora Community Correctional Centre and chaired the Victoria Sexual Offender screening committee. She also worked as a parole officer with a Nanaimo-based rehabilitation center for aboriginals from across B.C. The man sitting on her right was a part-time member of the National Parole Board. He had served as a member of the RCMP for 25 years with postings in Penticton, Maple Ridge, Coquitlam, and Surrey, B.C. The man sitting on the woman's left was a full-time member of the Board. He held two Masters Degrees and a Doctorate of Clinical Psychology. In addition to his private practice, he had worked in a forensic psychiatric setting preparing court-ordered psychological assessments and evaluations on individuals involved with the justice system. Prior to his work as a clinical psychologist, he had been a Detective Sergeant with the Ontario Provincial Police. Most of his 20 years with the OPP were spent conducting major criminal investigations involving homicide, sexual assault, and organized crime. This man seemed to act as chairman, calmly opening the discussion.

Early in the hearing, I was asked to read aloud from my three-page victim impact statement. The gist of it was my concern over the sexual molestation of my daughter, a crime that Anderson had never been charged with or convicted of. Subsequent to his admission of it to me and others, I had heard through a prison official at the same institution around the year 2000 that he had recanted that admission. His new version of events was that a prison psychologist who had worked with him early on in his prison sentence had pressured him into admitting it falsely in a handwritten autobiography, or else he would be sent back to maximum security prison. This latest revelation—to me at least—was perplexing and infuriating. I knew for a fact that Anderson had been enrolled in the High Intensity Sex Offender program and the National Sexual Offender Maintenance program. Why would he engage in such extensive therapy programs and not be a sex offender? As I read aloud my statement to the Board, I suggested that although it wasn't certain the sexual abuse of my daughter was the reason Anderson killed, by his own admission, it had something to do with it.

When Anderson's Institutional Parole Officer, who had worked intensively with him for the past two years, began to speak, he set the tone for the rest of the hearing. The IPO gave the distinct impression that Anderson was not forthright, that it was hard to keep him honest, noting that the offender's version of his crimes had varied over the years, and at one point, that he had recanted information he had previously provided to his case management team. He had some traits of borderline personality disorder. This IPO's analysis of Anderson's pre-offense and earlier post-conviction behavior led him to conclude that his sexual deviancy was not only a strong contributing factor in his crimes, *but that these murders were committed to silence the victims,* so that his sexual assaults on the children would not be revealed. He had a tendency for secrecy, for image management. He had fantasized for months about the homicides, while at the same time manipulating the leaders of a religious group into coercing his wife into returning to the marriage—against her will—and all of this while attempting to maintain the façade of a morally righteous and religious person. It was, in this man's considerable opinion, the fear of exposure, and not rage, that was the probable cause for murder. While recognizing that Anderson had made some progress within the prison context, some of his institutional behavior involving women and his recent reaction to new stimuli as a result of exposure to the community on escorted temporary absences left him cause for concern. He had challenged Anderson's lack of reporting in his sex offender logs about his true thoughts and fantasies with respect to two women who attended a community church he had accessed on his escorted temporary absences. While the IPO didn't believe the two women were at imminent risk, he did question Anderson's motives, his tendency for secrecy and his need for image management.

It was now time for Anderson to speak. The discussion was framed to him in three parts: What he did, what he had done, and what was his view of the future? To begin with, Anderson, in his courteous Texas drawl, expressed how nervous he was. He then asked the Board how much weight he should give to the first part of the discussion. The Board offered him as much time as he needed. He proceeded to tell in long, detailed fashion how marital difficulties had began immediately after marrying Kim in Houston, Texas in 1981. From the time he had met Kim in Maui, he had misled her about his employment and financial situation. His marital problems had increased in severity after he had subjected her to prolonged and painful sexual intercourse, exposing her to unwanted pornography, and then sexually assaulting her two children. These sexual assaults involved oral and digital genital contact against her daughter and genital contact against her son. His deviant behavior had involved urinating and ejaculating into the children's orange juice. Unable to tolerate his deviant behavior, Kim took her children and fled to Canada, leaving him in the United States. After that, he followed her to Canada and over time became increasingly obsessed with getting her back into the marriage. To that end, as he and his spouse belonged to the same religious organization, he persistently manipulated church authority figures to pressure Kim into returning to the marriage or face being ostracized by the group. Eventually, he rented an apartment of his own a short distance away from Kim's.

During the time preceding the murders, he had made three separate attempts to acquire a firearm. On one occasion, he attempted to purchase a .357 magnum handgun, but lacked the necessary legal documentation. Nevertheless, he managed to buy a shotgun which he sawed-off and concealed in his apartment. While away on a motorcycle tour of the United States, and fantasizing about venting his rage on Kim, his apartment flooded. His landlord, after discovering the weapon along with ammunition in his residence, had turned everything over to the police. Upon returning to Canada, a police officer confronted him about the shotgun that had been seized from his apartment. The officer stated that owning a sawed-off shotgun was illegal in Canada. He would be investigating Anderson, and depending on whether he found anything about him, he would come back and arrest him. That very same day, Anderson went out and purchased another 12-gauge shotgun with ammunition, sawing off the barrel of the gun.

At that point, as Anderson put it to the Board, he was afraid the officer would find out "something" about him and realized he had a "short timeline" in which to act. So on August 29, 1985, armed with the new sawed-off shotgun, he entered Kim's residence. She was on the telephone at the time, talking with her mother. The children were in their bedroom. She told her mother to notify the police. A short time later, a police officer telephoned the residence and spoke with Kim, who advised him what Anderson was doing. He then spoke over the telephone to this police officer that he was prepared to shoot both his wife and her two children, and then hung up. Within a short period of time, police officers who were outside the apartment heard the sound of gunfire. First, he shot his wife, then her daughter, then her son, and then he shot his wife again. All three victims were shot pointblank in the face. He was arrested by police after he made his way out of the residence.

While he had no previously recorded criminal history, he admitted to petty crimes, such as price-tag switching in a grocery store shortly after his marriage to Kim. He also admitted to sexually molesting his niece when he was young. Although admitting to the sexual assaults on Kim's two children, he was never charged with any of these crimes.

He reported several suicide attempts and had written a number of suicide notes over the years. Although the most serious suicide attempt took place during his incarceration, the suicide note on that occasion listed the types and quantities of the anti-depressant pills he had ingested.

According to information provided by his case management team, he had been raised by a single mother and had little contact with his biological father. After his mother remarried, he reported feeling anxiety as he was "accustomed to having things his way." In fact, he reported suffering separation anxiety when his mother dropped him off at a babysitter's home before going to work.

Anderson's assistant, the chaplain at the institution, told the Board that he had known the offender for about ten years and that the information provided at the hearing was consistent with information disclosed to him. The chaplain said he believed the offender had made considerable progress over the years and that he had gained considerable support from his new faith community.

At this point, Board members asked Anderson some probing questions. He was asked, for example, about the separation anxiety he had felt as a child when his mother had dropped him off at the babysitter's. Usually some core trauma suffered early on in a criminal's life—such as extreme physical or psychological deprivation, sexual molestation, or repeated beatings—can be determined as some basis for criminality later in adult life. It seemed incredible to the woman on the Board that Anderson cited the thing most children experience—that they are let off at a babysitter's, as the core, traumatic incident in his life. The question was clear: Was that all it took? Is that your excuse for destroying three lives as well as your own?

Board members were concerned about Anderson's past sexual depravity and deviancy, that he had sexually assaulted his wife's small daughter and had glossed over the sexual assault of her son. They were concerned about more recent reports that he had established a long-distance relationship with an older, wealthy divorced woman *on the internet* and that he had attempted to manipulate a woman by not fully revealing the details of his crime to her.

Another Board member, the man on the woman's right, asked Anderson about the certain "something" he was afraid the police officer might find out upon investigating his possession of an illegal firearm and his relationship to Kim. Could that "something" be the scandal and shame the sexual assaults against her children might bring to light? Was that the reason for the short "timeline" to carry out his plan of murder? Anderson glossed over that question by saying he had been concerned the officer might turn up something as innocuous as a speeding ticket and, as a result, he might have been deported.

The probable question on everyone's mind was, "Why did you kill the children?" Anderson's reason for killing the children was apparently "to get it over with as quickly as possible." But that didn't answer the question, and the Board differed with him. They cited an element of cruelty in his actions.

The Board asked about his current involvement in a faith community other than Jehovah's Witnesses. Given his history of manipulating religious authority figures, was this not already an established pattern and one to avoid? A recent report, given on January 7, 2009 from the NSOM (National Sexual Offender Maintenance) program stated, "However, it was also noted that you received feedback from the group about some of your pessimistic tendencies and inclination for hiding behind a false image." Anderson's involvement with another religious organization, it was said, could be somewhat zealous and he was cautioned to work diligently to maintain an open mind along with a balanced approach to his behavior and self-management. It had also been reported that he had a feeling of sexual attraction towards a female volunteer who occasionally visited the institution, along with her husband and children as part of a religious group. He glossed over that question too, saying earlier to his Institutional Parole Officer that it was just a fantasy about consensual sex with a woman of legal age.

Nearly three hours after the hearing commenced, the Board called for a recess so they could deliberate on their decision. When they returned, they told Anderson that he was denied his application for day parole. Citing reasons for this decision, here are some passages from the National Parole Board's pre-release decision document: near the beginning of the report, which addresses Anderson directly, it states, "Your score on the Statistical Information on Recidivism (SIR) scale suggests that 4 out of 5 offenders will not commit an indictable offense after release. Actuarially, you are assessed as posing a low-moderate risk for future violence or sexual offending."

However, in listing the factors identified as contributing to criminal behavior—including emotional instability—it was noted that "A reason you gave for not taking your own life was that you wanted to see your wife's family suffer."

It was reported that early on in serving his sentence, when Anderson was in therapy, "The psychologist also commented that after your conviction, you gave a number of self-serving interviews to the media in which you presented yourself as a 'normal, regular, law-abiding guy' who had endless love for his wife. It was also noted in this report that after you were confronted by your Case Management Team regarding this media attention, you apparently retracted some of the information you provided. In addition, this report also documented that you experienced violent and sexually deviant fantasies."

A 1990 psychological report commented "on the exploitation of your religious group in that you attempted to use them to pressure your spouse to return to the marriage. The psychologist also believed that your suicide attempts were not genuine, but were intended to elicit attention and sympathy from others. The report also highlighted your Narcissistic Personality Disorder, and pointed to your desire for media attention and your dysfunctional reaction to perceived criticism and rejection. In addition, the psychologist expressed concern that you maintained a deviant fantasy life that you are unwilling to disclose. Further, the opinion expressed in this report was that had the murders not occurred, your paedophilic behavior would have continued...

"A 1992 psychological report commented that your 'pathology' was beginning to surface. This report described you as passive-aggressive, grandiose, and pretentious. The writer also noted that you refused to do some photocopying work as you believed you were above such 'menial labour.' Concern was also expressed in this report that you had been sexualizing a young female undergraduate student who was working at the institution and that you were glorifying and romanticizing this woman.

"A 2007 psychological report underscored the narcissism that appeared to motivate your crimes. In his clinical opinion, the psychiatrist suggested that your spouse's refusal to return to the marriage resulted in you committing these murders. Moreover, the psychiatrist stated that your behavior was indicative of Borderline Personality Disorder and he cautioned that while personality dysfunction may subside over time, the potential to revert to earlier moods or functioning always exists, especially during times of extreme stress. In his clinical opinion, you are a low risk to re-offend, as he believes that you pose little risk outside the context of an intimate relationship.

"Reports from the psychologist indicate that you make good use of your sessions during your ETAs (Escorted Temporary Absences). The most recent report (December 19, 2008) indicates that you discussed experiencing sexual fantasies about the women who attend your religious group. The psychologist reminded you to deal with this issue in an appropriate manner, and not to fall back into 'black and white thinking,' as had been your tendency in the past.

"Specifically, your IPO's (Institutional Parole Officer's) analysis of your pre-offense and earlier post-conviction behavior has led him to conclude that your sexual deviancy was not only a strong contributing factor in your crimes, but that *these murders were committed to silence the victims* (italics mine), so that your sexual assaults on the children would not be revealed. Moreover, he puts little stock in your explanation that the reason you killed your spouse and her children was because your spouse did not afford you any emotional acceptance on the day you appeared in her residence brandishing a sawed-off shotgun.

"You admitted to have gone through periods in your life where you faked your religiosity. In addition, you admitted that you victimized your spouse spiritually, emotionally, and physically.

"When questioned about the concerns regarding your institutional behavior over the years, you told the Board that you made a poor decision in agreeing to talk to the media about your crimes; a decision, you said that reflected your egotistical nature and grandiosity. You also admitted that your numerous suicide attempts were not really motivated by your desire to die, but rather, they were intended to gain attention and sympathy. In addition, you acknowledged that during your incarceration, you were not fully disclosive about your crimes to a woman you were having a long-distance relationship with. With respect to you recanting your admission concerning your sexual assault of your spouse's daughter, you admitted that your claim about feeling intimidated by your therapist was a lie and that the actual reason for you recanting was that you were concerned about additional media exposure. The Board notes that this kind of deceptive and manipulative behavior is a longstanding pattern with you. Further, you admitted that this was another example of you lying and manipulating people."

In conclusion, the Board wrote that, "You accepted full responsibility for these 3 premeditated murders and the prior sexual assaults against both of your spouse's children. However, given your calculated pre-offence behavior, your longstanding pattern of engaging in secrecy and image management, and your concern regarding a 'timeline,' after speaking with the police officer about possessing an illegal firearm, the Board is not convinced that your 'rage' was the sole reason for these murders. *In spite of your denial, the Board believes that silencing your victims before they could expose you to the police as a sex offender was also a likely factor in the murders of all 3 victims* (italics mine).

The Board went on to say, "While you have made some progress towards the goals of your Correctional Plan, the Board is still concerned that your longstanding tendency to engage in image management and secrecy needs to be more extensively assessed by your CMT (case management team), specifically in relation to your sexual fantasy life, prior to you being granted any form of conditional release. While the Board noted that you do have a source of pro-social support in the community, *given your history of manipulating the members of another faith community, the members of your church are not in a position to adequately manage your risk* (italics mine)."

All three Board members registered their votes in this hearing as "denied."

Anderson's story seemed bewildering to everyone. The details of his behavior were so degrading, depraved, and deviant that I saw looks of horror and perplexity on Board members' faces as he spoke. There were looks of revulsion and disbelief as they questioned him about his motivations. At one point during Anderson's narrative, I looked over at the people alongside me, and Robertson had tears in her eyes.

My own impression of the hearing was that it was disturbing and, quite frankly, sickening to hear. Anderson rambled on and on as he provided the Board with a long and detailed account of his behavior prior to, during, and after the murders of Kim and the children. It was the same old sad story I had heard so many times before, but now instead of coming from other sources, it was coming directly from his mouth. I wondered how he had persisted in prison all these twenty-three years despite suicide attempts and repeated concerns about his safety. He must have endured because the narrative justified his existence— and was worthy of our attention.

When I asked Sarah Robertson about it later, she said, "Yes, but it's your sad story too, Jim." True, it has always been my sad story.

His reasons for pulling the trigger seemed contrived—he doesn't understand his own motives for killing. How could anyone explain away such actions when there is no defense for killing children? I've always wondered how Anderson can live with himself knowing what he's done. How could any normal person with a heart go on living with that on their conscience? And yet he continues to live in a cushy, minimum security facility like William Head, the so-called Club Med of Canada, for well over ten years now, demanding his rights, demanding and getting everything coming to him. He talks about remorse, but he doesn't sound or act very remorseful.

There's a disconnect between Anderson's rhetoric—he knows all the right psychological and institutional program buzzwords—and his feelings. As Carol Baldwin said, "He breezes through here every day as though nothing unusual has happened. I've seen other offenders who've killed their wives. They're all emotionally broken up inside and truly remorseful; he's not one of them."

What shocked me most during the hearing was the fact that not only had he sexually assaulted my daughter—which I already knew—but that he had done so with my son as well, something I didn't know. So many things, such as the sexual assault on his niece when he was young, had been hidden in his file until the day of his hearing. These new facts made me wonder: What else had Anderson been hiding? Was his narrative fact or fiction, or was it a blend of the two? There seems to be another, hidden layer to the story, one I'm afraid we'll never know.

Anderson's Statistical Information on Recidivism (SIR) score, cited on the front of the National Parole Board's decision document is, in my opinion, skewed. If he had been charged and convicted for his (admitted) sexual crimes against children, the outcome would have been much different. Had those crimes been accounted for, he would have undoubtedly scored at a higher risk. The reason, by the way, that he was never charged with those crimes was, first of all, that they originally occurred in the state of Texas—outside the jurisdiction of Canada—and secondly, by the time the RCMP had learned about these allegations during the murder investigation, the witnesses were all dead.

Anderson's return to fundamentalist Christian religion seemed self-serving. He began with a fairly closed religion—Jehovah's Witnesses—where he manipulated church authority figures, trying to force his spouse into returning to the marriage in a rather self-righteous way. Now a new faith group he subscribes to is busy advocating for Anderson's release from prison, while at the same time he has sexual fantasies about a married woman in their midst. It doesn't surprise me that the Board in their summary report said, "While the Board noted that you do have a source of pro-social support in the community, given your history of manipulating members of another faith community, the members of your church are not in a position to adequately manage your risk." I know that Christian groups mean well in their quest to save lost souls. Knowing what I know about Jeff Anderson, if I was a member of this new faith group, I would not be advocating for his release. Even if I was not a victim, I wouldn't want a self-confessed sexual offender out on the streets.

The National Parole Board, in their summary report, recommended seven conditions should Anderson ever be granted Day Parole:

1. Other—report all relationships with women to your parole supervisor.
2. Must Avoid Certain Places—not to frequent strip clubs.

3. Must Avoid Certain Persons—not to associate with sex trade workers.
4. Other—must maintain sex offender maintenance behavioral logs.
5. Other—not to access pornographic materials via the internet.
6. Must Avoid Certain Persons—not to be in the company of any person under the age of 18 without direct supervision of another adult pre-approved in advance by your parole supervisor.
7. Must Avoid Certain Persons—no direct or indirect contact with any family member of the victims of your index offense.

In Canada, a life sentence means life. Even if a life offender is granted full parole, it is always a conditional release, and he still must report to a parole supervisor and abide by certain restrictions, like the ones listed above, for the rest of his life. Not necessarily with Jeff Anderson. Why not? Because there is a deportation order in Anderson's file. It is my understanding that in July 2010, one month before the twenty-fifth anniversary of Anderson's index offense, he will be granted another parole hearing. If he doesn't succeed in his bid for day parole then, he will try again. It is my belief that he will eventually be granted full parole, in which case he will be deported to the United States. As he claims, he will probably live in Washington State, without any support or supervision from the National Parole Board of Canada. He won't be under any of the restrictions outlined above, other than an order not to return to Canada. Most importantly for Anderson, he won't have to tell his sad story any more. He can be somebody else for a change.

In that case, I pity the people of the United States. Americans, beware. Jeff Anderson may be coming to a community near you. It will be difficult, if not impossible, to learn of his true identity. Who knows what will happen then, without anyone keeping an eye on him and his activities?

* * * *

AFTER MARGE AND I returned home, I got a phone call from my editor at *The Carillon*, a Steinbach, Manitoba newspaper where I write a weekly column. After she finished reading her copy of *Wolves Among Sheep*, she surfed the web and happened to run across Jeff Anderson's photos and profile on a website called brothersinprison.com, a "Christian" website for prisoners seeking partners outside of prison. On the top of Anderson's webpage, basic details are provided such as his weight, eye color, hair color, race, religion, and education. He lists hobbies, such as large scale model railroading, and work skills, such as radio announcing. What he was really seeking through the website were "straight women only."

In the written statement that follows, he suggested that although he felt deep remorse for his crimes and had accepted full responsibility for them, the past could not be undone. He had done everything humanly possible to make amends and rehabilitate himself through the years, and there was nothing more to be done. After much soul-searching and prayer, the most important change occurred when he gave his life to Jesus Christ in 2001 and became a born-again Christian.

By his own admission, Anderson became an anti-terrorist, George W. Bush-loving Republican supporter, an avid fan of conservative talk show radio host Rush Limbaugh—and a fiery Southern White Christian through and through. No doubt, he would be a supporter of the National Rifle Association.

We were horrified to find out he was on the internet, searching for women.

Remembering what the CO had said at William Head Institution about not allowing inmates access to the internet, I contacted Carol Baldwin, who had Anderson's page taken off that particular website. How it got there in the first place, only Anderson knows for sure.

The main thing to remember about Jeffery Anderson is that, by all indications, he is probably out there, trolling for women. Why would he stop now?

Over the past 24 years, accounting for all expenses including police investigations, the courts, correctional services, and the work of the National Parole Board, Anderson has cost the Canadian taxpayer millions of dollars and still counting. Marge and I feel if Anderson could be truly rehabilitated and was no longer a threat to society, we would have no problem in having him deported to the United States, where he would no longer be a financial burden to Canada.

In that case, let him fend for himself.

James Kostelniuk
Winnipeg, Manitoba
July 2009

LaVergne, TN USA
19 November 2009
164729LV00005B/5/P